King and Court in Ancient Persia 559 to 331 BCE

DEBATES AND DOCUMENTS IN ANCIENT HISTORY

GENERAL EDITORS

Emma Stafford, *University of Leeds* and
Shaun Tougher, *Cardiff University*

Focusing on important themes, events or periods throughout ancient history, each volume in this series is divided into roughly equal parts. The first introduces the reader to the main issues of interpretation. The second contains a selection of relevant evidence supporting different views.

PUBLISHED

Diocletian and the Tetrarchy
Roger Rees

Julian the Apostate
Shaun Tougher

Rome and its Empire, AD *193–284*
Olivier Hekster with Nicholas Zair

Roman Imperialism
Andrew Erskine

King and Court in Ancient Persia 559 to 331 BCE
Lloyd Llewellyn-Jones

FORTHCOMING

The Family in the Roman World
Mary Harlow and Tim Parkin

Sex and Sexuality in Classical Athens
James Robson

Justinian and the Sixth Century
Fiona Haarer

The Emperor Nero
Steven Green

King and Court in Ancient Persia 559 to 331 BCE

Lloyd Llewellyn-Jones

EDINBURGH
University Press

For David
(& César-Phoebus and Maisie)

Edinburgh University Press Ltd
22 George Square, Edinburgh EH8 9LF

www.euppublishing.com

Typeset in 11/13 Minion
by Servis Filmsetting Ltd, Stockport, Cheshire, and
printed and bound in Great Britain by
CPI Group (UK) Ltd, Croydon CR0 4YY

A CIP record for this book is available from the British Library

ISBN 978 0 7486 4126 0 (hardback)
ISBN 978 0 7486 4125 3 (paperback)
ISBN 978 0 7486 7710 8 (webready PDF)
ISBN 978 0 7486 7711 5 (epub)
ISBN 978 0 7486 7712 2 (Amazon ebook)

Published with the support of the Edinburgh University Scholarly
Publishing Initiatives Fund.

Contents

Series Editors' Preface

This is a very welcome addition to *Debates and Documents*, broadening the series' scope to encompass ancient Greece's most influential neighbour and rival, Achaemenid Persia. Founded around 559 BCE by Cyrus the Great, the Persian Empire quickly expanded to cover an area roughly equivalent to modern Turkey, Syria, Lebanon, Jordan, Israel, Palestine, Iraq, Azerbaijan, Iran, and Afghanistan, extending south to include Egypt. A highly developed administrative system, as well as military strength, ensured the Achaemenid's dominance over this vast empire for over 200 years, until its conquest by Alexander the Great in 331 BCE.

Achaemenid Persia was immensely influential in Greek political affairs and more broadly on Greek culture; conquest by Persia effectively brought to an end 2,500 years of pharaonic rule in Egypt; and under Achaemenid governance the Jews returned from exile in Babylon to rebuild the walls and temple of Jerusalem. Such intersections with other ancient cultures provide a way into the study of Achaemenid Persia for many, but in recent years there has been increasing scholarly interest in Persian history for its own sake. The focus of this volume is on the king and royal court, the political and symbolic centre of Achaemenid culture, covering all its elements, from personnel and social organisation, political intrigue, and fierce struggles over succession, to the practicalities of the court's regular travels around the Empire.

As well as being a new area of study for many, Achaemenid Persia is particularly suitable for the *Debates* series because of a key methodological difficulty: much of our information has traditionally come via Greek writers, with varying degrees of knowledge of their subject, and with strong biases to distort the picture they present. Increasingly, however, the significance of other ancient texts has been recognised and material evidence from Persia itself has become available;

comparative evidence has also been supplied by recent studies of other court societies. The documents presented here include, in addition to Greek historiography, texts from the Hebrew Bible, Achaemenid (and Mesopotamian) inscriptions and images, archaeological material, and reconstructions. Taken together, and with careful analysis, this range of sources allows us a fascinating insight into an extraordinary culture.

Emma Stafford
Shaun Tougher

Preface

During the last thirty years or so, the study of Achaemenid Persia has developed into a rigorous discipline and has become an integral aspect of ancient history research and teaching at colleges, universities, and other scholarly institutions throughout much of the world. In this book the reader will meet with a number of the influential scholars who have turned Achaemenid history into that esteemed area of study, and I pay homage to the wisdom and energy they have brought (and continue to bring) to this burgeoning subject. But we stand, I think, on the cusp of another exciting period in the on-going study of the Achaemenid world in which newer scholars, secure in the discipline's scholarly recognition, are building on the foundations of their predecessors to engage with (and challenge) their findings, and advance diverse methodologies, themes, and subjects, which will only help to enhance our perceptions of both the ancient Persians themselves and of the sources through which we are obliged to find them.

This book does not attempt to offer a narrative or analytical account of the sweep of Achaemenid history, or to provide a study of any specific regions of the Empire, or a re-evaluation of the historical source materials; nor does it try to be exhaustive in its scope. A recent series of books and articles has already done these things – comprehensively (and no doubt more will follow). Pierre Briant's mammoth 2002 study *From Cyrus to Alexander. A History of the Persian Empire* (a translation of his 1996 French original) has become – and deservedly so – a cornerstone of modern Achaemenid historiography and it shares pride of place alongside the on-going publications of the Achaemenid History Workshop and Amélie Kuhrt's equally monumental and eminently useful 2007 publication *The Persian Empire* – an exhaustive sourcebook rich in commentary and detail and extensive in its choice of subject matter. This present study takes a far more polarised view of a central (but crucially important) element of Achaemenid culture, the royal court, and uses it as a focus upon which current trends in scholarly debate are projected.

There was a time when all 'proper' historians turned their critical and quizzical eyes to kings and courts, but court studies became unfashionable and by the 1970s courts were seen as moribund institutions and the study of kings and courtiers was thought of as old fashioned at best or, at worst, simply irrelevant. But modes change and, happily, studies of ancient courts are becoming fashionable again. A volume edited by Antony Spawforth, *The Court and Court Society in Ancient Monarchies*, went to press in 2007 (and has been released in a paperback edition too) and the *American Journal of Philology* has recently produced a special issue entitled 'Classical Courts and Courtiers' (vol. 132.1, 2011). In February 2011 the University of Edinburgh hosted a conference on the Hellenistic court and a publication is set to follow. In 2010 Bruno Jacobs and Robert Rollinger edited *Der Achämenidenhof/ The Achaemenid Court*, the first volume to be entirely dedicated to this subject. Here a rich collection of historical, archaeological, art-historical, and literary studies by leading experts in the Achaemenid field has already improved our general understanding of the structures and functions of the court and have whetted the appetite for future research. Kings are fashionable again in scholarship. Court studies are back too. The time is right, I suggest, to introduce less specialist readers to the rich and rewarding subject of king and court in ancient Persia.

Royal courts played a central role in ancient Near Eastern politics and culture, and it is not surprising that descriptions of courts infiltrate the literatures of many ancient societies. For its part, the Persian court – the ancient court *par excellence* – was so significant that it appeared in the writings and artworks of peoples who lived far outside the Persian heartland: the Greeks were fascinated by the structure, workings, and rationale of the Achaemenid royal court, so much so that, after the fall of the Empire, the court of the Great Kings became a familiar locale of Greek (and Roman) fairy tales and romances, and thereby maintained a presence in the western imagination. The Persian court was also a template for the numerous authors of the Hebrew Bible who, during the Exile and Second Temple periods, used it to create their own images of Hebrew monarchic splendour. For the most part, the legendary courts of David and Solomon were modelled on the Achaemenid archetype. With this in mind, it is worth noting that once the Queen of Sheba had seen the splendour of Solomon's ('Persian') court, 'his ministers, and their apparel, and his cupbearers', the Biblical author makes the point of telling us that 'there was no more spirit in her' (1 Kings 10: 4–7); in other words, she was flabbergasted. It is easy to understand why the Persian royal court commanded such feelings of awe, for it was a symbol of the king's authority, a physical manifestation of his god-given rulership. It is this vivid interplay of king and court which this book will highlight.

The book falls into two parts. Part I explores some of the central themes of monarchy and court society in ancient Persia and exposes some debates therein. Part II proffers a (limited but carefully chosen) selection of evidence: Classical and Near Eastern texts, archaeology, and material culture. References to these sources are cited in Part I in bold type, thus: **B7**. This refers to B7 in Part II, and you will find the exact page number for it in the contents list: 'B7. The creation of Darius' palace at Susa'. It is appropriate to consult the texts and images which make up Part II as they are encountered in Part I of the book.

Greek and Latin translations are largely my own or else are adapted and amended from the Loeb Library translations of the originals. I make no claim for the translations of other (Near Eastern) texts and I acknowledge the authority of others in these matters (for comments see 'Further Reading' in Part II and also on their citation in the 'Note on Abbreviations', p. xvii).

It seems that hardly a week passes by when Iran is not in the news – usually for negative reasons. Iran is vilified in the western press and other media as a harbinger of terrorism, the home of fundamentalism, or as the epicentre of the threat to world peace. This is the popular journalistic (and jingoistic) image of Iran. It bypasses the rich cultural heritage of the country, its deep and proud history and the diversity of its social institutions. Western media also do an injustice to the people of Iran, who are, in my experience of travelling to that country over many years, the warmest, most welcoming, and most cultured of peoples. They are intensely aware of – and rightly proud of – their Achaemenid heritage. I accepted the request to write this book shortly after returning from an extended visit to Iran, during which I undertook, for the large part, to follow in the Great King's migration from Ecbatana (modern Hamadan) to Persepolis (near the beautiful city of Shiraz), via Susa. The welcome and enthusiasm I encountered on my mini 'royal progress' encouraged me to write this book and so I want to thank my Iranian friends and fellow travellers: *kheily mamnoon va behtarin arezoohayemara bepazir.*

In preparing this book, I have encountered many people who have been helpful to me. Thanks go to Eran Almagor, Sandra Bingham,

Raphaëla Dubreuil, Keyvan Mahmoudi, Silvia Milanezi, Janett Morgan, Ricardo Pinto, St John Simpson, Emma Stafford, Shaun Tougher, Stephanie Winder, and Mark Woolmer. My colleagues in Classics at the University of Edinburgh (especially Ulrike Roth) have cut me the slack when I needed it most and I am grateful for their camaraderie. Students on several of my courses (*Ancient Persia: the Achaemenid Dynasty*; *Crowns and Concubines: Court Society in the Ancient World*, and *Persica: Greek Historians and the Persian Empire*) continue to motivate me. I want to mention in particular Chloe Anstis, Fran Armour, Leila Hedayat, Camilla Higgins, Elina Larravide, and Samantha Walker. Kourosh Afhami, Wolfgang Gambke, and the team at Persepolis 3d.com have kindly permitted me to use some of their remarkable and beautiful images; I am most grateful to them for their generous cooperation. Ralph Footring has been a thorough, communicative, and friendly copy-editor and I am deeply grateful for his keen insights. Last, but in no way least, Carol MacDonald at Edinburgh University Press has been a supportive and encouraging presence throughout the time this book has been in creation and I thank her warmly and sincerely.

My greatest debt of gratitude though is to David Pineau. I dedicate this book to him.

Lloyd Llewellyn-Jones
Edinburgh, May 2012

A Note on Abbreviations

In the Documents section (Part II) I have attempted to aid the reader who may be unfamiliar with standardised academic abbreviations by citing references to ancient authors (where known) and the titles of their works in full. The Debates section (Part I), however, omits the titles of works which were the sole output of an individual author (for example, Herodotus is used in place of Herodotus, *Histories* etc.). The use of full references applies to both Classical and Near Eastern texts, including the Hebrew Bible (for a comprehensive list of standard academic abbreviations see Kuhrt 2007: 910–18). But there are, nevertheless, some abbreviations used throughout this work:

Greek and Latin texts

F	Fragment
T	Testimonium
§	indicates a paragraph or section number

Achaemenid royal inscriptions

A^1	Artaxerxes I
A^2	Artaxerxes II
A^3	Artaxerxes III
Am	Ariaramnes
As	Arsames
C	Cyrus
D	Darius I
D^2	Darius II
X	Xerxes
B	Babylon (for the Cyrus Cylinder)

B   Bisitun (for the inscription of Darius I)
E   Elvend
H   Hamadan
M   Parsagade
N   Naqš-i Rustam
P   Persepolis
S   Susa
V   Van (Lake Van, Armenia)
Z   Suez

SC   Seal
VS   Vase
W   Weight

§   indicates a paragraph or section number

DPb §3 therefore means: Darius I's Persepolis inscription b, section 3.
DB II §4–6 means: Darius I's Bisitun inscription, column II, sections 4–6.
A³Pa §24–5 is: Artaxerxes III's Persepolis inscription a, sections 24–5.
D²Sb means: Darius II's Susa inscription b.
This system follows Lecoq (1997: 11).

Texts from Persepolis

PFT   *Persepolis Fortification Tablets* (Hallock 1969)
PF   siglum for Persepolis Fortification tablets published by Hallock (1969)
PFa   further Persepolis Fortification tablets published by Hallock (1978)
PF-NN   siglum for Persepolis Fortification tablets transliterated by Hallock, but as yet unpublished
PFS   Persepolis Fortification seal (cylinder seal)
PFS*   Inscribed Persepolis Fortification seal (cylinder seal)
PFs   Persepolis Fortification stamp seal
PFS-N   Persepolis Fortification seal only attested on PFa tablets

Timeline

Achaemenid Great King	Date	Royal women	Events in Persia	Events in the Empire	Key sources
Cyrus II (the Great)	559 BCE	Mother: Mandane (?) Wife: Cassandane and/or Amytis	Accession of Cyrus and establishment of the Empire		
	549 BCE			Capture of Ecbatana in Media	
	c. 559–539 BCE			Wars in Asia Minor. Fall of Sardis in Lydia	

Achaemenid Great King	Date	Royal women	Events in Persia	Events in the Empire	Key sources
	540 BCE			Elamite campaign and capture of Susa	Nabonidus Chronicle
	540 BCE			Attack on the Neo-Babylonian Empire. Fall of Babylon	Cyrus Cylinder
	540–530 BCE		Building of palaces and gardens at Parsagade		Deutero-Isaiah (Isaiah 40–55): 'prophesies' of Cyrus the Great
	530 BCE		Death of Cyrus II (in battle?)	Battle against Queen Tomyris (?)	
Cambyses II	530 BCE	Mother: Cassandane or Amytis (?) Wives: Roxane, two sisters, Phaidyme (Upandush), Atossa and Artystone (Irtašduna)	Accession of Cambyses		
	525 BCE			Conquest of Egypt	
	522 BCE		Death of Cambyses		

Achaemenid Great King	Date	Royal women	Events in Persia	Events in the Empire	Key sources
Bardiya	522 BCE	Mother: Cassandane or Amytis (?) Wives: Atossa (Udusana), Artystone (Irtašduna), Phaidyme (Upandush)	Accession and assassination of Bardiya		
Darius I (the Great)	522/1	Mother: Irdabama (?) Wives: Atossa (Udusana), Artystone (Irtašduna), Phaidyme (Upandush), Parmys, Phratagune and an unnamed daughter of Gobryas	Coup and accession of Darius I	Revolts suppressed by Darius. North-west India and Thrace added to Empire	
	519–515 BCE				Bisitun inscription and relief; building of Persepolis begins
	516 BCE			Consecration of the Jerusalem temple	

Achaemenid Great King	Date	Royal women	Events in Persia	Events in the Empire	Key sources
	506–497 BCE				Persepolis Fortification texts. Inscriptions from Persepolis and Susa
	499–493 BCE			Ionian revolt	
	490 BCE			Battle of Marathon	*Ganjnameh* inscriptions (DH); tomb as Naqš-i Rustam
	486 BCE		Death of Darius I	Revolt in Egypt	
Xerxes I	486 BCE	Mother: Atossa (Udusana) Wife: Amestris (and, according to Hebrew Bible, Vashti and Esther)	Accession of Xerxes I		From 486 onwards, inscriptions at Hamadan, Persepolis, Naqš-i Rustam, Lake Van

Achaemenid Great King	Date	Royal women	Events in Persia	Events in the Empire	Key sources
	484 BCE			Revolts in Babylonia	
	481 BCE			Battle of Thermopylae	
	480 BCE			Sack of Athens; Battle of Salamis	
	472 BCE				Aeschylus, *The Persians*
	465 BCE		Assassination of Xerxes I; execution of Crown Prince Darius		*The Babylonian Eclipse Lists* (BM 32234)
Artaxerxes I	465 BCE	Mother: Amestris Wife: Damaspia	Accession of Artaxerxes I		
	464/3–454 BCE			Revolts in Egypt	
	c. 450–420 BCE				Herodotus, *Histories*

Achaemenid Great King	Date	Royal women	Events in Persia	Events in the Empire	Key sources
Xerxes II [Sogdianus]	424/3 BCE	Mother: Damaspia (?)	Death of Artaxerxes I and accession and assassination of Xerxes II. Accession and assassination of Sogdianus		
Darius II	423 BCE	Mother: Cosmartidene (concubine of Artaxerxes I) Wife: Parysatis	Accession of Darius II		Aršama dossier (down to c. 410 BCE)
Artaxerxes II	405 BCE	Mother: Parysatis Wife: Stateira (I)	Death of Darius II; accession of Artaxerxes II		
	401 BCE			Battle of Cunaxa; death of Cyrus the Younger. Egypt secedes from the Empire	
	c. 400 BCE				Books of Nehemiah and Ezra; Book of Esther

Achaemenid Great King	Date	Royal women	Events in Persia	Events in the Empire	Key sources
	c. 394–385 BCE				Ctesias, *Persica*; Xenophon, *Cyropaedia*
Artaxerxes III	358 BCE	Mother: Stateira (I) Wives: daughter of one of his sisters; daughter of Oxathres	Death of Artaxerxes II; accession of Artaxerxes III		350s BCE Deinon, *Persica*
	348/7 BCE			Death of Plato	
	343/2 BCE			Re-conquest of Egypt	340s BCE Heraclides of Cumae, *Persica*
Artaxerxes IV (Arses)	338 BCE	Mother: (?) Wives: (?)	Death of Artaxerxes III; accession of Artaxerxes IV		
Darius III	336 BCE	Mother: Sisygambis Wives: Stateira (II); daughter of Pharnaces	Murder of Artaxerxes IV; accession of Darius III		
	333 BCE			Battle of Issus	'Dynastic Prophecy' from Babylon (?)

Achaemenid Great King	Date	Royal women	Events in Persia	Events in the Empire	Key sources
	331 BCE		Expulsion of Darius III from the throne by Alexander	Battle of Gaugamela	
	330 BCE		Murder of Darius III; Alexander of Macedon proclaims himself Great King		

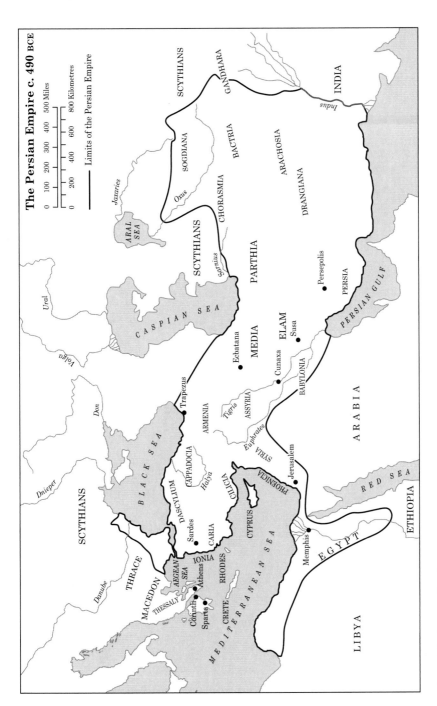

Map 1 The Persian Empire

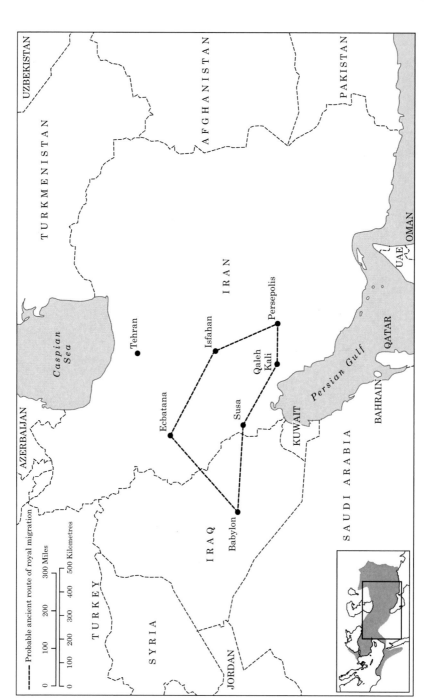

Map 2 Iran in the Achaemenid Period

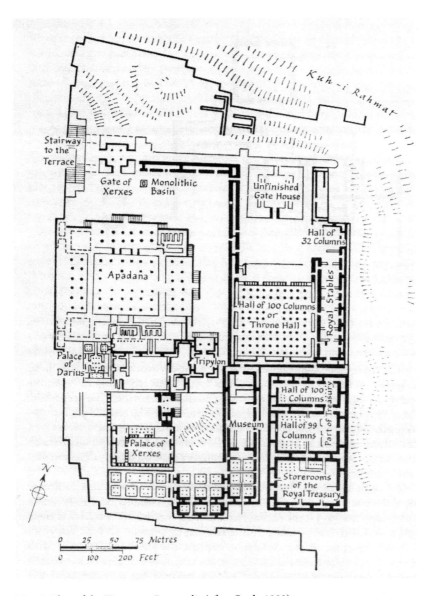

Map 3 Plan of the Terrace at Persepolis (after Cook, 1983)

Shahsenshahs of Ecbatana and Istakhr
All found glory and pride in this land.
This was the land of armies at the time of Cyrus –
The resting place of warriors and the camp of the king.
                    Mohammad-Taqi Bahar (1884–1951)

Part I
Debates

Costumed actors pose beneath a monumental doorjamb from the Hall of a Hundred Columns at Persepolis. The image (and others like it) was commissioned by Iran's Department of Tourism at the time of Mohammed Reza Shah's celebrations to commemorate 2,500 years of Persian monarchy in October 1971.

Introduction

In the court I exist and of the court I speak
but what the court is, God knows. I know not.
(Walter Map, *De Nugis Curialium*, 'Of Courtier Trifles', c. 1190)

Around 1190 CE Walter Map, a Welsh cleric at the court of Henry II of England, attempted to articulate the nebulous nature of the court in a treatise which, with its famous, if somewhat exasperated tone of phrase, has been much quoted by historians of court societies ever since in their own attempts to voice a definition of this most ambiguous of royal institutions. It is a fitting place start to this short work on the Achaemenid court, because in spite of recent sophisticated scholarly advances in the study of ancient courts (Spawforth 2007b; Strootman 2007; Jacobs and Rollinger 2010; Lanfranchi and Rollinger 2010; Duindam et al. 2011; Erskine et al. 2013), in our quest for the Persian court we ultimately share with Walter Map a frustration with the difficulty of defining what precisely a 'court' is.

Map was irritated by the fact that his contemporaries could interchangeably refer to the 'court' as a location (palace, castle, hall), an institution (the 'office of court'), a group of people (the royal retinue or entourage), or even an event ('holding court'). The court could also be a 'place' where myths and legends were created on the stage of monarchy, as well as a 'place' which was legendary in its own right (like King Arthur's court at Camelot). Courtiers in successive times and places have tried in vain to articulate the institution that created and defined them, but none has done it with such sublime irony as Walter Map (see further, Vale 2001). Let his experience stand as an exemplar for our own investigation of the court of the Achaemenid Persians.

Part of the difficulty in understanding the construction, functioning, and ideology of the Achaemenid court lies with the source materials available for our study: Iranian and other Near Eastern iconographic materials, fragmentary bureaucratic texts, repetitive and formulaic royal inscriptions, and scattered archaeological remains provide only piecemeal evidence for court structure, while, as we will quickly learn, Greek and Hebrew literary texts are as fulsome in their vivid descriptions of the court as they are judgemental or fantastical. Accessing the Achaemenid court is fraught with difficulties. It is logical to turn, therefore, to comparative court studies of royal cultures with richer source materials for models of how to think about ancient courts, and particularly that of the Achaemenid rulers.

For instance, the renowned modern historian of Tudor England Geoffrey Elton once wrote that 'the only definition of the court which makes sense . . . is that it comprised all those who at any given time were within "his grace's house"' (Elton 1983: 38) – suggesting that, predominantly, the court was seen to be a social space comprised of all the individuals who circled around the king, regardless of social rank. Elton contends that these varied individuals, the socially diverse members of the royal retinue should, *en masse*, be classified as 'courtiers'; their presence within the extended 'family' of the royal household qualified them as such. Can Elton's model of an extended entourage work for the Achaemenid court too? Perhaps, although David Starkey (1987: 5) has rejected Elton's hypothesis by suggesting that the 'court' consisted of the nobility and elite of the kingdom alone; therefore, Starkey has argued, 'lesser' persons such as guards, grooms, stablehands, servants, cooks, and all other labouring household personnel should not be incorporated into the definition of 'court' at all. Their occupations denied them the privilege of being a courtier. But Starkey's is a short-sighted approach. Certain individuals with regular (and on the face of it) menial labour tasks were in fact members of what can be termed an 'inner court'; they were servants with close access to the king (and even to the king's actual body in the cases of wardrobe officials, grooms, barbers, and beauticians, or even doctors and chefs), and even though they might be ignobly born, these individuals had the potential to wield great power and influence. Elton's definition of a 'courtier' is therefore more persuasive than Starkey's: membership of the 'court' should include all individuals with ready access to the monarch in any form, and regardless of high or low birth (or indeed of sex). This is the appropriate way to think about the Persian court as well.

However, there are nuances to take into consideration. In Tudor England, when the court 'occurred' in one of the monarch's official residences, household ordinances and rules of ceremony regulated who could gain sight of the monarch. Within the royal residences, access to rooms and spaces was successively more restricted as one progressed through the palace. Tudor historians can therefore speak of an 'inner court' (meaning the rooms occupied by the king on an intimate basis and the people who worked within that space, as both ministers of state and intimate body servants; see further Knecht 2008) and of an 'outer court' (meaning the public areas of the residence, including large throne rooms and banqueting halls, and the people who served the public functions or who were within the king's orbit only temporarily). Thus, under the Tudors only peers of the realm and the monarch's closest servants were allowed to enter the Withdrawing Room – an intensely private place reserved for the monarch's intimate relaxation hours. However, the barriers which restricted access were constantly being assaulted by courtiers who sought more intimate physical closeness to the monarch, for access to the monarch not only meant the opportunity to importune a favour, but also implied to all onlookers that the privileged gainer of access had social eminence. Tom Bishop (1998: 89) has perceptively noted that 'the court often functioned like a series of locked rooms, with those on the outside always trying keys, and those on the inside constantly changing the locks'.

As we will see, the concept of an 'inner court' and an 'outer court' is applicable to the Achaemenid royal household too, and the Persian court can best be understood as operating around these two axes. The people who naturally orbited within the Great King's inner court were members of the royal harem, in other words those people who were under his immediate protection, including his mother, wives, concubines, children (including royal princes who could, upon their maturity, be sent into the provinces as satraps and commanders to set up their own courts-in-miniature), siblings, personal slaves, nobles from the highest-ranking families of the realm, and those granted the honorific title 'Friend' of the king (see Chapter 1). Bureaucrats and administrators, ambassadors, eunuchs, and physicians made up the outer court. The Achaemenid court, just like that of the Tudors, obviously attracted individuals who sought access to the monarch, but it functioned as more than a place simply to catch the monarch's eye, because the court was the social and cultural epicentre of the kingdom as well as a recruitment office and seat of bureaucracy for the administration.

We can, however, look for an interesting alternative definition of 'court' to that provided by Elton in a proposition of Rodríguez-Salgado, who regards the court as the residing place of sovereign *power* but not necessarily of the sovereign *per se*. In other words, even when the king was *in absentia* his monarchic authority nonetheless remained present among a group of people or in a fixed locale, so that it was 'the monarch's residual authority, not his presence, [which] was the prerequisite of a court' (Rodríquez-Salgado 1991: 207). This probably holds true for the Persian king and court. The importance of the Great King's court was reflected in the fact that throughout the Empire, satraps replicated its forms, structures, customs, and ceremonies as the most effective symbol of a centralised royal authority. For its part, the Great King's power could be expressed in proxy, so that his physical presence was not needed. Courtiers, dignitaries, ambassadors, and even royal women might have deputised for the king's authority as they travelled around the Empire with their own courtly entourages in the name of the king (see Chapter 4).

Of fundamental importance to the development of court studies has been Norbert Elias' *Die höfische Gesellschaft* (1969; only partially updated from his 1933 *Habilitationschrift*), published in an English translation of 1983 (with revisions in 2006) as *The Court Society*. More of a Weber-inspired sociologist than a historian, Elias articulated a model of court society which focused sharply upon a study of Bourbon French monarchy at the palace of Versailles, and employed as a core text for his study the rich and detailed memoirs of the Duc de Saint-Simon (1675–1755), who lived as part of, profited from, and was ultimately almost destroyed by, the French royal court. Elias suggested that Louis XIV constructed his court as an effective political tool in order to consolidate and augment an absolutist rule through which the French nobility could be tamed and domesticated; stripped of effective power and occupied instead with the minutiae of etiquette and courtly ceremonial, the elite of French society became obsessed with their positions in the orbit of the Sun King, forgetting that they were prisoners within a gilded cage. Elias suggested that his model for the nature and workings of the French court could be utilised in the study of other courts.

However, Elias' model has not passed without criticism: Jeroen Duindam (2003) in particular has questioned Elias' image of Versailles and has challenged the strength of his argument, criticising especially the absence of a serious political dimension in Elias' work. Nonetheless, Elias' *Court Society* laid out the ground-plan for further research and his work has provided a stimulus for historians of court societies of other times and places, as we shall see in later chapters of this book.

While these European ideologies of court society provide much valuable material for consideration in our study of the Persian court, we must speculate if early-modern western courts like those of the Tudors and Bourbons really are the most apropos models to follow in our current study. After all, the Christian courts of pre-industrial Europe never fully experienced the true weight of an absolute monarchy in the way that courts of the pre-modern Middle East and Far East experienced absolutism (like that of the Achaemenids). Perhaps better comparative models for the Achaemenid court can be found in the structures, institutions, practices, and ideologies of the non-Christian court civilisations of the east, such as the dynastic courts of Mughal India, Safavid Iran, and Qing China (all dating from the seventeenth to nineteenth centuries CE). The Christian European courts moulded themselves around the figure of a king who, while undeniably authoritative, nonetheless had his power tempered by clergy and politicians. European Christian monarchy was counter-balanced by political groups from among the social classes and castes of the realm, whereas the absolute tribute-gathering rulers of the east tended to govern with greater independent autocracy as kings fused their political rule with their integral religious identity, so that they were not answerable to a clergy or an independent parliament.

Moreover, a Christian monarch could, at most, be a serial monogamist – marrying one wife and replacing her with another only upon her death or divorce – so that the number of legitimate offspring born to a king was hampered by the childbearing capabilities of his queen. Bastards born to a Christian king's mistresses might swell the royal nurseries, but these children (privileged though they might be) could never shake off the social slur of illegitimacy and the moral probity of the Church. Consequently, the royal succession and royal authority were sharply curtailed by the laws of the Church, as only legitimate sons could inherit the throne.

In contrast, the unions of eastern monarchs with their numerous wives and concubines resulted in multiple offspring who were free of the social stigma of bastardy; the sons of concubines had the potential to become kings, but even if they did not reach the giddy heights of rulership they could nonetheless serve their royal fathers by performing duties in the government or the military. In fact, this lack of social stigma over legitimacy propagated and unified the ruling eastern dynasties in tight family bonds, the mammoth scale of which was never experienced by Christian monarchies. Reproductive capabilities went hand in hand with dynastic success (Scheidel 2009). Oddly, in their comprehension of the Achaemenid court the Greeks – obsessed with issues of legitimacy – never understood the value of polygamous unions for the functioning and longevity of a monarchic house (see Chapter 4).

There can be no doubt that the pioneering work of Norbert Elias and other historians of western monarchies will continue to provide influential ways to examine court societies of antiquity (Maria Brosius' 2007 significant study of the Persian court benefits from such an approach), but an even better understanding of the Achaemenid court can be achieved if historians look to eastern civilisations for comparative models. Asking questions of the eastern courts will expose more of the nature of Achaemenid court ideologies, ceremonials, and rituals, of royal hunts and feasts, of marriage practices, and gender roles. As this book progresses, we will have occasion to use early-modern eastern and western comparatives with Achaemenid practices.

But there is another aspect of the study of Achaemenid court which demands our attention: the question of cultural influence. As the Persian Empire expanded its territory in the Near East through wildly successful military campaigns, so the ruling dynasty came into contact with pre-existing court structures, which proved to be influential in the formatting of a definable Achaemenid court society. Ancient Egyptian, Neo-Assyrian, Babylonian, Urartian, Levantine, and Anatolian courts all provided the Achaemenids with blueprints for constructing a courtly identity and, as with art and architecture, the Persians readily took from these mature royal societies the elements which they found most appealing or meaningful and blended them to create something definably 'Achaemenid' (on Near Eastern courts see Spence 2007; Lanfranchi and Rollinger 2010; Barjamovic 2011). This is not to deny though that the Persians had their own developing court style before the conquests of Cyrus II and that this might have already existed when the Persians were still only a tribal federation in south-western Iran, in the 'kingdom' of Anšan. The sophisticated Neo-Elamite court based as Susa had an especial hold on Anšanite identity, and it is also feasible that a northern Assyrian-inspired courtly tradition based in Media infiltrated its way into the Persian heartland before Cyrus' take-over of Median territories.

Just as the Achaemenids drew inspiration from the older court societies of the Near East, so too the fully codified Persian court structure went on to influence successive empires. Following his overthrow of Darius III, Alexander of Macedon enthusiastically embraced important Achaemenid court rituals and structures and, in turn, some of these entered into the Hellenistic world through the practices of the Seleucid monarchs (Spawforth 2007a). Of course, there was a gulf of around 230 years between the reigns of the Persian kings Cyrus II and Darius III, and some 250 years separate the reign of Alexander III and the fall of the Seleucid kingdom; the political and cultural worlds of these monarchs might have changed considerably, and while they may have utilised the same palaces, we cannot say with any certainty that their courts remained unaltered over the centuries. Court reforms (in ceremony, personnel, and etiquette) are known to have occurred under King Artaxerxes I's watchful eye, and there may have been many deliberate (or haphazard) changes to the Persian court system over the centuries of the Achaemenid dynasty's existence, but nonetheless, in the essential elements of ritual and presentation, the *longue durée* of the Achaemenid court's influence could still be observed in many prominent Roman and Byzantine court practices (Maguire 2004; Paterson 2007; Smith 2007). Within Iran itself, Achaemenid influences on the rituals of royalty, aspects of the presentation of monarchy (including elements of palace architecture), and imperial ideology survived into the Sasanian period (third to seventh centuries CE), and in fact could still be felt in the Safavid, Qajar, and Pahlavi courts of the sixteenth to twentieth centuries CE (see, for example, Babaie 2008; Huff 2010). A schematic representation of the way in which the Persian court drew on, and then influenced, other ancient court societies can prove informative (Figure 1). In addition to utilising early-modern comparative evidence, this book will also acknowledge the influence of neighbouring Near Eastern court cultures on the Achaemenids.

The definition of the court in its Persian context can be encapsulated in several important and interrelated ways. As we will go on to explore, the court was a circle of elite people and attendants ('courtiers') in orbit around a monarch (see Chapter 1; Briant 2002: 302–54; Brosius 2007: 30–40, 53–6) as well as being a larger environment of political, military, economic, and cultural structures which converged within the monarch's household; the court was therefore the vibrant contact point between the Great King and the ruling classes (satraps and elites) at regional and local levels of the Empire (see Henkelman 2010a). The court was also an architecturally defined series of permanent and portable spaces: the private rooms, the bureaucratic quarters, and the public halls and courtyards of the royal residences, wherein the rituals of royalty were enacted and where the monarch received homage (Chapter 2), threw banquets, entertained, and relaxed (Chapter 5). In the case of the Achaemenids it is especially important to remember that the court was not a single place *per se* – the court moved (Chapter 3). The court was the setting of royal ceremonial and a place wherein

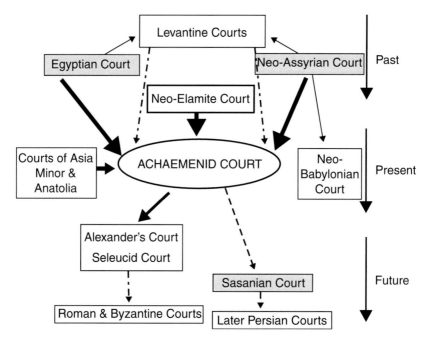

Figure 1 The development and legacy of the Achaemenid court.

a theatrical display of power was created and presented through audiences, feasting, and even hunting (Chapter 5).

Taken together, the people of the inner and outer courts constituted the royal *viθ*, an Old Persian word meaning 'house', 'household', and (by extension), 'court' and 'palace' (see Chapter 2 for further discussion). In Greek texts, individuals in the orbit of the Great King, his 'courtiers', were termed 'the people of the court' (*hoi peri ton aulōn*; literally 'those around the court') or *aulikoi* ('those of the court'), although the word *aulē* ('court') itself was rarely used by the Greeks as a synonym for 'palace' or 'residence' (the possessive noun *basileion* or *basileia* – roughly, 'the king's habitation' – was used instead; see for example Herodotus 1.30; alternatively, Ctesias F9 §13 used *ta oikēmata*, 'household'; see further comments in Brosius 2007: 25). The Romans usurped *aulē* (Latin, *aula* – 'courtyard', 'court') and thus its compound meaning enters into modern European languages (court, *cour*, *Hof*) with all the nebulous connotations found in the definition of the institution itself.

The royal court influenced many of the key areas of Achaemenid culture and society. It was the epicentre of politics, bureaucracy, and administration, the military, and perhaps even a religious centre, with rituals enacted around the person of the Great King (de Jong 2010); the court was also the intellectual, artistic, and cultural centre of the Empire, and artisans of all sorts flocked to court to receive patronage from the monarch. The court was without doubt the hub for the creation of imperial royal ideology and the dissemination point for all forms of official Achaemenid dogma. In ancient Persia the royal court mattered; without it there would have been no Empire.

CHAPTER 1

The Great King and His Men

Suddenly the Queen shot a look across at me.... For an instant we had eye contact and I thought with utter horror, 'Oh no! She's going to talk to me!' I wanted the ground to swallow me.... Why should one individual have this capacity to strike awe? I have interviewed presidents and prime ministers, murderers, and generals – even, once, a living god (the Dalai Lama...). What was it about this diminutive grandmother that induced paralysing tension? 'Majesty' is one of those words almost meaningless through its overuse. It is part of the explanation, perhaps. The uniqueness of a king or queen has something to do with it – there is only one of them. (Jeremy Paxman, *On Royalty*, 2006: 45)

Between 12 and 16 October 1971, Mohammad Reza Shah, the last Pahlavi monarch of Iran, held an international gathering of heads of state in the ruins of the Achaemenid palace city of Persepolis to celebrate what he regarded as the anniversary of 2,500 years of unbroken rule by the Persian monarchy. Criticised at the time (and by generations since) for its extravagant hubris, for the Shah the Persepolis celebrations confirmed his belief that he was ruling as the direct descendant of Cyrus the Great, the founder of the first Persian Empire.

However, in his commitment to the Persepolis celebrations, the Shah managed to ignore centuries of Islamic rule in Iran, provoking contempt from many Iranians and outpourings of scorn from Ayatollah Khomeini, the father of the 1979 revolution which overthrew the Shah and brought a swift and crushing end to the monarchy itself. 'Islam came in order to destroy these palaces of tyranny', the Ayatollah insisted as he contemplated the ruins of Persepolis from his exile in Iraq: 'It is the kings of Iran who have constantly ordered massacres of their own people and had pyramids built with their skulls' (see Milani 2011 for Khomeini's reaction to the Shah's anniversary celebrations).

The Iranian monarchy continues to have a hold on the public consciousness within the Islamic Republic of Iran, and whether the past kings of Iran are deplored or ridiculed, exalted or revered, there is no denying that the depth of history embodied in the institution of the Iranian monarchy is still overwhelming. Mohammad Reza Shah believed in the ancient Iranian concept of a demi-mythical force wherein God bestowed upon the kings of Iran a mystical light (*farr-ī īzadī*) that legitimised their rule. This notion of *farr* persisted in Iran for thousands of years and some might argue that it continues to influence Iranian concepts of leadership in the modern Islamic Republic. Even without a monarchy, it would seem that monarchic ideology still structures, moulds, and underpins contemporary Iranian society. This chapter explores the deep-set fundaments of that ideology and examines the Achaemenid origins of Iranian governance.

The king is dead! Long live the king!

When, in the centuries immediately before Alexander's conquest of Iran, a Great King of Persia died, his body was mourned, prepared for burial, and finally interred in a rock-cut tomb. Then the ceremonies of a royal investiture could begin and a new monarch could take his place upon the throne and begin the process of governing his gigantic Empire. Greek authors knew something of the cultic rituals that surrounded this important ceremony, but many of its details were lost to them, and therefore to us too (**A1**). It is clear from the writings of Plutarch (probably following Ctesias' observations) that some kind of accession ceremony was enacted at Parsagade, the traditional tribal homeland of the Persian monarchy and the site of the palace built by Cyrus the Great and subsequently embellished by Darius I (and probably later kings also). It was here that Cyrus himself was buried in an impressive free-standing chamber tomb placed high on a step platform, and it was here within the tomb that the accoutrements of Cyrus' kingship were stored (Arrian 29.1–11). It was a fitting locale at which to celebrate the unbroken lineage and continuity of the Persian monarchy.

At the shrine of the warrior goddess Anahita, and in the presence of a few select courtiers and priests (Magi), certain rituals were enacted which conferred the legitimacy and sanctity of kingship upon the monarch. At the royal investiture, the new Persian king adopted an official throne name and stopped using the familial name by which he had previously been known (before his accession, for example, Darius II was called Ochus, and Artaxerxes II had been called Arses or Arsaces; Ctesias F15 §47, 55). While we cannot be sure that every Achaemenid monarch used this policy, the concept of a throne name would help explain the preponderance of a particularly strong onomastic tradition throughout the dynasty's history, where certain names appear with regularity: Darius (Old Persian, Dārayavauš – 'holding firm the good'), Xerxes (Old Persian, Xšayāršā – 'ruling over heroes'), and Artaxerxes (Old Persian, Artaxšaçā – 'whose reign is through truth'). With their rich symbolic meanings, these were the Achaemenid dynastic names *par excellence*, although, interestingly, the name Cyrus (Old Persian, Kuruš – 'humiliator of the enemy'[?]) was sparingly used in the latter part of the dynasty's history (see further Schmitt 1977a, 1977b).

In addition to adopting a new name, at the investiture, in the presence of the Magi, and through their agency, a prince was transformed from heir designate to Great King and symbolically took on a new 'body'. Since the dynasty lacked any basic laws of primogeniture, succession struggles and other forms of harem politics played a role in determining who the heir to the Achaemenid throne might be (see below), so it was the investiture ceremony rather than physical birth – or even the death of the previous king – that marked the moment when the king became a different, more august, person. Accordingly, during the ritual he was 'given' a different anatomy and underwent a classic rite of passage of 'exclusion–inclusion' which was expressed through his undressing, his donning of symbolic garments, his eating of specific foods, and his imbibing of ritual liquor (terebinth, milk, *homa*), another undressing, followed by his dressing in new garments to symbolise an altered state of being. The drinking of the sour milk and the acts of ingesting humble foods and hallucinogenics confirmed the initiate's liminal status (Sancisi-Weerdenburg 1995; McGovern 2009: 110–20), as did the new king's dressing in the pre-monarchic (peasant?) clothing of Cyrus the Great. Humility and humbleness were stressed in the ritual as the monarch was reminded of his tribal nomadic ancestry, and only afterwards, when the king donned a robe of state, were his new monarchic brilliance, strength, and vitality confirmed (Binder 2008: 111–22; Binder 2010). It is little wonder that the Greeks read the initiation ceremony as a significant *teletē* or 'mystery rite' in which the ruler underwent a true metamorphosis of being.

If at the completion of the *teletē* the king was publicly acknowledged as undisputed sovereign by the courtiers who assembled at Parsagade, then we have no record of it. It is unlikely though that some kind of prayer was not performed in honour of the occasion, comparable perhaps to the hymns intoned by priests and nobles at Neo-Assyrian investiture ceremonies which lauded the kingly virtues and where the blessing of the gods was invoked (**A2**).

It should be noted, however, that the Persian investiture ceremony cannot be classified as a 'coronation' as such, given that crowns or a ceremony of crowning do not seem to be a focus of the ritual in any way, even though there can be no doubt that Achaemenid monarchs wore ceremonial crowns (see Chapter 2); nor, incidentally, can the ceremony be called an 'enthronement', since no throne is mentioned *per se*, although the royal throne was certainly an icon of majesty too (see Chapter 2). Emblems of sovereignty can generally be divided into two categories: those handed over to the sovereign during the accession ceremony which are subsequently worn or used by the monarch on other important occasions; and those which are emblems of sovereignty, with the purpose of augmenting and enhancing the image of monarchy. Clearly, Cyrus' robe falls into this latter category, although it was the royal clothing of the first category that the new king subsequently donned, which thereupon became imbued with particular symbolic significance and was infused with the spiritual essence of the Persian kingship (see Chapter 2). Crowns had little direct symbolic value for the Achaemenids. How can we explain that? It is possible that the Great King's head was considered sacrosanct (see Chapter 2) and that for anyone of lesser status to touch it was highly inappropriate; it might have been inappropriate for a hand or even a shadow of a subject to appear above the ruler's head, which might help explain the emblematic use of parasols, which in official palace art are repeatedly held over the king's head (**F1**). In such a situation, rulers may have crowned themselves after being formally presented with a crown by a high-ranking courtier, and when in October 1967 Mohammad Reza Shah Pahlavi held an ostentatious coronation ceremony in Tehran (**F2**), he crowned himself with his own hands following what he declared to be an ancient Persian precedent (Milani 2011: 322; Mackey 1996: 231–2), although this was not known to be an Achaemenid ritual.

A prince among men: gaining the throne

What qualified a man to be king? What role did lineage play in the royal succession? Persian kingship was hereditary and the right to rule was kept strictly within the Achaemenid family and thereby a king's possession of the blood-royal was the very basis of the monarchy; this is why the Old Persian title *Haxāmanišiya*, 'an Achaemenid', is reiterated time and again in the official texts of successive kings.

While there is little doubt that the birth of a king's first son was a cause for court celebration and that this prince continued to hold a position of prestige throughout his life (Plato, *Alcibiades* 121c; Athenaeus 12.515a), it does not mean to say that he was automatically destined to follow his father to the throne. Primogeniture did not operate at the Persian court (after all, the king was not subject to any constitutional law), and in this the Achaemenids followed a practice witnessed in the courts of Egypt, Assyria, and Israel, where on several occasions we learn that kings chose younger (more favoured or more able) sons to succeed them. For instance, David of Israel was succeeded by Solomon, his youngest (known) son (1 Kings 1) and Sennacherib selected his youngest son Esarhaddon for the kingship (Kwasman and Parpola 1991: xxix–xxxiv). Both of these succession decisions triggered fierce rebellions at court (which reveals that there was perhaps an *expectation* that the first-born or elder son would succeed his father). Sennacherib's choice of heir resulted in his assassination (see further Chapter 5), prompting Esarhaddon, when his time came to appoint a successor, to take steps to secure a smooth succession for his chosen relative, his grandson Ashurbanipal, who ascended the throne backed by powerful nobles who had been forced to swear an oath of loyalty to him (**A3**).

Some Persian monarchs named their heirs in a more timely fashion (as Darius II did with prince Arsaces, the future Artaxerxes II), but others did not. When Xerxes left for his military expedition against the Greeks, he had not designated an heir and consequently his uncle Artabanus was left in charge of the court (but was not appointed regent); this begs the question, what would have happened had Xerxes died on campaign? Pierre Briant (2002: 567) provides a frank answer: 'Dynastic wars, already frequent during anticipated successions, would have raged'.

To avoid this chaos a king appointed his successor while he was still strong enough to defend his decision and provide the heir-designate with the support and instruction he needed. We know for instance that upon his appointment to office, the Assyrian crown prince moved into the so-called 'succession palace' (a distinct physical space separated from the main royal residence) and began his grooming for power. He acquired a harem and a wife (or wives – the 'ladies of the house'; see Svärd and Luukko 2009) and proceeded to take on royal duties both at the seat of government and in active military service in the provinces (Montero Fenollòs 2006). A similar situation might have existed for the Achaemenid crown prince, since we know that he could acquire his own household of wives, ministers, and servants (although there is no direct evidence for a Persian 'succession house'), and was provided with appropriate robes, a crown, and a chariot and horses (which are depicted on the walls of Persepolis; see generally Sánchez 2006) befitting his exalted status. He also received expert tuition in government from the Magi and other royal tutors (although he shared this privileged education with his bothers and the sons of courtiers – **A4**; see further Xenophon, *Anabasis* 1.9.2) and Briant (2002: 522) makes the important observation that, given the high infant mortality rate, it would be unwise of a king not to educate all of his sons to a high standard – any one of them had the potential to become king.

It is possible that the crown prince was known by a specific title, **visa-puthra* ('son of the clan'), which set him above the other 'princes of the (royal) house' (Aramaic, *br-byt'*), although in a text recalling his succession to the throne (XPf §4–5) Xerxes allies himself to his father's memory and designates himself *maθišta* (literally, 'the greatest [after him]'):

> Darius had other sons, but – thus was Ahuramazda's desire – my father Darius made me the greatest [*maθišta*] after him. When my father Darius went away from the throne, by the grace of Ahuramazda I became king on my father's throne.

In the visual programme of Persepolis, the crown prince is sometimes represented at the side of the Great King wearing similar garments, crowns, and hairstyles to his father (**F3**); there is also is a tiny but exquisite lapis lazuli head of a beardless, crowned youth (**F4**), perhaps (but by no means certainly) representing a young crown prince.

Xerxes' statement that he was made the 'greatest' of Darius' sons is full of confidence and bravado, but is perhaps more hyperbole than reality, at least if we choose to follow the story of Darius' succession as told by Herodotus (**A5**), who reports a 'violent struggle' which erupted between Darius' many sons. Xerxes emerges victorious because he pulls rank over his brothers, the sons born to Darius while he was still a private man, but also because, as Herodotus insists, his mother, Atossa, Cyrus' eldest daughter, 'had all the power'. Female intervention in the politics of succession is not at all infeasible (see Chapter 4), although Herodotus' foregrounding of Atossa's power and influence does not sit well with the scant mentions of her in authentic Persian sources. Only two texts from Persepolis refer to 'Udusana' – Atossa – and they can be dated to 500/499 BCE, but there is no mention of her beyond that date; the evidence from the tablets suggests that 'she did not rise to real prominence before 493 BC (the end of the archive) and probably not until after the accession of Xerxes' (Henkelman 2010b: 33). Perhaps

Herodotus was developing a trend in Greek literature which traditionally depicted Xerxes' mother as influential and calmly authoritative
(consider Aeschylus' portrayal of Atossa – called simply 'the queen'
– in his tragedy *Persians* of 472 BCE; see Sancisi-Weerdenburg 1983,
although perhaps she overestimates the idea of the Greek 'construction'
of Persian women; see further Chapter 5).

Moreover, enticing (if somewhat tentative) evidence has recently
emerged from the Persepolis Fortification archive (PF-NN1657; **A6**)
which opens up the possibility of a new reading for a co-regency
between Darius and Xerxes. It is the earliest known document of
Xerxes and can be dated to May/June 498 BCE. It suggests that he was
serving as a military commander in Parthia a full twelve years before
his mention in Herodotus as Darius' heir. While PF-NN1657 does not
categorically state that he was a joint ruler, the document shows Xerxes
taking full responsibility for the chain of command in Parthia, and, as
Henkelman notes:

> Since the Parthian men were travelling from the king to Parthia, and were
> carrying a sealed authorisation from the king, they may have been initially
> dispatched by Xerxes to report to his father. Having done so, they were
> now heading back with the king's response. The context makes the scribe's
> silence on Xerxes' title (or the fact that he was Darius' son) eloquent: his
> position was apparently well-known. (Henkelman 2010b: 31)

Text PF-NN1657 perhaps confirms Calmeyer's once controversial
thesis that Xerxes was 'king and co-regent' for twelve years before
Darius' death and that his reign began in 498 BCE (Calmeyer 1976: 83).

Borchhardt (1976: 121–3) has also argued for a co-regency between
Artaxerxes II and his son Artaxerxes III, who, as a young joint
monarch, decisively put down the satraps' revolt, but this interpretation is dubious (Briant 2002: 996), as is the question of a co-regency
between Cyrus II and Cambyses II. Although Cambyses was awarded
the title 'King of Babylon' following his father's conquest of the city,
we should not regard this as evidence of a co-regency between the king
and his eldest (known) son (the Babylonian title was, however, Cyrus'
recognition of Cambyses as his heir). The late epitomist Justin also
comments on Persian co-regencies (**A7**) and he insists that Artaxerxes
II took great delight in appointing his son Darius (who was already
fifty years old) as his co-ruler, although he also suggests that this was
an unusual situation: 'Artaxerxes broke with Persian custom, amongst
whom there is a change of king only at death'. Before his sole accession to the throne, however, Darius plotted against his father and was

sentenced to death and executed, allowing Ochus eventually to ascend to imperial power as Artaxerxes III (Plutarch, *Artaxerxes* 27.5–28.5, 29.1, 29.8–10; cf. Justin 10.2.5; the chronology of the events is not precise but they might be dated to 362 or 361 BCE; see further Chapter 5 and **E26** and **E27**).

Briant (2002: 522) suggests that the sacred office of kingship could not accommodate the notion of co-regency and that 'the official recognition of a crown prince in no way signified a sharing of power: the king was One'. Indeed, it is important to realise that, in spite of his status at court, a crown prince could fall victim to royal disfavour, as Prince Darius learned when his father, Artaxerxes II, accused him of treason. The evidence for co-regency is scant and contradictory, and the question of whether the Achaemenid monarchs ever employed the co-regency system must remain open.

The Great King and his gods

Three key features identified kingship in the ancient Near East. First and foremost was the fact that monarchy belonged to heaven and that earthly kingship was vested in the gods so that the men who ruled on earth did so as mediators and intercessors of a divine agency. Second, but as an extension of this god-given status, kings had a judicial responsibility to guard and protect their subjects from war, want, and terror. Third, kingship was sacred, and ceremonies like the royal investiture often involved a ritual of humiliation followed by reinstatement, as an expression of the regeneration of cosmic order encoded within the monarch's being. As Henri Frankfort (1944: 3, 12) summarised:

> The ancient Near East considered kingship the very basis of civilization. Only savages could live without a king. Security, peace, and justice could not prevail without a ruler to champion them. Whatever was significant was embedded in the life of the cosmos, and it was precisely the king's function to maintain the harmony of that integration. . . . For the truth about their king affected their lives in every (even the most personal) aspect, since through the king the harmony between human existence and the supernatural order was maintained.

There was no doubt in the Near Eastern mind that the universe was divinely ordered and that kings and their appointed courtiers were the mundane earthly reflections of a heavenly hierarchical ideal. On earth the reality was that kings were confronted by all sorts of political upheavals, ranging from succession challenges to international rebellions, but the ideological picture of kingship created and promoted by king and court was one of cosmic harmony maintained only through the centralised position of the throne. Rituals of monarchy and the royal ideologies from which they emerged were designed to articulate the complex interconnection between the cosmological and earthly aspects of rulership.

Hugo Gressmann's influential 1929 work on the concept of ancient sacred kingship has suggested that in the religious and political thought of the Near East the royal body was generally perceived to have taken on a new form of semi-divine being at the investiture, so much so in fact that Gressmann argued that this transformation of the royal body was part of a region-wide *Hofstil* ('court style'). If this is correct, then it is logical to see the ancient Persian investiture ritual examined above as part of the same Near Eastern theological system. Certainly, in Achaemenid iconography the Great King shares his appearance with that of the supreme Iranian deity, Ahuramazda, echoing a *Hofstil* which was already identifiable in a proverb of the Neo-Assyrian period: 'Man is a shadow of God [but] the King is the perfect likeness of God' (Parpola 1970: 112–13, no. 145).

Created under imperial auspices for predominantly Persian spectators at the heart of the Empire, the monumental Bisitun relief (**F5**; dated to just before 519 BCE) is a vivid depiction (although not necessarily a 'portrait' as we might use the term) of Darius the Great. The high relief compresses into one tableau the essence of the dramatic events of Darius' accession to power, as described in the accompanying trilingual inscription. Darius, attended by two courtly Persian weapon-bearers, treads upon the prostrate Gaumata as nine rebel leaders, securely bound in fetters, approach the king. They wear elements of regional dress and are identified by name. Darius, bow in one hand, lifts his other hand in a gesture of salutation to Ahuramazda, who hovers over the scene and offers a ring (perhaps representing the kingship itself) to Darius. (On the Bisitun monument see Briant 2002: 122–7; Kuhrt 2007: 141–58; of course, there is no consensus that the anthropomorphic figure emerging from the winged disk *is* Ahuramazda; for debates see Briant 2002: 248.)

It is clear from Achaemenid royal iconography that just as the king and the god share close intimacy of space (**F3** and **F5**), so they share a physical form. The Great King encodes in his appearance the best physical attributes of the anthropomorphic divinity, Ahuramazda; the Great King is the deity's doppelganger. They adopt the same hairstyle and beard shape, the same crown, the same type of garment, and they 'emit' the same *xvarnah* or 'brilliance' (in terms of luminosity or glory; Battesti 2011). The iconography stresses that reciprocity between king and god is guaranteed, and thus, in an inscription from Susa, Darius can state with confidence that 'Ahuramazda is mine; I am Ahuramazda's' (DSk). Even if Persian kings were not gods, they could be understood only in their intimate relationships with the divine (Lincoln 2012).

We have already seen that Xerxes attributed his success in the succession struggle which followed the death of Darius I to the divine favour and celestial support of Ahuramazda: 'by the grace of Ahuramazda I became king on my father's throne' (XPf §4–5). But who exactly was Xerxes' helpful deity?

The earliest reference to Ahuramazda ('the Wise Lord') is actually found in an eighth-century BCE Assyrian text, in which *as-sa-ra ma-za-aš* is named as one god in a list of many gods. It is clear that Ahuramazda was one of the Elamite pantheon, although it is difficult to know for sure if he was Cyrus the Great's god. Nevertheless, there are numerous references to this deity in the Achaemenid royal inscriptions, and especially those of Darius the Great, who lauded the god as creator: 'A great god is Ahuramazda, who created this earth, who created yonder sky, who created man, who created happiness for man' (DNb §1–3). In other words Darius envisaged the Wise Lord as a creator only of what is good, and he expresses over and over again his faith in Ahuramazda and his belief that he serves the god as a divine instrument for establishing order and justice on earth: 'When Ahuramazda saw this earth turbulent, then he bestowed it on me. . . . By the will of Ahuramazda I set it again in its place' (DNa §31–6); and 'After Ahuramazda made me king in this earth, by the will of Ahuramazda all (that) I did was good' (DSi §2–4). Commenting on the close affinity between the king and his god encoded in the royal texts of Near Eastern antiquity, Leo Oppenheim (1964: 149) observed:

> One gains the impression that these inscriptions were written for the king himself. The scribes and poets at court created for him his own image as hero and pious king; they show him in the texts as he wanted to see himself.

It is little wonder that the Greeks mistook the Great King's intimate relationship with Ahuramazda to mean that the king himself was divine, and a text by Plutarch attempts to articulate what was perceived to be a *bona fide* Persian point of view (**A8**). The Great King held, by virtue of his office, a mystical position and he was, if less than a god, still more than a man. Therefore in his tragedy *Persians*, Aeschylus calls the dead Darius *isotheos* ('equal to the gods'), *theion* ('divine'), and *akakos* ('knowing no wrong'), and while the Athenian playwright must not be taken literally on these points, he was capable, nonetheless, of thinking of the kings of the Achaemenid dynasty in this way (Aeschylus, *Persians* 651, 654–5, 671, 711, 857; see further Garvie 2009: 73–80; on later Classical Greek conceptions of the Great King see Llewellyn-Jones 2012). Indeed, some Greeks described the Great King as having a divine *daimon*, or spirit. Plutarch (*Artaxerxes* 15.5), dependent for much of his information upon Ctesias and Deinon, says that courtiers revered the *daimon* of the king, while Theopompus (*Histories* F17 = Athenaeus 6.252B) went so far as to say that the Persians piled tables high with food for the pleasure of the king's *daimon*. This Greek belief in the king's *daimon* is a reasonable interpretation of the Persian belief in the *fravashi*, or 'soul' of the monarch. Moreover, Herodotus (1.131–2) says that the Persians were duty-bound to pray for the king and his sons during their private acts of worship, which demonstrates that the Greeks understood the Persian 'intertwining of god(s), king, and Empire' (Kuhrt 2007: 473).

It is clear that Ahuramazda was conceived of as the king's god *par excellence* and the intimate relationship between the two is reiterated repeatedly; the king was expected, under the auspices of the Magi, to pray and carry out rituals in Ahuramazda's honour, or to tend to the god's sacred fire (Briant 2002: 246–50). In the early Achaemenid royal inscriptions Ahuramazda alone is named, although occasionally he is mentioned alongside 'all the gods' or as the 'greatest of the gods' (DPh §2; DPg §1). On one of the Elamite tablets from Persepolis dating to Darius I's reign, he appears with 'Mithra-[and]-the Baga' (that is, 'gods'; PF 337) and towards the end of the Achaemenid period, under Artaxerxes III, the same occurs (A[3]Pa §24–5). The Persepolis texts amply testify to the presence of 'the other gods who are' and show how the royal administration supplied cultic necessities for the worship of numerous Iranian, Elamite, and Babylonian deities (Henkelman 2008, 2012). In addition to Ahuramazda, the Persepolis texts name other gods worthy of ritual offerings, including Zurvan (a weather god), Mizduši (a fertility goddess), Narvasanga (a fire deity), Hvarita (Spirit of the Rising Sun), and Visai Baga (a collective entity of deities).

It was Artaxerxes II who conspicuously invoked a new triad in the official inscriptions of his reign – 'Ahuramazda, Anahita and Mithra' (A[2]Sd 3–4) – and these latter two gods proved to be popular in the Sasanian period alongside the ever-present Ahuramazda. Artaxerxes' texts suggest that they stood close to Ahuramazda in the monarch's esteem, probably for good reason: Mithra was a sun god and a deity closely associated with horses (see Chapter 3), while Anahita was an important water goddess as well as a warrior and fertility deity, likened by the Greeks to Athene, Artemis, and Aphrodite (Briant 2002: 250–4; on Persian religion and Iranian traditions see Briant 2002: 93–4).

Titles and qualities of kingship

When in the Bisitun inscription, Darius states that 'I (am) . . . the Great King, King of Kings, King in Fars, King of the Countries, Hystaspes' son, Arsames' grandson, an Achaemenid' (DB I §1–3), he utilises the full panoply of titles available to any Persian king (Old Persian, *xšayaθiya*, hence Middle/New Persian, *šāh* – 'king'). The monarch's three pre-eminent titles, found time and again in official rhetoric, were:

- 'King of Kings' (Old Persian, *xšayaθiya*, *xšayaθiyanam*; Akkadian, *šar*, *šarrani*), which was derived from Urartian usage although originally of Mesopotamian origin and was used by the Achaemenids to claim their legitimacy as the heirs of the Babylonian, Assyrian, Urartian, and Median kings.
- 'Great King' (Old Persian, *Xšayaθiya vazraka*; Akkadian, *šar rabû*), a title first encountered in Mesopotamia but readily used by the Persians.
- 'King of the Countries' (Old Persian, *Xšāyaθiya dahyūnām*) or its variations: 'King of the Countries Containing All Races' (Old Persian, *Xšāyaθiya dahyūnām vispazanānām*) and 'King of the Countries Containing Many Races' (Old Persian, *Xšāyaθiya dahyūnām paruzanānām*) (see further Chapter 3).

To these can be added another title, less commonly used but nonetheless instructive:

- 'King on this (Great) Earth (Even Far Off)' (Old Persian, *Xšāyaθiya ahyāyā būmiyā (vazrkāyā) (dūraiy apiy))*, suggesting a development in the Achaemenid conception of their own territorial expansions.

Unsurprisingly, in foreign territories under their control, Great Kings adopted and adapted indigenous titles for their own use; thus in Babylon Cyrus II claimed for himself the grandiose Babylonian title 'King of the Universe, the Mighty King, King of Babylon, King of

Sumer and Akkad, King of the Four Quarters of the World' (CB §20; see Kuhrt 2007: 71), while Darius I portrayed himself as the legitimate pharaoh of Egypt by adopting a series of important and ancient hieroglyphic titles, including 'King of Upper and Lower Egypt', 'Lord of the Two Lands', 'Supreme Ruler of the World', 'Son of Amun', and 'Living Image of Rē' (DS a, b; Kuhrt 2007: 477–9).

The topic of the ideology of ancient Persian kingship (Old Persian, *xšaca*) has attracted much attention and clear developments in the ways in which scholars have conceptualised the fundamental nature of Achaemenid royal ideology can be identified. Geo Widengren, a prominent comparative historian, strongly argued that Achaemenid kingship was essentially an Indo-European construction and that a title such as 'King of Kings' was an expression in a Persian belief that the monarch was *primus inter pares*, or a king who ruled over other sovereigns, which was regarded as a fundamental Indo-Iranian trait (Widengren 1959, 1965, 1968). His work was challenged by Gherardo Gnoli and his Italian school of thought, which argued for a Mesopotamian root to Iranian kingship, suggesting, for instance, that a New Year festival at Persepolis derived from the Babylonian *akitu* festival and that Persian gods should be regarded as natural extensions of Babylonian deities: Ahuramazda was thus an aspect of Marduk of Bablyon, Anahita was Ishtar, and Mithra was the Persian incarnation of Shamash. Moreover, the support given to the Great Kings by a supreme god was interpreted by Gnoli to have come directly from Assyrian and Babylonian ideologies, which had nothing to do with an Indo-European background (Gnoli 1974a, 1974b).

Scholars now have little doubt that Mesopotamian ideologies of kingship did help to inspire certain Achaemenid traditions, but into the mix we must place other influential components: first, an indigenous Iranian element (see below); second, a pharaonic Egyptian ideology that had an increasing hold on the Persians following Cambyses' conquest of the country in 525 BCE (Root 1979); and finally, and most importantly, some Neo-Elamite elements. The last had entered early into the developing Achaemenid ideological thought processes and scholars are increasingly recognising Elamite cultural and theological ideologies as a key to understanding early Persian conceptions of monarchy (see especially Potts 2010).

As kings of Anšan, the early Persian rulers of south-western Iran were easily pulled into the culturally dominant orbit of the sophisticated Elamites and scholars are becoming increasingly aware of a geopolitical interdependency which emerged between Elam and southern

Iran in the centuries immediately before the growth of Persian power in the Near East (Álvarez-Mon and Garrison 2011). The very name 'Kuruš' (Latinised, 'Cyrus') is probably Elamite and, as Daniel Potts (2011: 47) has recently posited, 'if this is the case, then . . . [it] would suggest that the empire created by Cyrus was an Elamite one that only became "Persian" or "Achaemenid" with the accession of Darius'. Even then there is a likelihood that Darius' own ancestry, at least on his mother's side, was Elamite too (Chapter 4), and that Darius seems to have readily embraced his Elamite past. His vast relief sculpture at Bisitun for instance is closely modelled on the so-called Sar-i Pol relief of the Elamite king Anubanini, at nearby Luristan (**F6**), which depicts the victory and inauguration of the Elamite warlord, who, like Darius, stands on one of his captives in his role as a military hero while the goddess Ishtar, proffering the ring of kingship, leads naked and bound prisoners before the victorious sovereign (Potts 1999: 319).

Xerxes followed in his father's footsteps and continued to employ Elamite ideologies in his royal policy; in the Elamite version of his so-called Daivā inscription (XPhe §29–32) he claims to rule through the power of his '*ki-te-in*', a magico-religious term meaning 'divine aid' or 'divinely bestowed royal power' – a supremely Elamite concept which had long been central to their theology and royal ideology but was straightforwardly used by Xerxes. The presence of *ki-te-in* in such an important Achaemenid religious text as the Daivā inscription suggests that even the conception of Ahuramazda, the supreme Persian royal god, was modelled on an Elamite theological idea (Henkelman 2011b: 97).

There can be little doubt that the Elamites form the 'missing link' in the chain of Persian royal ideological development and the Persians have now been revealed as the true heirs of the Elamites, and not of the Medes as has long been supposed (Henkelman 2011b: 91). But nonetheless, this must not overshadow the fact that the Persians had their own distinct identity. In the royal texts Persian uniqueness is repeatedly emphasised and the Great King is shown to be a Persian, the descendant of generations of Persians, ruling over Persians and the conquered lands beyond Persia. For its part, Persia is shown to be 'good, containing good horses and good men' (DPd §2) and under the especial care and attention of the king: 'If the Persian people is protected, for a long time unending happiness will rest upon this [royal] house' (DPe §3).

And what exactly were the Persian people to be protected from? As was common to all ancient societies, the threat of famine, pestilence, or enemy attack was ever present and the Great King, in his role as heaven's viceroy on earth, was obliged to repel them (DB I §14; for a detailed discussion of this theme see Lincoln 2007) . Therefore Near Eastern royal imagery frequently cast the king in the role of the shepherd of his people: the Israelite King David was a shepherd ruler *par excellence*, a man whom Yahweh 'took ... from the sheepfolds ... to be shepherd of ... his people' (Psalm 78:70) and the Hebrew conception of Cyrus the Great depicted the Achaemenid monarch in the same light (Isaiah 44:28). The shepherd image was also effectively used of Sargon II of Assyria:

> May the king, my lord, the good shepherd ... truly tend and shepherd them [his people]. May Ashur, Bel, and Nabu add flocks to your flocks, give them to you, and enlarge your spacious fold; may the people of all countries come into your presence! (Tomes 2005: 79)

Rooted deep in the sheep–shepherd relationship, the image of the shepherd king stresses his care and compassion for his people and, simultaneously, the dependence of the people on the ruler to meet their needs. In addition, the metaphor of people as sheep emphasises their passivity – an ideal state of being in ancient royal ideology, because it was wilfulness and disobedience that kings most feared.

The king was also the judge of his people, serving as an agent of both civil and divine order, and by the fact of his very 'being' he was a natural law-giver and law-upholder: 'when a king sits on a throne to judge, he winnows out all evil with his eyes' (Proverbs 20:8). A responsive and able ruler received his wisdom and his ability to judge his people and ensure the rule of justice and law directly from the gods, who dispensed mercy, justice, faithfulness, and righteousness through the person of the king. In the Hebrew Bible this concept is expressed through prayers addressed to Yahweh by his worshippers:

> Give the king your justice, oh God,
> and your righteousness to the royal son!
> May he judge the people with righteousness,
> and the poor with justice!
> Let the mountains bear prosperity for the people,
> and the hills, in righteousness!
> May he defend the cause of the poor of the people,
> give deliverance to the children of the needy,
> and crush the oppressor!
> (Psalm 72:1–4)

The Assyrian god Shamash was viewed as a 'lofty decider ... [the] judge of all ... who makes decisions for men in their settlements. ... Judge incorruptible, governor of mankind', and consequently when the god intervened in earthly affairs he routed out evil-doing: 'the wicked and violent man you admonish, [you] pronounce their condemnation' (Cumming 1934: 151). Corruption and resistance to moral judgement therefore had no place in good kingship, since they contravened divine purpose and godly example. This important theme is stressed in a Babylonian text from the eighth century BCE which admonishes an earlier monarch (probably Merodach Baladin) for his abuse of royal privileges and the misdeeds he committed to the peoples of Sippar, Nimrud, and Babylon. Composed as an omen of warning, the text (**A9**) lists the monarch's misdemeanours and warns all future kings of the consequences of acting in an ungodly manner.

It was the Persian king's duty, under the auspices of Ahuramazda, to maintain the status quo, to act as shepherd and judge, and to bring order out of potential chaos. It was his obligation to uphold the truth (Old Persian, *arta*) and to dispel the lie (Old Persian, *drauga*); in the Persian mind the concept of *drauga* was best represented by the chaos of rebellion and insurgence against the throne (or, in purely visual terms, a lion or hybrid monster may represent the essence of chaos, which the king slaughters in his guise of Persian hero; **F7**). In an Old Persian inscription on the façade of his tomb at Naqš-i Rustam, Darius I confirms that his Empire was won by military prowess: 'the spear of a Persian man has gone far; then shall it become known to you: a Persian man has delivered battle far indeed from Persia' (DNa §4). This is the logical conclusion to the first official pronouncement of Darius' reign contained on the Bisitun monument in which his initial fight for Empire is inscribed (DB; Kuhrt 2007: 141–59). His tomb contains another interesting statement which focuses on the strength of the king's body and his ability as a warrior king and is, incidentally, the most verbose surviving Achaemenid text (**A10**). Darius depicts himself as rational and considered monarch (he never acts in haste or in panic) and it is his sheer force of personality that guarantees his Persian subjects will receive the benefit of his considered and learned judgements. Being a judge of the people was a quality expected of a Near Eastern ruler and Darius expertly portrays himself in that role in his tomb inscription, as Amélie Kuhrt (2001: 109) describes:

> Ahuramazda has equipped the ruler with insight and ability to distinguish right from wrong, making him the guarantor of justice and maintainer of

social order. Because he does not react unthinkingly and is able to control his temper, the king metes out reward and punishment absolutely fairly, and only after due consideration of a case. He judges services rendered according to the potential of the individual, and is ready to reward loyalty.

But while ethical and moral qualities are central to the ideology of the tomb inscription, brute force is stressed there as well. Darius is strong enough to endure the hardships of campaigning on horseback and on the march, and his arms have strength to draw the bow and wield the lance, and these skills, he emphasises, come *directly* from Ahuramazda. Near Eastern texts frequently suggest there was a special connection between the king's weapons and the deity, for, after all, it was the god who made powerful the royal weapons and imbued the royal body with strength enough to wield them, and, at Darius' insistence, in his inscription Ahuramazda is portrayed as the god who empowers the king with martial valour.

The Iranian deity is therefore as much a warrior god as he is a god who upholds (and loves) truth, peace, and justice. Civic order and equilibrium are achieved through the dual forces of divine law and brute force. Might we therefore think of all Achaemenid military activity (wars of territorial expansion, conquest and reconquest, suppression of rebellions) as a type of holy war? This clearly had its *Sitz im Leben* in the Near East as a whole (Jones 1989; von Rad 1991) and it is possible to read Ahuramazda as the type of warrior god regularly played by other Near Eastern deities, such as the supreme Israelite god:

> Yahweh is a man of war;
> The Lord is his name!
> (Exodus 15:3)

Texts from Egypt, Ugarit, and Mari and from the Hittite and Neo-Assyrian kingdoms repeatedly stress this divine motif, and rulers take delight in praising the military prowess of their gods. Sargon calls Nergal 'the king of battle' and 'the all-powerful amongst the gods, who goes at my side, guarding the camp', while Ishtar is the 'lady of conflict and battle whose delight is warfare' (Jones 1989: 300). Kings were champions of the gods, doing the bidding of heaven and carrying out divine will to the letter. Saul of Israel was instructed to fight against the Amalekites and annihilate them completely because it was the express command of Yahweh (**A11**).

An interesting incident recorded in the Assyrian royal annals shows a sickly Ashurbanipal, unable to fight in one of his wars, directing the campaign from his palace. The scene is set in the city of Arbela, where the city's goddess, Ishtar, is receiving the honours of a state festival. The king hears the news that the Elamite ruler, Teumman, is preparing for battle and so Ashurbanipal quickly enters the shrine of the goddess and, with tears in his eyes, beseeches her to destroy the Elamite foe on his behalf. His report stresses the deity's willingness to come to the Assyrian monarch's defence (**A12**; see Stevens 1995: 14).

That Darius' bow is so clearly visible in the Bisitun relief (**F5**) strengthens the notion that force has played a major role in the victory of *arta* over *drauga*. It is the strength of Darius the warrior king (a prowess which he ultimately derives from the god floating above him) which is eulogised on the monument. Here the relief sculpture depicts a victorious Darius. He stands in sharp contrast to the humiliated bodies of his enemies paraded before him; the texts which accompany the scene tell how each of the defeated rebels was pursued, captured, and killed, but notable is the fact that Darius himself is never represented (in text or image) being pursued or hounded by the rebels. While the narrative account demonstrates that his grip on power was certainly challenged, he is never shown weakened, let alone fleeing from his enemies. Instead Darius charges across his realm (or sends a proxy to do so), quelling rebellion after rebellion and enacting his just and premeditated revenge on the fleeing and captured traitors. Subsequently, in the relief, as the rebel leaders fall before Darius they offer him their necks. For it is they, not he, who are men of violence; it is they who are followers of 'the lie', so that the moral ambiguity of warfare and internal strife vanishes in the face of the legitimate Great King of Persia. The enemy are therefore justifiably abased, mutilated, and killed, and the king chains them by their necks, steps on their bellies, and then orders their executions; the upshot of this makes Darius the undisputed head of all lands.

Achaemenid nobles were expected to participate in actual warfare and fighting skills were a prerequisite of elite identity (many of the Persian nobility died in action) and although Great Kings did not necessarily regularly participate in battle, imperial royal ideology propounded that Great Kings were skilled fighters: 'as a warrior, I am a good warrior' is Darius' bold claim. In order to be an effective ruler, the king had to be a thought of as a brave soldier first, and court propaganda (later picked up in Classical traditions) reiterated the image for successive Achaemenid monarchs (**A13**; **A14**).

The image of the Great Kings' noble bravery needs to be balanced

by the fact that the Persian monarchs could prove to be merciless over-
lords if crossed. Rebellious subjects could be treated with ruthlessness:
entire populations were uprooted and deported across the Empire, and
their holy shrines were burned and destroyed. Herodotus (6.19, 8.53)
records the Persian destruction of the sanctuaries of Apollo at Didyma,
and of Athena in Athens, and Artaxerxes III's reputation for harshness
and cruelty was perhaps justified by his treatment of the population
of Sidon (**A15**; see also **D13**). His violent reconquest of Egypt was
recorded on the stela of an Egyptian nobleman named Somtutefnakht:
'The Asiatic (i.e. the Persian king) . . . slew a million at my sides' (Kuhrt
2007: 458).

The longevity of such a vast empire as the Persians managed to
sustain is testimony to the Achaemenid policy of both tolerance
towards its conquered peoples and its ruthlessness in maintaining
power. The royal rhetoric recorded in the inscriptions, visualised in
official art, and disseminated widely across the Empire emphasised that
all conquered nations were united in service to the Great King, whose
laws they were required to obey and whose majesty they were obliged
to uphold.

Bound to obey and serve: Persia's hereditary elite

As we noted in the Introduction, royal courts were the 'households'
of monarchs and the attractions of court life for the nobility of the
realm were obvious – power, prestige, and remuneration could all be
obtained through service to the Great King. There was clearly a hierarchy of rank among the many groups who made up the Achaemenid
court, although trying to decode the precise function of every royal
office within the Persian court is difficult and frustrating. Something
of the rich mixture of jobs which comprised an ancient Near Eastern
royal bureaucracy is reflected in the Biblical list of officials who served
under King David of Israel (**A16**). For their part, the Greeks found
Persian court hierarchy puzzling and their writings on the Persian
court fail to provide us with a clear picture of the multitudinous
range of court offices. But the Greeks were certain of one thing: the
Persian Great Kings needed to be surrounded by a variety of courtiers,
ranging from satraps to stable boys, because they were too grand to
bother themselves with the mundane tasks of governing the Empire
themselves (**A17**). Greek sources suggest that in his youth Cyrus had
held several court positions – 'master of the wand-bearers', 'master
of the squires', and 'cup-bearer' (Athenaeus 14.633d; Ctesias F8d* §5;

see also Xenophon, *Cyropaedia* 1.3.8–9); Darius the Great had been 'quiver-bearer' to Cyrus II and was Cambyses' 'lance-bearer' (Aelian, *Historical Miscellany* 12.43; Herodotus 3.139); and, before his accession, Darius III had held the title 'letter-bearer' (Plutarch, *Alexander* 18.7). The Persepolis texts record office-holders such as a 'chair-carrier' and 'footstool-carrier' (PF 0830) as well as a 'bow-and-arrow-case carrier' (PF 1011) who were given sizeable food rations, indicating the high rank of the courtiers who bore these titles. The entire inner court was under the watch of a powerful official known as the *hazāra-patiš ('master of a thousand') or chiliarch (Keaveney 2010), who (it seems) commanded the royal bodyguard and was responsible for all elements of court security and enjoyed the complete confidence of the ruler, controlling access to his personage through the protocol of the royal audience (Chapter 2). Other prominent inner-court dignitaries included the steward of the royal household (perhaps *viθa-patiš), the royal charioteer, and the king's cup-bearer (see Chapter 5).

It must be noted, however, that court titles did not necessarily have a bearing on the duties expected of the courtier who held them and that nobles with courtly titles perhaps only 'acted' the prescribed roles at state ceremonies. The Vulgate book of *Tobit*, set at the Neo-Assyrian court, notes that a single courtier could, of course, hold multiple offices, ranging from king's body servant to palace pen pusher: 'Now Ahikor was chief cup-bearer, keeper of the signet, and in charge of the administration of the accounts under King Sennacherib' (*Tobit* 1.22).

Two of the most prominent nobles at Darius I's court, Aspacana (Greek, Aspathines) and Gaub(a)ruva (Greek, Gobryas), were honoured by Darius by being represented on his tomb at Naqš-i Rustam. Between them they were provided with several court titles – 'lance-bearer,' 'garment-bearer' (or possibly 'weapon-bearer'), and 'bow-and-arrow-case carrier' – but, as Henkelman (2003a: 120) has stressed:

> these designations are probably not expressions of actual duties, but, given the status of Gobryas and Aspathines, honorary titles bestowed on privileged court officials, possibly implying some ceremonial obligations. From this perspective 'garment-bearer' should not be taken too literally, but be interpreted as 'chamberlain'.

It is clear that the Achaemenids created a complex court structure which in general can be regarded as pyramid-like, with the Great King at its apex and the workers (servants and slaves) at the base. A comparatively small group of nobles occupied a high place in this pyramidal structure, for these were the hereditary Persian nobility, whom the

Greeks called the 'People of the Gate' (Plutarch, *Themistocles* 26.6), and who were obliged – because of blood and status – to serve at court and wait on the king (Briant 2002: 326–7). A multitude of middle-ranking officials operated in the social pyramid's space in between the nobles and the workers, and they communicated between all the other ranks. Any individual who had rendered important service to the king was a 'benefactor' (Greek, *euergētai*), and his name was recorded in the royal archives (Herodotus 8.85.90; Josephus, *Jewish Antiquities* 11.6.4). Briant (2002: 302–20) has carefully explored how royal benefactors were rewarded by the king with gifts of clothing, jewellery, livestock, and land, and has noted that even foreigners who worked at court could benefit from this gift-giving system (see Chapter 2 for further details of the king's gifts). Xenophon (*Anabasis* 1.2.27) also records the way in which a Great King expressed his favour to a courtier: 'Cyrus presented him with the customary royal gifts – that is to say, a horse with a gold bit, a necklace of gold, a gold bracelet, and a gold scimitar, [and] a Persian robe'. This formalised gift-giving of 'unequal exchange', as Briant (2002: 316) terms it, was an important tool for the monarchy, as it established as system of debt and dependency on the part of nobles and other courtiers (for gifts to the king see Chapter 3). Moreover, courtiers designated as 'relatives of the king' and 'friends of the king' had the right to eat from the royal table or assist the king as a body servant, and these were highly prized and ferociously policed privileges (discussed by Briant 2002: 308).

The title 'friend of the king' had a long pedigree in the Near East, and it is particularly well attested in the Hebrew Bible (2 Samuel 15:37; 1 Kings 4:5, 16:11; de Vaux 1961: 122–3, 528) and in Akkadian texts as *rukhi šarri* (van Selms 1957). The title does not seem to have implied any specific function, but being a 'friend of the king' was clearly a closely guarded privilege and a source of pride for those who bore it; thus Tiribazus, the powerful satrap of Armenia, was a particularly favoured 'friend of the king' (Artaxerxes II), and, when resident at court away from his satrapy, 'he alone had the privilege of mounting the king upon his horse' (Xenophon, *Anabasis* 4.4.4; see further Curtius Rufus, 3.3.14.21; and Briant 2002: 321).

It was important for hereditary nobles to make regular appearances at court, and satraps like Tiribazus were expected to leave their satrapies to pay their respects before the Great King. Masistes was at court at the time he quarrelled with Xerxes (Herodotus 9.108–13), even though he was satrap of far-away Bactria, and, starting in 410 BCE, Aršama, the long-serving satrap of Egypt, took a two-year leave of absence from his official post in Memphis to visit the royal court and to survey his Babylonian estates (Driver 1956: 5–6). It should be noted that Aršama is never specifically called a 'satrap' in the diverse texts that name him, but this is not problematic: he is 'Aršama who is in Egypt' or 'Aršama who is in Egypt as [. . .]' or 'lord' or 'son of the house' – Aramaic *br-byt*; this is the only address he needs, and his satrapal position is implicit.

The court was a locus of practical political decision-making and imperial power, and the hereditary nobility of Persia made an important contribution to policy-making and the governance of the realm (**A18**; Herodotus 3.80–4). The monarch and the royal family formed the nucleus of the court, and the Empire was regarded as the Great King's inheritable personal possession; the interests and honour of the dynasty were propelled by the ruling dynasty and its chief adherents, who were drawn from Persia's great noble houses (Briant 2002: 334–8). For their part, the nobles organised their own households based on the template of the royal court, by employing the same types of staff and celebrating the same rites and rituals as the king (*Xenophon*, Anabasis 1.6.10). Moreover, the satraps stationed in provinces far away from the heart of the Empire fashioned themselves after the royal model. Satraps should not be thought of simply as high-ranking civil servants, because, throughout the Empire, they represented the king by proxy and, as such, they imitated his behaviour and emulated his taste (Briant 2002: 345–7). But being a satrap was a hazardous business, for satraps depended personally on the king's good favour and had to watch their behaviour accordingly, and there can be no doubt that in their provincial courts they were carefully scrutinised by the central authorities for any hint of self-aggrandisement or potential treason (Briant 2002: 338–45).

The letters sent between Aršama in Egypt and the royal court in Iran at the beginning of the fourth century BCE demonstrate that even when absent from the imperial centre, court nobles in the service of the king kept up a steady dialogue with the central authority (Driver 1956; Lindenberger 2003). The so-called Passover edict from Elephantine (**A19**), for instance, should be viewed as the transmission of a command of Darius II via his Egyptian satrap, and therefore a reflection of how political decision-making at court was disseminated to the provinces (Kuhrt 2007: 854 n.1). Satrapal courts engaged in the same political discourse articulated in the royal court, and a series of Aramaic texts from Bactria (such as **A20**) offer a rare glimpse of a very distant part of the Empire to balance the richer Aršama dossier from

Egypt and the abundant Persepolis archive, and help demonstrate that the official language of a centralised policy travelled far and wide (Shaked 2004). These sources, coupled with extensive Greek texts, show us the imperial administration at work across the Empire and remind us that Achaemenid courtiers were first and foremost political animals.

Courtiers were also bureaucrats. As Elias (1983: 3) noted, the royal court was 'both the first household of the extended royal family, and the central organ of the entire state administration', and there can be no doubt that the Achaemenids revelled in administrative red tape (a love affair they shared with their Assyrian and Elamite forbears). Their system of government from the highest level to the lowest depended on tight communication, record-keeping, and archiving – as witnessed by the Persepolis archive, the Aršama documents, and the Bactrian files, the vast dossiers of administrative material which make up only a tiny percentage of Achaemenid documentation which originally existed but which has not survived to the present day.

The Persian monarchical system was based on a highly trained bureaucratic elite, recruited on the principle of merit. One courtier in particular stands head and shoulders above all others in respect of his role in the Achaemenid administration: Parnaka, a 'son of the house' and (probably) the uncle of Darius I. He was the chief overseer of the entire Persepolis administrative system as well as its larger integration in the region of Fars province, and he seems to have had free and open access to the king. He is frequently cited receiving his orders directly from Darius. It was Parnaka who oversaw the distribution of foodstuffs and other goods from the royal storerooms and it was he who conveyed the king's orders in writing and whose personal seal-impressions (PFS 9*, PFS 16*) ratified the communication. A typical order for a ration of wine (PF 665; see further **D10**), for instance, runs like this:

> 9 marriš wine, allocations by Karkish, Parnaka received for rations. For a period of 1 day, at a village named Hadarakkas. Hishbesh wrote. Mannunda communicated its message. In [regnal] year 23; month 2; on day 25 the sealed document was delivered.

Working directly under Parnaka was a man named Ziššawiš (who also had his own seals – PFS 83*, PFS 11) who was also in charge of recording and issuing ration orders; he sometimes deputised for Parnaka but he is usually seen working as his chief aid. Between them Parnaka and Ziššawiš supervised numerous storeroom and ration managers, as well as the range of officers in charge of provisions for the court when it went journeying on its regular trips around the Empire (see Chapter 3), each of whom looked after departments of wine, beer, fruit, grain, livestock, poultry, and numerous other food and drink supplies. The two chief administrators also worked alongside the head scribe and his vast workforce of secretaries and translators, the head of royal messengers and his army of staff, and the chief treasurer, who took charge of all of the court's financial transactions and reported directly to the king.

Outsiders as insiders

Bureaucrats, grooms, and translators constituted some of the essential elements of the outer court, as did ambassadors and emissaries (called 'secretaries' of the king). However, a few disparate, but significant, groups of courtiers fit less easily into the pyramidal hierarchical structure of the court proposed above; physicians, bodyguards, and eunuchs could in theory interweave themselves into each of the different court strata, so that positioning them securely into one place within the hierarchical structure is difficult.

The Persepolis texts show that many of the servants at the Achaemenid court (bakers, cooks, wine stewards, stable-hands, and so forth) were recruited from the peoples of the Empire, and foreigners certainly made up a significant portion of the court. But none of the court's foreign personnel were as important as the Greek physicians who were brought to Persia to serve the medical needs of the royal family. The Great Kings had long esteemed the skills of Greek doctors, even more so than Egyptian physicians, who are also attested as medical practitioners at the Persian court (individuals such as Udjahorresnet, Semtutefnakht, and Wenen-Nefer), and they actively sought Greek doctors from around the Empire (see Stronk 2004–5: 105; Griffiths 1987; on Greeks at the Persian court see Hofstetter 1978; Brosius 2011). During the reign of Darius I, the celebrated Democedes of Conon had been captured as war booty and had been coerced into serving as a doctor within the inner court (Herodotus 3.122–5, 129). He had reset Darius' sprained ankle (the result of a fall during a royal hunt) when Egyptian court physicians proved useless, and later he cured Atossa of an abscess in her breast (Herodotus 3.130). Darius richly rewarded Democedes for his skills: he lived in a fine house in Susa, 'took his meals at the king's table', and purportedly had great influence over Darius (Herodotus 3.130).

Another fêted Greek doctor was Apollonides of Cos, who worked as a court physician during the reign of Artaxerxes I. But his glory turned to infamy when he behaved 'unprofessionally' with one of his royal patients, Princess Amytis, the king's sister, and he was executed for his misconduct (see Chapter 4 and **D9**). The doctor-cum-author Ctesias of Cnidus certainly worked as a court physician during the reign of Artaxerxes II and it appears that he cared for the king himself as well as for the king's much loved wife, Stateira, and his revered (and feared) mother, Parysatis (Ctesias T7a; Llewellyn-Jones and Robson 2010). He may well have been tasked with caring for the royal family in general, although perhaps these duties were shared with another Greek doctor, one Polycritus of Mendes, who also seems to have served Artaxerxes as a personal physician – although Polycritus is a particularly shadowy figure (Plutarch, *Artaxerxes* 21.2).

How far the office of royal physician was a voluntary one is debatable. We know that the Egyptian physician Udjahorresnet returned to his native country with the blessing of the Great King (and perhaps a handsome pension) after serving many years at the court of Persia (for the inscriptional evidence from his statue found at Sais, see Lichtheim 1980: 36–41). However, Democedes arrived, like Ctesias perhaps, as a prisoner of war and later escaped the court and fled to Croton, where he was protected by the citizens of the city from being taken back to Persia (Herodotus 3.136–7). Whatever their level of personal freedom might have been, foreign doctors clearly served an important function at the Persian court. However, if we choose to believe him (and there is no obvious reason not to), Ctesias' own account of Apollonides' punishment for unethical behaviour served as a warning that, no matter how valuable a service they might perform, doctors were nonetheless merely servants of the Great King.

In the context of caring for the Great King's welfare, it is worth mentioning here something about the monarch's personal security and the military personnel who formed the so-called 'Immortals' (Greek *athánatoi*, 'those without deaths'), an elite corps of 10,000 Achaemenid Persian infantry soldiers tasked with defending the life of the monarch. Much of our information about the Immortals derives from Herodotus' *Histories* (7.82–3) although later attestations are found in Athenaeus' *Deipnosophistai* (12.514c, quoting Heraclides of Cumae), Hesychius' *Lexicon*, and Procopius (1.14.31), although the Herodotean passages are our most valuable source for the Immortals' involvement in Xerxes' Greek campaign of 480–479 BCE.

Unfortunately the *bona fide* Persian sources for the Immortals are elusive. It is generally assumed that the bearded and richly liveried soldiers represented in the beautiful faience tiles from the Achaemenid palace at Susa and the wall reliefs at Persepolis represent the Immortals (**F8**; Olmstead 1948: 238; see further comments in Head 1992), but there is nothing categorically to support this idea. More importantly, there are no references to a corps of Immortals in the Persian written sources. Probably Herodotus heard the Old Persian word *anûšiya* ('companions [of the King]'), which certainly is located in Persian texts, but confused it or associated it with the phonetically similar Persian word *anauša* ('immortals'). Nick Sekunda has argued that *Amrtaka* was the Old Persian word for 'Immortals', but there is little to support this (Sekunda and Chew 1992: 6). All in all, there are more questions surrounding this special corps of the Persian army than there are answers: their exact tasks, and even their Iranian name, remain unknown because authentic Achaemenid sources with this information no longer exist.

But what might we expect of a cohort of royal bodyguards? What were the duties of the Great King's elite soldiers? Perhaps we can answer that with reference to a remarkable Hittite text known simply as 'The Instruction for the Royal Bodyguard', which illustrates the details of a royal procession (with the king well guarded) as well as providing a vivid description of court ceremonial:

> [They] are to be walking in front of the king . . . [. . .] are standing holding spears. . . . They are to be walking in front of the king. . . . The guard sets up the stool. The king comes out (of the palace) while the chief-of-the-palace-attendants is holding his hand. The king sits down (in a light chariot)... the high-ranking spear-men bow, then they run and walk in front. But the palace-attendant-of-the-spear gives the whip to the chief-of-palace-attendants and (he) gives it to the king. In front of the chariot walks the chief-of-grooms . . . but when the chariot begins to move off, the chief-of-palace-attendants . . . entrusts the king to the chief-of-guards. When the guards march, two guards are marching in front and hold spears. . . . [To their] left . . . the guards and the palace attendants march in three files. . . . They are wearing good festive garments. . . . The soldiers . . . keep the peaceful (population) lined up on the sides: the left ones keep it lined up on the left, the right ones on the right. If (any soldier) lets anything in – either horses or a raging ox – then it is (his) fault. (Excerpts from §15–28; Guterbock and van Hout 1991: 33)

As with the Hittite king, it is likely that the Achaemenid monarch was accompanied by special attendants and a defence force of elite guards

– a physical representation of his ideological strength, as well as a practical measure for his security.

Debate and doubt also surround the historical validity (and subsequent study) of royal eunuchs, the (supposedly) castrated males who served at court as high-ranking officials, bureaucrats, and attendants (in Assyria they also seem to have been military personnel). If these individuals were indeed castrati, then as a kind of 'third sex' they were able to negotiate the permeable barriers of the inner court and outer court in their crucial capacities as messengers and trusted body servants (Llewellyn-Jones 2002). Briant, however, has vehemently rejected the notion that all individuals identified as 'eunuchs' in the context of the Achaemenid Empire were castrated males and suggests instead that 'eunuch' was how 'Greek authors transmitted a term that the court of the Great King considered a court title' (Briant 2002: 276–7). His debate centres on the problem of whether the Akkadian term *ša rēši* (literally, 'of the head') should be translated 'eunuch' (see further Oppenheim 1973). The translation 'eunuch' for *ša rēši* has been open to considerable scholarly debate among Assyriologists and, given that the same term is found in Achaemenid-period Babylonian sources, its interpretation continues to be an issue for the study of the Persians too.

Were eunuchs more figments of the overheated imaginations of Greeks, like Herodotus and Ctesias, than a reality of Persian court life? Did the Greeks inflate the importance of court eunuchs to demonstrate the unmanliness of the Persians? Were 'eunuchs' really 'eunuchs' at all? Perhaps, it has been suggested, there were two 'types' of 'eunuch' at the Persian court: the castrati, who served the needs of the court at large and (for a minority) tended to the Great King himself as body servants, administrators, or even as advisers; and those courtiers who performed the services expected of eunuchs but without the need for castration. For the latter, 'eunuch' was a court title not a physical state of being. But this idea remains mere speculation (for recent overviews of the debates see Jursa 2011; Pirngruber 2011).

Shaun Tougher in his major study of eunuchism in antiquity has wisely warned that Greeks knew what castrated eunuchs really were and, therefore, 'being too sceptical [about the sources and hence the presence of eunuchs in the Persian court] can be as dangerous as being gullible' (Tougher 2008: 20). Briant and others find it difficult to accept that castrated males could be powerful courtiers and elite officials, or even military men, but this is to do a grave disservice to a wider knowledge of eunuch history, because eunuchs are attested in other Near Eastern courts (Guyot 1980; Grayson 1995; Deller 1999; Pirngruber 2011), and they became hallmarks of the royal courts (and noble houses) of Ottoman Turkey, Mughal India, Ming and Qing China, and Safavid and Qajar Iran (Lal 1988; Peirce 1993; Tsai 1996, 2002). It would seem odd to write Achaemenid eunuchs out of a world history of castrati.

According to Greek reports (and here we clearly see the Greeks trying to come to terms with an alien practice) the Persians allegedly valued eunuchs for their honestly and loyalty, since the process of castration made men, like gelded horses and dogs, docile and more malleable (Herodotus 8.105), and Xenophon (*Cyropaedia* 7.5.60–4) unambiguously affirms that Cyrus the Great had first introduced eunuchs into his guard for just this reason – although in reality the pliancy of castrated men cannot be asserted. Herodotus recounts an interesting tale of how a Greek-speaking youth, Hermotimus of Pedasa, was captured and sold to the slave-dealer Panionius, who specialised in trading beautiful boys to elite customers in Asia Minor, having first castrated them. Hermotimus subsequently found himself at the Persian court, where he quickly caught the eye and gained the favour of Xerxes, who charged him with the privileged and trusted task of tutoring the children of the royal harem (Herodotus 8.103–5; see Hornblower 2003). Herodotus (3.92) further ascertains that Babylon was required to send the Great King an annual tribute of 500 boys, who were to be castrated and turned into eunuchs, and by implication it is possible that the five boys he mentions being sent every three years from Ethiopia and the 100 boys sent by the Colchians to court as tribute were castrati also (Herodotus 3.97). There may be truth in Herodotus' report (certainly human tribute was demanded in the Ottoman, Safavid, and Qing empires). He also points out that at the suppression of the Ionian revolt, the Persians emasculated the prettiest boys and shipped them off to Iran (6.9, 32). It is clear that Herodotus found the practice of castration abhorrent and the creation of eunuchs perverse, yet he nonetheless finds stories of them compelling, for, after all, the Persian creation of eunuchs gave Herodotus an opportunity to comment on Persian moral laxity, albeit subtly and unobtrusively, while still describing the realia of Persian life.

Perhaps it is more logical to accept the presence of genuine castrati at the Persian court and we need not look for excuses to exonerate the Achaemenids of the practice of castrating boys and men. If we accept the logical presence of *bona fide* eunuchs within Persian society then we can note that some of them clearly rose to positions of high influence, prestige, and outright power at court. The roles eunuchs played at court were as diverse as they were complex. Ctesias (probably using authentic Iranian sources for his history) begins his examination of each successive Great King's reign with a kind of litany which lists the key eunuchs at court, and implies that their names and deeds were remembered for generations after their deaths alongside the monarchs they served:

> Artasyras, the Hyrcanian, held the greatest sway with him [Cambyses II], and of the eunuchs Izabates, Aspadates and Bagapates were influential: the latter was also influential with Cambyses' father. (Ctesias F13 §9)

> So Ochus, who was also called Darius [II], ruled alone. There were three eunuchs who held sway with him: the foremost was Artoxares, second Artibarzanes and third Athöus. (Ctesias F15 §51)

If we follow the fourth-century Greek sources then we are alerted to the idea that, from the end of the reign of Xerxes, eunuchs began to acquire increasing power at court, and that they routinely entered into plots and even became involved in regicide (see Chapter 5). But how much of this can be taken at face value is difficult to know, given, as we have noted, a certain Greek penchant for using eunuchism to disparage Persian values and traditions.

Interestingly, all known court eunuchs (with the exception of Hermotimus) have identifiably Iranian names, which perhaps puts into doubt the stories Herodotus recounts of foreign eunuchs being sent to Persia as tribute. However, it might be expected that, upon their arrival at court, any foreign eunuchs were required to abandon their ethnic names and adopt ones more suitably Persian. It is also possible that the beardless youthful-looking servants depicted on some of the doorjambs at Persepolis are eunuchs (**F9**) but this is by no means certain, nor is the traditional interpretation that Artaxerxes I's cupbearer, Nehemiah, who was later appointed governor of Judah, was also a eunuch (Olmstead 1948: 314; Cook 1983: 136; on the physical repercussions of castration and issues of beard growth see Bullough 2002, and below, Chapter 2).

The study of eunuchs in the Achaemenid court is far from simple and the question of their presence at court is very far from being resolved. Scholars remain sharply divided over the presence of eunuchs in Persian society and even over the meaning and appropriateness of the word 'eunuch' and how it might be applied (if at all) to Achaemenid courtiers.

Concluding thought

There is hardly a grander or more widespread image found in Achaemenid sources than that of the king. He was the dispenser of protection, justice, and authority and his presence was woven into every strand of ancient Persian culture.

Yet the king was not a law unto himself. He was subject to the will of Ahuramazda and 'the other gods who are' and his major function was to be an example of a humble (if honoured) servant of the gods. Concerning the security of Persia and its people, it was Ahuramazda himself who was a 'divine warrior' and he empowered the king with the strength and skill to fight in battles and bring about the 'truth' which he had created at the dawn of time. This Persian concept, shared with other Near Eastern monarchic ideologies, was so deep-set that Hebrew prophets were able to transfer the intimate relationship between the Persian king and Ahuramazda to the Isrelite god Yahweh and the Persian king. Thus, Cyrus the Great was addressed by Yahweh as 'my shepherd' and 'my anointed one' (Isaiah 44:28, 45:1).

In circuit around the king were his many courtiers, the hereditary nobles of the realm as well as the administrators, civil servants, guards, doctors, and body servants who made up the royal household. The study of these nobles and servants provides rich insights into discourses of power. The Great King needed courtiers for both practical and symbolic reasons, because these individuals performed important and menial tasks, kept the large and complex imperial household smoothly functioning, and influenced imperial law and policy. Achaemenid rulership required that the king maintain a lavish lifestyle and his court had to be bigger, grander, and more complex than anything lesser mortals could devise. In many respects the Achaemenid court is analogous to the divine courts of the gods we read of in Mesopotamian, Levantine, and Egyptian mythological texts (Brettler 1989) and the hierarchical structure of the Achaemenid secular court placed the Persian ruler in the role of the god in a parallel heavenly court.

CHAPTER 2

Pomp and Circumstance:
Monarchy on Display

On Wednesday, Michelle Obama briefly put her hand on the back of Queen Elizabeth II as the two chatted at a reception. . . . Etiquette is quite stern about this: 'Whatever you do, don't touch the Queen!' The sight of anyone apparently touching the Queen with anything more than a limp handshake is enough to send the British twittering. (Howard Chua-Eoan, *Time Magazine*, April 2009)

This chapter explores the use of display, ceremony, and etiquette at the Achaemenid court, and also examines the issue of the king's 'visibility' and 'invisibility'. Court ceremonial, whether it is a splendid one-off investiture ritual or the daily routine of the royal audience, was no shallow display of pomp and circumstance, but the eloquent demonstration, in a condensed and intensely ritualised form, of the Achaemenid ideology of rule. When a courtier participated in a court ceremony and was granted an audience with the king, or was even permitted to join the royal dinner table, the wider court might read that alignment of the monarch's favour as a change in government policy or as heralding the rise of one noble house at the cost of another. Court ceremonials and the intricacies surrounding them were the micro-language through which imperial politics were articulated.

Why ceremony?

It was through the complex series of symbolic ritualised acts that majesty was made (see Geertz 1983: 124). In any monarchic system, ceremony naturally revolves around the figure of the ruler; in fact, ceremonies have always been the favourite way for a regime (in our case the Achaemenid dynasty) to exhibit its political clout and, when properly employed, ceremony nearly always produces the desired results, by appealing to people of diverse backgrounds and beliefs. Alongside promoting the regime's power and stability, ceremony served to reveal its ideological basis and world-view to its targeted population. Therefore the study of Achaemenid ceremony (as far as can be achieved, given the limitation of the sources) offers clues as to the dynasty's self-definition.

If we examine certain aspects of Persian court ceremonials then it becomes apparent that intended messages lie encoded in various components of the rituals. The architectural venue for ceremonies (such as the Apadana or 'throne hall') and the route of imperial processions (delineated by rich carpets so that the king never stepped on the bare floor), for example, can offer the scholar clues about the meaning of ceremonies, about the life and ideology of the dynasty. Similarly, the study of objects used in ceremonies can be a rich field of exploration: thrones, footstools, parasols, fly-whisks, sceptres, crowns, and robes had symbolic implications, although many of the subtleties of these objects' symbolic importance still require scholarly exploration. Moreover, the identity of courtiers participating in ceremony, reflected in their attire – from headgear to garments – as well as their position and stance throughout the ceremony, imparts a mass of information about the self-perception of the ruling elite. However, the codes still need to be unlocked.

Since ceremonies operated around the figure of the Great King, he was always distinguished from the other participants in the ceremony by his dress, posture, or his isolated or somehow unique position; indeed, without such distinctions it would (in theory) have been impossible to differentiate the monarch from some of his high-ranking courtiers. Therefore, carrying out the ceremonial roles of his office meant that the ruler cloaked his mortal body within the sacred garments of kingship and came to be regarded by his inner circle of courtiers and by his subjects at large as embodying within himself the sanctity of his office. This was how Achaemenid majesty was created.

In addition, Achaemenid court ceremonies maintained and reinforced hierarchy within the ruling elite and delineated power relations between courtiers, the royal family, and the monarch himself. After all, imperial majesty required the strict observation of hierarchy at all times and it is highly likely that the royal chiliarch acted as a sort of 'master of protocol' and was responsible for arranging and setting the hierarchical order of all ceremonies.

The royal residences of the Empire witnessed a constant traffic of diplomatic emissaries: Persian satraps and officials as well as foreign ambassadors and envoys could potentially obtain an audience with the Great King provided that they brought the required tribute or gifts. The staircases of Persepolis' Apadana show diplomatic gift-giving on an imperial scale (see below for a discussion), which alerts us to the idea that court ceremony was not just an act staged for 'home spectators' but that its audience included 'outsiders'. Perhaps the actors in the drama of ceremony were more careful to play their parts well and to avoid *faux pas* when foreigners appeared at court, because receptions for envoys served both to signal the smooth running of the realm and to enhance the prestige of the territories of the Empire.

It is highly likely that the reception ceremonies of individual states reflected current twists and turns in Achaemenid foreign policy and that an envoy's royal audience was shaped by politics. A country which expressed its loyalty to the crown and paid its taxes on time might have enjoyed the special attention, indulgence, and favour of the king, while an envoy arriving from a troublesome country at a time of political tension might have experienced nothing but disfavour and even humiliation should the king have wished to degrade him as an example to other bothersome parts of the Empire. Territories outside the borders of the Empire experienced similar situations, and stories of Greek ambassadors at the Persian court testify to the barometer-like relationship between the court and the various *poleis* of Greece (Miller 1997: 109–14).

Unseen but all-seeing

In spite of the ceremony which surrounded Great King (see further below), he was a shadowy figure even to longstanding courtiers. Indeed, limited access to the person of the sovereign was actually the prerequisite of Achaemenid monarchy. Under Darius I, only six Persian dignitaries allegedly enjoyed freedom of access to the ruler, but otherwise the physical separation of the king from his courtiers permeated every aspect of royal life, including dinners and feasts, where only a few individuals were permitted to interact with the king (**B1**). Both Xenophon and Plutarch suggest that the king carefully manipulated seating prerogatives at the dinner table to highlight the social worth of a few honoured members of the court (**B2**; see also Chapter 4, **D7**). Because these favoured individuals were, presumably, able to address the king directly as they ate and drank, they were perceived by other courtiers to be in a position of favour and therefore of influence (this in turn could lead to envy and outright rivalry on the part of others; see Chapter 5). While some high-ranking courtiers no doubt often saw and spoke with the monarch (we can imagine that Parnaka, as head of the

Persepolis administration, had frequent occasion to converse with the king), for most members of court the king was inaccessible, and seeing and speaking to the sovereign were tightly controlled. Courtiers had to follow certain formulations of etiquette and most would not have dared to speak directly to their sovereign (the king, however, could permit a courtier to speak and express an opinion – see Nehemiah 2:1–6, 8).

This notion of an 'invisible' sovereign flies in the face of the ideology of monarchy that Norbert Elias (1983) understood to have been promoted at Versailles: Louis XIV was constantly on display to his court, whether he was dressing, eating, or praying (only sex and defecation were private acts for the Bourbon monarch), so in this respect Elias' concept of court society is at loggerheads with the Achaemenid model. However, while Louis XIV was undoubtedly a great Christian king, his form of sacred kingship fell short of the ancient Near Eastern models of monarchy, or for that matter the form of kingship adopted in East Asia and the Middle East in later periods. These were all formatted on the idea of the hidden monarch's inaccessibility. The Achaemenid kings followed a practice adopted by Mughal and Qing emperors, Safavid and Qajar shahs, Ottoman sultans, and a myriad of African rulers; as late as the 1940s the Japanese emperor was a hidden monarch, and even today His Majesty King Bhumibol Adulyadej of Thailand carefully rations his civic appearances, guards his public image with meticulous laws of *lèse-majesté*, and strictly rules over a formal court stiff with ceremonial (Handley 2006).

Perhaps as a result of this region-wide courtly concept of royal invisibility, texts from across the ancient Near Eastern world speak of the ardent desire of courtiers to behold the faces of their kings. The Assyrian Bel-ibini, for instance, writes to his ruler, Ashurbanipal, stressing that 'I long for the sight of the king my lord, that I might see the face of the king my lord' (Tomes 2005: 82), while the governor of Calah addresses the same ruler imploring 'Let an order be given to the Palace Overseers. . . . Let them allow me to see the face of the king, my lord, and may the king look at me' (Tomes 2005: 82). These are nothing short of expressions of dependence on the king's majesty, and they articulate clearly the desire (even desperation) felt by many courtiers to bask in their sovereign's gaze. Most desperate of all is the plea of the courtier Barhalza, located some distance away from his lord and master Esarhaddon in a province far west of Nineveh: 'Like sunshine, all countries are illuminated by your light. But I have been left in darkness; no one brings me to see the king' (Tomes 2005: 81).

The smugness of individuals regularly admitted into the royal presence is just as palpable, as demonstrated by a tomb inscription of Ineni, a favoured courtier of the New Kingdom pharaoh Thutmose II:

> I was a favourite of the king in his every place; greater was that which he did for me than for those who preceded (me). I attained the old age of the revered, I possessed the favour of seeing His Majesty every day.
> (Breasted 1906: vol. ii, §117; see further Tomes 2005: 81)

Courtiers who regularly served in the royal presence were therefore to be congratulated:

> Happy is the man whom you have chosen to approach you
> And to live in your court!
> (Psalm 65:4)

> Happy are they who live in your house,
> Who are always praising you!
> (Psalm 84:5)

Kings were hard to see and difficult to access. Herodotus, in his (essentially fantastical) 'Median history', attributes the creation of this kind of 'invisible monarchy' to the Medes (**B3**). Clearly he is wrong but, regardless of historical accuracy, Herodotus seems to understand well enough what motivates a monarch to opt for this sort of rule, as well as realising the effects of royal detachment: Deioces opted to be inaccessible to his nobles to enhance the place of the monarchy in society. Ctesias, however, disagrees with Herodotus and not only advocates an earlier formulation of the practice, in Assyria, but proposes that Ninyas wished to be secluded from the whole population of his realm and not just his courtiers (**B4**). Of course, it is impossible to give a historical date to either Deioces or Ninyas (given that they are, at best, merely amalgamations of genuine historical figures) and thus Giovanni Lanfranchi's careful analysis of this discrepancy concludes by noting:

> the descriptions given by Herodotus and by Ctesias of the invention of the first shaping of royal inaccessibility or invisibility are the exemplary models of the etiquette that they believed, or pretended to be current at the Persian (or better 'Oriental') court. Either of Median or of Assyrian origin, this was the character which they wished to stress in their picture of the royal court etiquette in Persia. (Lanfranchi 2010: 52)

So, should we believe the Greek sources on the inaccessibility of the Great King? We probably should, while nevertheless recognising that the Greek fascination with the image of the invisible king served a negative agenda: the remoteness of the ruler helped sanction the Hellenic stereotype of the degenerate Oriental despot. Thus the anonymous Greek author known to us as Pseudo-Aristotle envisaged the Great King as a luxury-loving demi-god hidden away in the depths of his court and he conceived of the royal palace itself as a series of thresholds, with the palace gate, walls, towers, guards, and multiple doors functioning as a sequence of barriers between the outer world and the inner sanctum of the royal chamber, where the divine king sat unseen but all-seeing (**B5**).

Interestingly, from at least Herodotus onwards, there is something in the Greek discourse on the nature of the Persian Empire which is fixated on the Great King's ability to control his own public visibility as well as the sight of others (Llewellyn-Jones forthcoming a). Cyrus the Great, at least as portrayed by Xenophon, modelled his kingship on the premise that 'the good ruler [has] eyes for men, [so that] he is able not only to give commandments but also to see the transgressor and punish him' (*Cyropaedia* 8.1.22), although, on a less positive note, Xenophon also evokes the image of a somewhat paranoid Great King policing his realm by utilising a tight network of spies, the 'Faithful' (*pistoi*), throughout the length and breadth of the Empire, to report back to the central authority any hint of threat or rebellion in the satrapies (*Cyropaedia* 8.2.10–12; see also Briant 2002: 344). A court official bearing the (curious) title of 'King's Eye' (Old Persian *Spasaka*?) – beautifully lampooned by Aristophanes in his comedy *Acharnians* of 425 BCE (lines 61–129) – was in charge of intelligence-gathering and reported directly, and perhaps even daily, to the king (Herodotus 1.114; Ctesias F20: 12).

Greek sources emphasise how the Persian king had power over the sight of others, so much so, indeed, that he put out the eyes and directly managed the gaze of his subjects. In Ctesias' *Persica* the gouging out of eyes is not infrequently cited as the punishment for treason: the rebellious eunuch Petisacas, for instance, had his eyes gouged out prior to his crucifixion (F9 §6 and F9a) and the braggart Mithridates was deprived of his eyes before molten lead was poured in his ears (F26 §7). Ctesias also recounts the cruel practice of pricking the eyeballs of tortured prisoners (F26 §4 = Plutarch, *Artaxerxes* 14–17). Xenophon likewise recalls that, as he marched through the Persian Empire, he often saw along the roads people who had lost eyes because of some crime against the Great King's law (*Anabasis* 1.9.11–12; on imperial punishments see Rollinger 2010).

The Greek authors are correct to identify this particular form of punishment, for there is good evidence for this practice of blinding rebellious traitors from Old Persian sources too. In the Bisitun inscription, Darius boasts of how the Median pretender Phraortes (Fravartish) 'was captured and brought to me. I cut off his nose, his ears, and his tongue, and I tore out one eye, and he was kept in fetters at my palace entrance, and all the people beheld him' (DB II §32). The same fate is reserved for the traitor Tritantaechmes (Cicantakhma) the Sagartian (DB II §33). In this, Darius is consistent with a general Near Eastern practice, since successive civilisations regarded blindness as the lowest type of degradation that could be inflicted upon an individual. Of particular interest in the Bisitun inscription, however, is Darius' report that the mutilated heads of the rebellious prisoners were placed on display – probably at the gates of the royal palace in Ecbatana. This was a standard practice, since the public display of rebels – either as mutilated corpses or as living prisoners still awaiting the final death blow – signified the serious nature of rebellion and acted as a warning to other subject peoples. That 'all the people beheld him' highlights the notion of the active gaze of the population, who must look and learn from the decapitated head with the hollow eye sockets, and underscores the paradox of the seeing and unseeing eye, as well as the powerful image of the palace in royal propaganda.

The architecture of majesty: the royal residences

The ideology of royal inaccessibility was promoted in the space which monarchs inhabited, and the palaces of the Empire were carefully designed, on the one hand, to separate the king from his subjects but, on the other hand, to display him to the eyes of the court on specified ceremonial occasions.

The Achaemenid Great Kings were builder kings. Dynastic and imperial structures were their speciality, as between them they erected architectural complexes – fortresses, royal residences, and tombs – on a grand scale. Several of them allude to their construction projects in their official inscriptions, often in an attempt to demonstrate dynastic longevity through the exhaustive planning and creation of palaces, tombs, and fortresses as symbols of royal power and imperial harmony (**B6**; in the inscription note how Xerxes presents himself as his father's heir in his desire to add to the palace site and to ask for Ahuramazda's blessing).

The Persian palaces were part of the royal *viθ* (Akkadian, *bītu*; Elamite *ulhi*) – the Old Persian equivalent of the complex Greek term *oikos*, meaning 'dwelling', 'household', 'economic entity', and 'people of a household' (Morgan 2010). The king's servants and officials – those who comprised the royal *viθ* – are recorded in the Persepolis texts, but we should be aware that even the king's animals formed part of the royal household.

When Darius I prayed that Ahuramazda would allow 'happiness [to] rest upon this *viθ*' (Dpe §3) he was alluding, of course, not just to the individuals who made up the royal household but also to the physical space which they occupied: his hope was equally that 'happiness will rest upon this *palace*' (see Kuhrt 2007: 487, n. 4; in the Bisitun inscription likewise, *viθ* is used in the sense of 'house', 'palace', and 'household'; see DB §61–70). The *viθ* was the seat of Persian kingship, for the word certainly refers to the palace or royal residence, which itself was imbued with a deep symbolism reflecting monarchic power. The palace was a centre of active power and, given that the court was the administrative hub of the Empire, archives, libraries, and offices demonstrated that the court was a working machine of royal legislation. Interestingly, in the recent wars and revolutions across the Middle East, the palaces of rulers such as Saddam Hussein in Babylon and Baghdad and the palaces of the Gaddafi family in Libya were attacked in the aftermath of the downfall of their regimes, demonstrating that the intimate symbolic relationship between the ruler, his administration, and his palace still exists.

Drawing on the rich resources and the gargantuan labour force of their vast Empire, the Achaemenid kings built lavishly throughout the realm (Briant 2002: 165–70), although the chief palatial sites, crafted from fine stone, mud brick, glazed brick, and wood, were clustered in the ancestral regions of Fars (the palaces at Parsagade and Persepolis), Media (at Ecbatana) and Elam (Susa), or in areas of early conquest (Babylonia). With the exception of Persepolis, which was the brain child of Darius and built almost from scratch (there are *some* indications that the area around Persepolis already had a governmental presence under Cyrus and Cambyses), Achaemenid royal residences tended to be built on top of earlier areas of habitation (Susa in particular had a rich and renowned Elamite heritage – see Potts 1999 – while Babylon had a deep antiquity) and each palace site essentially duplicated the other in form and function, if not in scale. At Susa, Darius was clearly so proud of his newly built fortifications and palace that he instructed the creation of a fine text to testify to the multi-ethnic labour of love which went into its construction (**B7**). Archaeology also testifies to the presence of skilled foreign craftsmen and builders working at the heart of the Empire, as do the many bureaucratic texts discovered in Persepolis' Fortification and Treasury archives (Boardman 2000: 62–9; Tavernier 2008; Brosius 2011: 69). Yet these sources – the Susa inscription in particular – underplay an important if (to us) unpleasant aspect of Near Eastern civilisation, namely the ancients' dependence upon slavery or other forms of forced labour. After all, palaces, fortresses, city walls, and roads did not build themselves and the Great King expected all his subjects to serve the throne whenever he ordered, and just as he could conscript able-bodied men into his army, so too he could draft them into corvée labour. As Douglas Knight and Amy-Jill Levine (2011: 337) remind us:

> Edifices from antiquity which impress us today with their beauty and size were constructed not only by labourers earning a living wage and not only by slaves and war captives, but generally by peasants and farmer who were compelled to spend months away from their families and fields for state building projects and receive, at best, only enough food to survive.

Persia did not have an extensive slave economy and, as Dandamayev (1988) emphasises:

> on the whole, there was only a small number of slaves in relation to the number of free persons even in the most developed countries of the Achaemenid empire, and slave labour was in no position to supplant the labour of free workers.

We know from the Persepolis texts that the majority of the royal *kurtaš* ('workers') were foreigners, but, as Henkelman and Stolper (2009: 281) ask, 'were they seasonal workers on corvée duty or rather a dependent and even exploited part of the heartland population including large permanent communities of deportees?' It is hard to imagine that the peasant population was not recruited in some way for the Great King's large-scale building projects. (More generally on Achaemenid slavery see: Dandamayev 1984b, 1988; Briant 2002: 433–9, 505–7, 940–2.)

Inge Nielsen reminds us that when trying to understand the layout and meaning of ancient palaces it is important to remember that 'form follows function' (Nielsen 1999: 13), that is to say, royal architecture was intended to conform to, highlight, and even augment the needs of monarchy, whether in a ceremonial or in a domestic sense. To quote

Norbert Elias (1983: 9): 'every kind of "being together" of people has a corresponding arrangement of space'. The primary function of the Achaemenid royal palaces was to serve the ceremonial and official needs of Persian kingship and the Persian court and therefore they were places where audiences were granted, business was concluded, embassies were received, judgements were pronounced, petitions were heard, and councils were held. Moreover, the palaces were hierarchically charged sites for monarchic display, where the king appeared in the full panoply of state, surrounded by his court. The palaces also functioned as residential spaces and each one must have included, to a fuller or lesser extent, living quarters of the king and some of his family, and maybe even of members of the court (around the stone palaces, tented cities accommodated the bulk of the court; see Chapter 3). To sustain the royal household, slave dormitories, service quarters, and kitchens were needed and to ensure the king's protection guard rooms must have been present too. Finally, the palaces had an important administrative function, represented by treasuries, offices, and archives, all of which needed space. What we see in Achaemenid palace architecture is the idea that space is constructed by the way it is occupied. Our mental maps of the palatial structures of Persia stem from our understanding not only of the physical and material elements of the spaces but of how their occupants functioned within them.

The creation of the Empire went hand in hand with the erection of stone palaces. Cyrus II began construction of a palace complex in his tribal territory at Parsagade (Elamite, *Batrakataš*) early in his reign and yet the full extent of the enormous, sprawling site is yet to be completely understood, although the official palaces, built in stone and decorated in marble, have been well documented and studied (see Matheson 1972: 116–19; Stronach 1978, 1997a, 1997b). The official complex includes a 'private' palace, a hypostyle hall for public audience ceremonies, and a magnificent gatehouse which served to control access to the monarch's court. The decorative scheme used for the palace reliefs (such as survive) drew heavily on Assyrian, Babylonian, Egyptian, and Elamite motifs and merges them to make something harmoniously and distinctively 'Persian'. Surrounding the palaces were formal gardens fed by a myriad of water channels and a large park for hunting. All in all, Parsagade suggests that early on in his reign Cyrus had a sophisticated appreciation of the trappings of kingship and understood the effective use of architectural space; the separation of the public areas of the palace (the throne hall and gateway) from the private areas (and we can assume that garden was for the use of the royal family alone) already fostered that deep-set Achaemenid penchant for controlling access to the king.

Following the conquest of Babylon in 539 BCE, the Persians began construction of a large ceremonial palace next to the old residence of Nebuchadnezzar II (a clear political statement to the Babylonians), but little remains of it today and only a hypothetical reconstruction of its once august appearance can be attempted; nonetheless, there is evidence for the use of Achaemenid-style column bases and bull capitals, and at least part of the palace was decorated with fine glazed brickwork which shared motifs with examples found at Susa. In fact, the influence of Babylonian culture on Achaemenid art and architecture is apparent in various remains, and is seen in the use of terraced platforms in palace construction, wall decoration, and repoussé technique in metalwork (André-Salvini 2009: 241–5).

Little remains of the once-famed Achaemenid residence at Ecbatana (Old Persian, *Hamgmatāna*) near Hamadan – and much controversy surrounds even its archaeological location (see Boucharlat 1998). The palace at Susa (Elamite, *Šušan*), and its adjacent *ville royale* is archaeologically better preserved, with good traces of monumental gateways, columned halls, and staircases. Finds have included glazed brick reliefs and enormous columns with bull capitals (Harper et al. 1992; Curtis and Tallis 2005: 86–91; Perrot 2010), although perhaps the most remarkable discovery (in 1972) was the unearthing of a statue of Darius I (originally there were probably two) at the palace's main gate (**F10**). Larger than life size, the statue is a very rare example of Achaemenid royal sculpture in the round, and while its upper part is missing, the statue nevertheless tells us much about imperial ideology. The king wears the court robe (see below), but the posture – one foot forward, one arm held close to the chest, the other hanging straight at the side – is purely Egyptian in style. The folds of the robe carry an inscription in Egyptian hieroglyphics and three Near Eastern cuneiform scripts: 'Here is the stone statue which Darius ordered to be made in Egypt, so that he who sees it in the future will know that a Persian man holds Egypt' (DSab). The statue's base is carved with the Egyptian symbol of unity and the sides are adorned with the representation of the peoples/countries of the Empire, each of which is identified by local dress and a cartouche tag (Azarpay 1994: 177; Curtis and Tallis 2005: 99; Perrot 2010: 256–87).

Persepolis (Old Persian, *Pārsa*; Greek, *Persis*, whence *Persia*), some 500 km east of Susa, lies in the heart of Fars and is by far the largest and most spectacular of the Achaemenid palaces (see especially Mousavi 2012). The structures there were chiefly built by Darius I, Xerxes, and Artaxerxes I but were still being added to until 330 BCE, when they were destroyed by Alexander of Macedon (although enough of the site was still sufficiently complete for it to be described by Strabo 17.1–2, 71.1.3–8). Remarkably there is still no scholarly consensus about the aims of Darius in building the palace, and the basic function of Persepolis is still debated (for a succinct précis of the deliberation see Briant 2002: 185–6; and, importantly, Mousavi 2012: 51–6). Was the palace primarily a site for celebrating Nowruz, the Persian New Year festival? This has been well argued for, from the time of Herzfeld's excavations onwards, even though some scholars repudiate the claim that Nowruz was celebrated in the Achaemenid period at all (see Mousavi 1992: 206; Mousavi 2012: 52–3). Some have seen Persepolis as a temple-like religious centre and not a working palace at all (Razmjou 2010), although the presence at the site of a huge bureaucracy overseeing and recording the day-to-day economic manoeuvres of the central Empire seriously challenges this. For other scholars, though, Persepolis is the ultimate illustration of royal power (Root 1979: 153–61) as well as a political, economic, and administrative centre of the Empire. This is perhaps the best way to regard the palace, although the case for considering Persepolis as the site of the Nowruz festival should not be dismissed lightly because the remarkable images of tribute-bearers from across the Empire carved into two regal staircases at the palace's throne hall certainly suggest their participation in some kind of imperial celebration (**F11a–d**; Briant 2002: 175–81), and a Nowruz festivity might fit the bill nicely.

The same palatial configuration found at Susa is repeated at Persepolis (see Wilber 1969; Matheson 1972: 122–8; Koch 2001; Mousavi 2002; Shahbazi 2004). The palace is built on a high terrace platform (fortified and permeated with drainage channels) and is entered via a grand double-flighted staircase, whose steps are shallow enough to be comfortably ascended by horses and other animals; this might endorse the theory that the palace was used for a great gift-giving festival in which animals were presented to the king (the Apadana reliefs show goats, sheep, rams, horses, bulls, camels, lions, and even a giraffe – or possibly an okapi – being presented to the ruler). At the top of the staircase stood the mighty portal known as the 'Gate of All Nations', built by Xerxes, which was flanked by monumental stone bulls (**F15**) and human-headed winged bulls (for a ground plan see Kuhrt 2007: 582, fig. 12.1); official access to the palace was via this gateway (although a service gate at the southern end of the terrace was also maintained).

The terrace was essentially divided into two areas: a public space (a physical manifestation of the outer court) for group gatherings, parades, and state occasions; and a more private area (the corresponding inner court), catering to certain ceremonial events as well as residential and administrative needs. The largest and most imposing part of the public space was the audience hall (Apadana), which, at a height of nearly twenty-two metres, stood on a podium three metres higher than the huge open courtyard that surrounded it to the north and east. It consisted of an immense square hall with thirty-six columns supporting an enormous roof of cedar wood; it had three porticos (each with twelve columns) on the north, west, and east sides, four four-storey corner towers, and a series of storage and guardrooms on the south. It is estimated that the Apadana could hold 10,000 people. This was clearly the main site of the most important royal ceremonies, and entering into the darkened hallows of this majestic hall must have been an overwhelming experience for any diplomat, courtier, or suppliant.

Other official buildings included the magnificent 'Hall of a Hundred Columns', an immense banqueting vestibule (or an alternative throne hall), and the Tripylon or 'Central Palace', a small but lavishly orna-mented structure with three doorways and four columns, which may have served as a council chamber. The jambs of the eastern doorway show foreign throne-bearers lifting high the Great King (**F12**); this might be a purely symbolic image, but it has been suggested that this may reflect an actual court ceremony in which, at some great festival at Persepolis, twenty-eight courtiers representing subject nations of the Empire lifted the royal throne seating the king and prince, and carried them into the main hall of the Tripylon, where they received guests (L'Orange 1953; Root 1979: 153–61; Shahbazi 2009).

The buildings of the inner court, situated to the rear of the Apadana, were made up of Darius' *taçara* (literally, 'suite of rooms') and Xerxes' *hadiš* (literally, 'seat of power'), two smaller palaces used as 'private' residences by the kings (Shahbazi 2004: 160) and incorporat-ing (perhaps) dining areas and even bathrooms; it should be noted, however, that Lindsay Allen (2005a: 62) has rightly pointed out the dangers of attempting to pin these Old Persian words to specific palace locations. Other 'palaces' were located in this area, including the so-called Palace H, perhaps originally built by Artaxerxes I, and the completely destroyed palace G (dating, maybe, to Artaxerxes III). At the southern end of the platform, on a level below these small private palaces, was the harem (see Chapter 4 for a discussion). The managerial heart of the palace was based in the private part of the terrace as well: the treasury was located here, and it contained not only the vast wealth of Persepolis brought there by foreign dignitaries, satraps, and an unending herd of middle men, but it also housed the state bureaucracy's army of scribes, secretaries, and other administrative personnel. It was here, as well as in the surrounding fortification wall, that the archival documents relating to the running of the Empire were discovered. At the foot of the platform, to the south, were gathered several mud-brick and stone pavilions (buildings A–H) which might well have served as royal dwelling places, including one (building H) with a sunken stone bath.

Perhaps the most striking feature of Persepolis, though, is the profusion of finely carved stone reliefs which seem to cover every available inch of space. Once brightly painted and even embellished with overlays of precious metal, the reliefs are now bleached of colour and stripped of ornament, yet their beauty and elegance, made most apparent in the formulaic regularity of their subject matter and detail, are a wonder of artistic creativity and planning. Armed guards, court dignitaries, foreign ambassadors, a menagerie of animals, and a host of magical creatures jostle for space on the palace walls, but all of them take second place to the many images of the Great King which dominate the scenes. He is shown calmly walking from one room to another, eyes fixed on the middle distance; he holds a long sceptre (**F1**; Salvesen 1998: 136–7; Brettler 1989: 80–1), and is followed by two courtiers (always depicted on a smaller scale), one of whom holds a parasol above the king's head while the other holds a fly whisk (see **F2**; some examples show a folded towel-like strip of linen or else an unguent pot); sometimes the king is more active and is depicted slaying real or mythical animals, his sword plunging into the belly of the monster (**F7**; Root 1979: 285–9). Occasionally the monarch strangles a lion in the crook of his left arm. In these combat scenes, where the wild beasts represent chaos, disorder, and 'the lie', it is possible that the king represents 'every man' and takes on the form of 'the Persian hero' restoring order to his country (Root 1979: 303–8).

Remarkably, though, certain artistic themes are notable by their absence: in all of Persepolis there is no representation of the king engaged in warfare or the hunt – yet we know both to have been integral components of Achaemenid kingship and its ideology; neither is the king represented feasting or in worship (although tomb reliefs do represent the latter act). Hunting scenes, feasting scenes, war scenes, and religious scenes are all represented in the minor arts (especially seal images) but for some reason they do not enter into the repertoire of official monumental Achaemenid iconography. Why? Briant (2002: 185–6) puts forward a valuable suggestion:

> Persepolitan art is not a simple quasi-photographic reflection of reality. Though it does capture reality, it does so in order to transform it and make it sublime; it relates less to a scenic scenario than to an ideological discourse on royalty and imperial might organized around themes particularly evocative of the power of the Great King: the king in majesty . . . armed forces . . . the cooperation of the aristocracy . . . and imperial dominion.

'Beautiful to behold is the king'

The Great King might have enjoyed the security and prestige of 'invisibility' but when he was viewed by members of his court he was a sight worth seeing. Look at any conventional Persian-made image of an Achaemenid Great King (**F1**, **F3**, **F5**, and **F7**) and notice how perfect he is. (Azarpay 1994 suggests he is even mathematically perfect, thanks to an Egyptian-style grid system employed by artists when depicting the human frame.) The monarch's clothed body emanates strength and vitality; his posture encodes military prowess and sportsmanship; his hair and his beard are thick and luxuriant and radiate health and vitality; his face, with its well defined profile, large eye and thick eyebrow, is as noble as it is handsome.

These images are imperial pronouncements. We must read them as codes through which the king's body takes on cultural meaning: the manliness, wholeness, beauty, and physical fitness of the monarch's body guarantee his right to rule. As we noted in Chapter 1, the Great King's body was special, sharing in appearance the best physical attributes of the anthropomorphic divinity he worshipped (see Bertelli 2001; Hamilton 2005; Sommer 2009; Llewellyn-Jones forthcoming b). The origin and significance of the tradition of the handsome king is unclear, although it is probably connected to the connotation that the ruler is superlative in all respects, for, as Briant (2002: 225–6) has pointed out, 'a man did not become king because he was handsome. . .; it was because of his position as king that he was automatically designated as handsome'.

Greek texts do seem to fixate on the body of the Persian monarch, however, and they take an obvious delight in his splendid appearance, making him into a handsome, if nevertheless inherently despotic, opponent. Successive kings are noted for their valour, handsome demeanour, and their impressive stature (and coincidentally, as we have observed, a hallmark of Achaemenid art is that kings are made taller than their subjects). They are all 'the most valiant of men' or 'the best-looking of men' and their wives and daughters are equally beautiful – a 'torment' for Greek eyes no less (see Herodotus 7.187; Plutarch, *Artaxerxes* 1.1) – and together Persian kings and queens are habitually tagged as being 'the best looking in all of Asia' (**B8**; see further Llewellyn-Jones forthcoming a). Even Plato could not resist speculating on the striking beauty of the royal Persian physique, which he explained by suggesting that infant princes underwent a strict regimen of massage therapy in which their young oiled limbs were twisted into perfection by their doting eunuch slaves (**B9**; see also Pliny 24.165). Of course, every prince and monarch aspired to match the standard of masculine good looks set by Cyrus the Great – his aquiline nose was allegedly the benchmark of beauty for generations of Persians: 'Because Cyrus was hooked-nosed, the Persians – even to this day – love hooked nosed men and consider them the most handsome' (Plutarch, *Moralia* 281e).

Xenophon's Cyrus understood the benefit of what might today be termed a good 'makeover': he saw the beauty of 'Median' dress, considering it to be stately and becoming (**B10**), and he realised also the effectiveness of cosmetics in enhancing a person's appearance (on the term 'Median' see below). The story goes that Cyrus especially admired his grandfather Astyages' use of eye-liner, rouge, and wigs (**B11**). Of course, reading between the lines we must note Xenophon's disparagement of the Persian penchant for garments and cosmetics that are intended to trick the observer: Cyrus finds 'Median' dress suitable for the Persians for the very fact that it conceals physical imperfections and makes the wearer look 'tall and handsome'. From a Greek perspective, this was unmanly and uncivilised; the Greeks prided themselves on the display of nudity (in controlled situations: at the gymnasium and sporting events, even on the battlefield), so that to cover the body conspicuously *à la perse* was categorically cowardly. For the Greeks, the wearing of cosmetics was strictly the prerogative of women and for Xenophon even that was unacceptable. His work on household management, *Oeconomicus*, includes a diatribe (10.1–13) instructing a young bride to set aside her powders, rouge, and eye-liner because of their connections to trickery. For Xenophon's readers, the implication is simple – Persians wear concealing robes and cosmetics because they are womanly and untrustworthy.

Of course, Xenophon fails to understand the long history of dress and cosmetics in the ancient Near East, especially the role given to kohl in ornamenting the eyes. The Persian use of kohl is attested in iconography, where make-up lines drawn around the eyes are sometimes delineated (**F4**), but also in Achaemenid-period archaeological finds from north-west Iran which have yielded delicate kohl tubes made of coloured glass (Dayagi-Mendels 1989: 46). In common with many courts of the Near East, the Achaemenids also created a stratum of specialist slaves who were trained as beauticians, some of whom could become influential at court – no doubt because of their close proximity to the ruler or his family (**B12**). The Biblical text of Esther records that new recruits into the royal harem at Susa underwent six months' intensive beauty therapy as they were massaged with oil of myrrh in what B. W. Jones (1977: 175) has called 'conspicuous consumption in the extreme' (on cosmetics in Esther see further Albright 1982; Baldwin 1984: 68–9; De Troyer 1995).

There can be little doubt that Achaemenid kings and courtiers wore wigs and false hair pieces and their images at Persepolis and other palace sites certainly suggest that false tresses could be plaited into natural hair and beards. This fashionable caprice must have made hair expensive. Strabo (15.3.21) notes that hair was therefore a taxable item in the Persian Empire, while Pseudo-Aristotle suggests that the Great King demanded a 'tribute' of hair from provinces specifically for the creation of wigs (**B13**).

In the ancient world, hair and beards were highly significant and were surrounded by rituals and symbolic undertones; elite men grew their hair long, full, and luxuriant as a supreme mark of high social status and women's beauty was judged by their luxuriant hair (Llewellyn-Jones 2011). At the most mundane level, hair signalled a person's state of health or lack of it (poor-quality hair could signal disease or uncleanliness and the tearing out of the hair was a symbol of grief or distress), and therefore men of the warrior elite carefully grew and cared for theirs to represent their strength and virility (after all, the greatest heroes of Near Eastern antiquity were long-haired: consider Gilgamesh and Samson). They were careful to dress it and arrange it, thereby symbolically 'taming' and 'civilising' it. Excessive hair growth had overtones of the barbaric, so that when the Babylonian king Nebuchadnezzar went into mental decline his courtiers read the external sign when 'his hair grew as long as an eagle's feathers, and his nails were like birds' claws' (Daniel 4:33).

Egyptian pharaohs had an age-old tradition of wearing carefully dressed wigs and Neo-Assyrian monarchs also took extreme care with the plaiting, braiding, and ringletting of their hair and beards into elaborate coiffures (see Madhloom 1970: 83–9; and images in Dayagi-Mendels 1989: 66–7; Bahrani 2003), and it was this fashion which was wholeheartedly adopted by Achaemenid rulers, who carefully had themselves depicted in the artworks with every curl and wave of hair clearly delineated. In reality, the hair and the beard were carefully dressed by skilled hairdressers, who twisted the curls into shape and fixed them in position by the use of perfumed oil, which helped control the hair, in addition to keeping it shiny and fragrant. Anointing the hair and beard with oil was probably a ritual practice for the Achaemenid monarchs as it was for other Near Eastern kings (1 Samuel 16:1–13; 1 Kings 1:39), but it was also a beauty ritual in its own right, and one associated too with festivity and hospitality. Great Kings lavished their wealth on costly perfumed hair oil, and one particular sort, *labyzos*, was even more expensive than myrrh (Deinon F25a = Athenaeus 12.514a).

A full, well set, fragranced beard was a sign of manhood and a source of pride for Persian men. It was the ornament of their machismo. In Near Eastern cultures the beard was symbolically loaded: it was the object of salutation and the focus of oaths and blessings, although, conversely, the beard could also be a locus of shame, for an attack on the beard was an attack on the individual who sported it. Because the beard was the superlative symbol of manhood, it was a great insult to degrade it; to humiliate them, prisoners of war might have half their beards shaved off. Thus Israelite prophets threatened the people that the king of Assyria would 'shave your head and the hair of your legs and . . . take off your beards also' (Isaiah 7:20; see also 2 Samuel 10:4–5). Not surprisingly then, given the close association between the beard and physical power and martial ability, the Great King was depicted with the most impressive beard of all; it far outstripped those of his courtiers in terms of length, fullness, and elaboration and it clearly demarcated him as the Empire's alpha male.

Ctesias tells a story (which perhaps has at its core a genuine Iranian version) of the time a powerful court eunuch, Artoxares, attempted to overthrow the throne of Darius II and establish himself as Great King. To do this, Ctesias says (F15 §54), he asked a woman to procure for him a beard and moustache of false hair, 'so that he could look like a man'. At a time when beards were *de rigueur* for all elite men, eunuchs (who, if castrated before puberty, could never sprout facial hair) must have appeared very incongruous – at best 'half-men', at worst sub-human (for eunuchs see Chapter 1; on eunuchs and beards see Tougher 2008: 23), and Ctesias' point is to confirm that, to rule as a king, one must look the part. The vital accoutrement for the job was the luxuriant royal beard. Since Artoxares was incapable of growing his own, he would seize on the fashion for false hair and wear a counterfeit one (see Llewellyn-Jones 2002: 39). Preserved in Ctesias is a genuine Persian belief that the monarch was the first among men and that his ability to rule and to preserve cosmic order was signified through his appearance. Interestingly, Pirngruber (2011: 283) expresses doubts that Artoxares was a eunuch *castrato*, suggesting that it was his *wife* who helped procure for him the false beard; if he was married, Artoxares could not have been a castrated eunuch. This thesis is fundamentally flawed, however: Ctesias' Greek refers only to an anonymous 'woman', not specifically to 'his wife' (see Llewellyn-Jones and Robson 2010: 195).

One further symbol of monarchy needs to be examined in the context of the king's head – the crowning glory, quite literally, of monarchy – for on top of the Great King's coiffured and oiled locks sat a crown, weighty with symbolic authority. In antiquity, as in later eras, the crown signified some kind of state of honour or dignity for those who wore it because a kind of divine aura emanated from a monarch's crown and raised the wearer up to the most exalted position. Whether children in make-believe play, beauty queens, athletic victors, or royal heirs, aiming for the crown, with its lofty ritual and ancient symbolism, secures glory even today.

The Old Persian word for 'crown' is not known, although various contemporary Greek terms like *kidaris* or *kitaris*, *tiara*, and *kurbasia* were possibly derived from Old Persian vocabulary. In the Achaemenid period there is evidence to suggest that rulers might wear two very different kinds of crown. Most common (and more in keeping with the standard image of a crown) was a rigid metal cylinder with or without crenelated decoration (it is not known whether the king's crown was of a special colour or metal, like gold). While it is possible that Achaemenid kings adopted different forms of crown (crenelated crowns certainly changed shape over the decades), they cannot be considered 'personal crowns' in the way that Sasanian crowns are understood (Berghe 1993: 74; see also Root 1979: 92–3; Henkelman 1995–6); after all, the Achaemenid crown prince is usually depicted wearing the same crown as his father (**F3**) and members of the court at Persepolis sometimes likewise wear crenelated and fluted crowns (although less tall than royal examples; see Tilia 1978: 53–66; see further Kaptan 2002: 58–60).

Greek texts suggest that an alternative 'crown', the *tiara*, was commonly worn by Great Kings. This was a soft headdress, a kind of *bashlyk* (a cap with lappets for wrapping around the neck) made from treated leather, felt, suede or cloth. It was a form of headdress worn by nearly all Iranian tribesmen and was constructed with long ear flaps and neck flaps, which could be draped in a myriad of styles. The form of this 'crown' varied considerably from tribe to tribe but, according to the Greeks, only the Great King wore the upright (*orthē*) *tiara* or *kidaris* (Hebrew, *keter*?), although it must be stated that this headdress is *never* encountered in indigenous Iranian royal iconography (Salvesen 1998: 126–30, figs 2 and 3, suggests otherwise, but she is confusing the *tiara* with the crenelated crown and *diadem* – see below). Nevertheless, the Greeks fixated on the royal upright *tiara* so much that it must have its basis in reality (see further Tuplin 2007c). The *tiara* was usually worn in conjunction with a *diadem* – a purple and white cloth band – which was wrapped around its base. When Darius I prayed to Apollo, however, he took off his *tiara* and wore only the *diadem* (Polyaenus 7.12), suggesting that the latter had a special symbolic importance of its own; certainly the honour of wearing the *diadem* was also bestowed on the king's most high-ranking courtiers, who wore it knotted on the forehead. Interestingly, of all the elements which made up the Persian royal crown, Alexander adopted only the *diadem* (Arrian, *Anabasis* 7.22) and it remained the primary symbol of royalty for all Hellenistic rulers.

Royal robes

Clothing was an important element of ancient Persian court culture. Its significance could be physical, economic, social, or symbolic and the function of clothing, moreover, was multiple. Clothing could protect, conceal, display, or represent a person's office or state of being and the fact that garments could wear out or tear is also important. After all, in the ancient world handmade fabrics were costly, scarce, and valuable and dyes and decorations added to their worth, so their disintegration or loss was a serious blow to a household economy and personal wealth (see Cleland et al. 2007: 40–1, 205).

In our discussion of the royal investiture (Chapter 1) we noted that the new king went through a symbolic rite of separation and reincorporation that was signified through the use of ceremonial clothing as the ruler stripped off his fine garments, put on the humble garb that Cyrus II had worn before taking the throne, and was then re-clothed in a robe which indicated both his illustriousness and his right to rule. The imagery of undressing and dressing is usually symbolic of bigger issues, and in the case of the Achaemenid investiture ritual the transference of clothing harked back to Persia's humble beginning (and, in a sense, by donning Cyrus' clothing every subsequent Great King became a Cyrus reborn) while simultaneously celebrating its current glories.

The Greeks generally regarded Persian dress as beautiful (Herodotus 1.135, 7.61–2) and expensive, and indeed Cook (1983: 138) estimates that by modern standards Artaxerxes II stood up in nothing short of £3 million worth of clothing and jewellery. But what did the royal robe look like? Members of the Achaemenid court wore two distinct types of clothing (Llewellyn-Jones 2010b). The first sort can be called 'riding habit' or 'cavalry costume' (**F13**; see Widengren 1956; Vogelsang 2010): made up of five items of clothing – a felt cap, a sleeved coat (Greek, *kandys*; Old Persian, *gaunaka*), sleeved tunic (Greek, *ependytēs*), trousers (Greek, *anaxyrides*), and footgear – this sort of dress was ideal for a people so dependent on horses for transportation and warfare (see Chapter 3). On the Persepolis Apadana reliefs it is worn by peoples from the Iranian plateau and related groups (Vogelsang 2010). The Greeks erroneously called this 'Median dress' – for there is no evidence for it being limited to the Medes, although unfortunately the tag has stuck in much contemporary scholarship (see for instance Sekunda 2010). The labelling of this type of outfit as 'Median' needs to be overturned in favour of 'riding habit' or 'cavalry costume' or some other suitably equine-related idiom. Interestingly, Achaemenid iconography never depicts the king wearing the riding habit, although it is probable that he did so. Indeed, four groups of Iranian delegates are represented at Persepolis bringing coats, tunics, and trousers to their ruler, and the motif is repeated on the Nereid monument from Xanthos in Asia Minor. The message is clear: the Great King is an Iranian horseman as well as the foremost Persian courtier.

Aspects of court etiquette operated around the *kandys*, which is usually shown draped over the wearer's shoulders with the sleeves (Greek, *korē*) hanging loosely at the sides. These ultra-long sleeves were supposed to be used in the presence of the Great King and the suppliant was expected to place his arms in the sleeves but (probably) allow the excess fabric to fall over his hand, thereby rendering his hands harmless (since they could not grip weapons). Failure to do this was read as an insult to the monarch or his representative, and Prince Cyrus the Younger used such an affront as an excuse to execute two of his powerful –and potentially troublesome– kinsmen (**B14**).

The second form of Persian clothing is known as the 'court robe' (**F14**) and may have been of pure Persian invention, although it does bare resemblance to Egyptian-style royal tunics of the New Kingdom period (Root 2011: 426–9 argues that the garment originated in Elam but there is nothing to support this). Constructed from a huge double square of linen or wool (or perhaps cotton or even silk), and worn over baggy trousers, the tunic was tightly belted at the waist to form a robe with deep folds which created an overhang resembling sleeves (see Goldman 1964, 1991; Beck 1972; Kuhrt 2007: 532). The court robe (Greek, *sarapis, serapeis, kalasireis* or *aktaiai*) was richly decorated with woven designs and ornamented appliqué decorations made from gold and semiprecious stones; it was as costly as it was beautiful (Athenaeus 12.525d–e). This was the costume of the Great King *par excellence* and he is represented wearing it repeatedly, whether sitting on his throne or actively fighting in battle or killing an animal (mythical or otherwise). In reality the court robe would have been a highly impractical garment for any form of active combat, so the choice to depict the monarch wearing it with such regularity can only be explained by the fact that it was symbolically important. The court robe represented Achaemenid power.

In daily life, kings and courtiers could wear either the court robe or the riding habit as situation required, although it is next to impossible for us to understand when and why the two types of dress were worn. It is not beyond possibility that some court positions required a specific form of livery. On the tomb of Darius I, for instance, Aspathines, the king's bow-bearer, wears the riding habit, while Gobryas, the spear-bearer, wears the court robe (both courtiers, incidentally, were Persian, strengthening the argument that the riding habit was not Median at all).

It is probable that the royal robe worn at the climax of the investiture ceremony was a court robe since we know that it was richly dyed and beautifully worked with exquisite designs (Xenophon, *Cyropaedia* 8.3.13–14; Curtius Rufus 3.3.17–19). Ctesias (F41) recalls that one sort of royal robe was known as a *sarapis* and here, remarkably, he seems to preserve an authentic ancient Elamite term for a royal garment since the word *sarapi* is found in Middle Elamite texts from the acropolis at Susa, suggesting a long continuity of tradition in ceremonial dress in southern Iran (see Henkelman 2003b: 228–31; for Elamite royal robes in the Achaemenid period see Álvarez-Mon 2009).

Given that the investiture ceremony was a rite of passage or, as Plutarch would have it, a *teletē* ('mystery rite') in which the ruler underwent a metamorphosis, the royal robe worn by the king was thereafter imbued with religious symbolism. Curtius Rufus (3.3.17–19) notes that it was purple, white, and gold and decorated with the 'motif of gilded hawks attacking each other with their beaks' – no doubt his interpretation of the winged Ahuramazda symbol. It was this ensemble which, Ctesias (F45pγ) notes, struck the Persians with an almost religious awe (*thaumaston*).

The Great King's robe was a talisman. When Cyrus the Younger plotted to kill his brother Artaxerxes II, he refused to strike the death blow while the king was wearing this garment (**A1**) and the true significance of the robe as a manifestation of the kingship itself is the key to understanding the story Herodotus tells about Xerxes' robe (**E14**), behind which no doubt lies a Persian account of Masistes' attempt to usurp the throne (Sancisi-Weerdenburg 1983: 28–9); moreover, Herodotus' audience would probably have known that Xerxes himself was assassinated in a court coup, thereby adding significance and irony to the story (see Chapter 5). The very real paranoia lying behind the idea of usurpation and its relationship to the royal robe is likewise encountered in a Persian story told by Deinon which has the ambitious and treacherous Assyrian queen Semiramis trick her weakling husband into lending her his royal garment, which she subsequently refuses to return (**B15**). When in the Hebrew Bible Prince Jonathan, the son and heir of King Saul, gifted David his robe and belt he was effectively relinquishing his claim to the throne and announcing David as a more fitting (God-chosen) successor to Saul (1 Samuel 18:1–4).

Even when ripped or tattered, the king's robe possessed extraordinary powers. One courtier, Teribazos, managed to get hold of one of Artaxerxes II's cast-offs and wore it openly in front of the court. But he escaped the death sentence which naturally accompanied such a rash act because of the king's benevolence and because Teribazos was prepared to debase himself by playing the fool in front of the king and was thus exonerated of treason (Plutarch, *Artaxerxes* 5.2).

The king's robe was uniquely his. An aetiological legend recounted by Xenophon tells how Cyrus the Great received the prototype royal robe from the daughter of the Median king, whom he then took as a wife (*Cyropaedia* 8.5.17–19), and the robe, it is suggested, bestowed the kingship of Media on Cyrus. Thus there is little doubt that the Persians believed the Great King's robe to have possessed the supernatural powers of monarchy. Xerxes, troubled by dreams, instructed his uncle Artabanos to put on royal clothes and to sleep in the king's bed; as he slept, the same apparition that had visited Xerxes came to Artabanos too, now decked out in the paraphernalia of royalty and imbued with the requisite aura of majesty (Herodotus 7.17). Alexander of Macedon's careful employment of articles of Persian royal dress following his defeat of Darius III is best understood in this light and suggests that he wanted to be acknowledged as a legitimate Great King (Plutarch, *Alexander* 45.2; Diodorus 17.77.4–5; Fredricksmeyer 1997).

Garments played an important part in the wider culture of court society and in particular the act of a superior (especially the ruler) bestowing a robe on a subordinate (a courtier) as an indication of special favour and as a rite of investiture has a very ancient pedigree in the Near East. The Hebrew prophet Isaiah records the promotion of a man named Elyakim to the position of master of the Jerusalem palace and notes how he was clothed by the king with a robe and a sash as a signal of his new authority over the royal household (Isaiah 22:20); most famous is the story of Joseph and the gift his father made him of a well dyed multi-coloured coat as a sign of favour in Genesis 37. In Iran this custom can be traced in unbroken lineage from antiquity to the late twentieth century, where it has long been known as *kheilat*, an Islamic-period term referring to both the act of gift-giving and the robe of honour itself (see Gordon 2003, 2010; Baker 2010). The bestowing of a *kheilat* was a chief signifier in the political process: deserving loyal followers were rewarded with clothing and even erring courtiers who humbly repented received a *kheilat* to signal renewed loyalty.

Kheilat is certainly attested for the Achaemenid Empire (although the Old Persian expression is unknown). The Great King often gifted robes to his satraps, military officers, and courtiers as an expression of personal favour or for services rendered to the crown and the act served to sustain courtiers' loyalty as the robe-giving ceremony was held publicly at court or, for those not present at court, the robes were received at public ceremonies in the provinces (even cities could be honoured with the gift of a robe – see Herodotus 7.116). Mary Boyce suggests that even in the Achaemenid period the New Year celebration was the time for *kheilat* ceremonies, the most lavish displays of royal gift-giving (Boyce 1983: 799–800). The Greek sources suggest that the sleeved riding coat (*kandys*) was especially valued as a royal gift, and that the colour and decoration of the coat could reflect rank and status (not every robe was equal, and neither was its recipient; Herodotus 3.84; Xenophon, *Cyropaedia* 8.3.3–5). Those honoured with the gift of a royal robe would show it off in public, as Mithradates did when he had received a handsome coat from Artaxerxes II after the Battle of Cunaxa (Plutarch, *Artaxerxes* 15.2) or as Mordechai did when he was paraded through the streets of Susa on the back of the king's horse

(Esther 6:11). Decked out in their finery, Achaemenid courtiers clearly cut fine figures; all the more humorous therefore is Xenophon's vivid account of them, all bedraggled and mud-splattered, attempting to free baggage wagons from the quagmire of an impassable road (**B16**).

The idea that a magical sympathy exists between an individual and his clothing was acknowledged by James Frazer (1911: 207), who noted a primitive belief that 'whatever is done to clothes will be felt by [a] man himself'. This might explain an Achaemenid ritual whereby instead of scourging the bodies of an erring courtier, his clothes were whipped as a substitute. This was a highly emblematic act that at once humiliated the victim and made an example of him to others of his rank (**B17**). As Keaveney (1998: 240) notes, 'the intent seems clear enough. Those punished were meant to feel pain through their clothes . . . in a real sense, clothes made the man'. Of equal significance was the symbolism of the belt, which on a practical level could be used to tighten the tunic of the riding habit or to pull in the voluminous folds of the court robe. But the belt also indicated a bond of loyalty to the king and figuratively bound the wearer to the throne. If the king grasped a noble by his belt (presumably to pull it off) it meant that the bond between them was broken (Nepos, *Datames* 10.1–2; Diodorus 17.30.4; Briant 2002: 325).

Ceremony and etiquette of the royal audience

Like kings in other ancient Near Eastern societies, the Achaemenid monarchs relied upon formalised etiquette and court ceremony to create a special aura around the throne (see above and Brosius 2010a, 2010b). The separation and distancing of the king from the gaze of his subjects, even from the majority of his court, meant that elaborate rituals were enacted through which courtiers and visitors might get limited access to the royal personage during a tightly controlled audience ceremony, where matters of security and etiquette were paramount (Esther 1:14 highlights the notion of having 'privileged access to the royal presence'). To enjoy the benefits of a royal audience courtiers and visitors had to undergo (we must assume) tight security checks and had to be conversant with palace protocol to ensure that they behaved with dignified decorum and observed preordained rules in the presence of the monarch.

We might think of the Great King, costumed in his finery, as an actor in a great royal drama and his courtiers as both players and spectators. Thinking about the court in terms of theatre is, of course, not new. Historians and others writing about the Hellenistic court or the court of Versailles (or many other early modern courts) have found the metaphor of theatre irresistible (Burke 1994; Strootman 2007: 10). The metaphor is perfectly apropos. No less a person than Elizabeth I of England once declared that 'We princes . . . are set on stages, in the sight of the world duly observed' (Neale 1958: vol. II, p. 119), implying that monarchs could regard themselves as performers in the drama of court life. The social theorist Erving Goffman has argued that the word 'performance' refers to 'all the activity of an individual which occurs during a period marked by his continuous presence before a particular set of observers and which has some influence on the observers' (Goffman 1956a: 22). Events at court, like investiture ceremonies, royal audiences, and imperial parade reviews, were clearly focused on a more limited kind of 'performance', since they were set apart from everyday life by being 'scripted' or turned into ceremony. But nevertheless, Goffman's exploration of the notion of 'ceremonial' and its relation to deference, demeanour, and etiquette suggested that 'the self is in part a ceremonial thing, a sacred object which must be treated with proper ritual care and in turn must be presented in a proper light to others' (Goffman 1956b: 497). While here Goffman is writing about everyday behaviour patterns in the twentieth century, his observation, if anything, is even more pertinent to an earlier society which was more rigidly and hierarchically ordered, such as the Achaemenid court. Indeed, the ceremonies of the Persian court arose precisely out of a heightened concern for establishing and reconfirming the place of each individual within a structure of both bonds and boundaries.

In addition, the close association between etiquette and ceremony must not be dismissed lightly as a mere frippery of a privileged aristocratic lifestyle, for, as Elias was keen to demonstrate in his work on Versailles:

> Etiquette had a major symbolic function in the structure of . . . [court] society and its form of government. . . . [Etiquette] served as an indicator of the position of an individual within the balance of power between the courtiers, a balance controlled by the king and very precarious. . . . What gave [etiquette and ceremony] their gravity was solely the importance they conferred on those present within court society, the power, rank and dignity they expressed. (Elias 1983: 94)

Moreover,

> Each individual was hypersensitive to the slightest change in the mechanism [of etiquette and ceremony], standing watch over the existing order,

and attentive to its finest nuances. . . . In this way, therefore, the mecha-
nism of the court revolved in perpetual motion, fed by the need for prestige
and by tensions which, once in place, endlessly renewed the competitive
process. (Elias 1983: 97)

In other words, 'doing the right thing' was expected at court. The laws
of protocol, the knowledge of employing the correct formulae (spoken
and non-verbal) for greeting, showing respect or deference, and the
arts of obsequiousness had to be mastered by courtiers who were
eager to maintain court positions or to climb the ladder of success.
Conversely, failure to 'do the right thing' could be used as a weapon to
bring about the fall of an enemy at court and courtiers (at Versailles as
much as in Persia) carefully observed the actions and speech of others
to measure their knowledge of the correct courtly behaviour.

An extreme example of a courtier who did not 'do the right thing'
is that of Intaphrenes, a historically verifiable figure who in the Bisitun
inscription was entrusted with putting down the Babylonian revolt in
the autumn of 521 BCE. Herodotus tells his story (although there are
novelistic folk motifs within it which are shared by many cultures)
and his narrative pivots around Intaphrenes' misreading of his courtly
privilege (**B18**). Insisting that he, like the other killers of the Magus,
should have unlimited access to the monarch, Intaphrenes doubts the
protestations of the king's security personnel (who tell him that the
king is in bed with a woman), attacks them and, as a result, is thought
by the king to be behaving treacherously. He is imprisoned and then
executed. Intaphrenes plays fast and loose with the rules of correct
court procedure and he dies for it.

The Intaphrenes story also highlights the careful demarcation
of space inherent in Achaemenid royal architecture, ideology, and
ceremonial (Herodotus appears to have a secure grasp of this). The
inner court/outer court polarity is central to the tale, in that while
Intaphrenes violates the boundaries of space and self-control, his
(unnamed) wife understands all too well the rules of space and the
efficacy of playing by the rules. Her persistent appearance at the king's
gate solicits the king's curiosity and ultimately his benevolence, a situation which occurs elsewhere in the literary tradition (Esther 4:1–5;
Herodotus 3.140).

The king's gate, a genuine Near Eastern expression (Akkadian, *bāb
šarri*; Hebrew, *s'r 'hmlk*), actually refers to an imposing building always
a short distance from the main palace. The term nonetheless became
a synonym for the palace and court as a whole; 'those of the gate' was

likewise a kind of court title (see Esther 2:21, 3:2), just as in the Ottoman world the term 'the sublime porte' referred to both the physical palace gateway and to the court itself. At Persepolis, Xerxes' 'Gate of All Nations', with its huge apotropaic bull figures (**F15**), served its purpose as the magical portal between the brutal outside world and the rarefied universe of royalty (**B19**), while at Susa the gateway was flanked (as we have seen) with over-life-sized statues of Darius I, which perhaps served a similar magico-religious function as the Persepolis bull figures. The gate was the place where all suppliants and petitioners waited for an appointment with the monarch; they were questioned by security here and only after satisfying the guards were they admitted into the court-yard beyond. Here messengers (including eunuchs) conveyed missives back and forth between the courtyard and the audience hall. Briant (2002: 261) notes that in the Parthian period every visitor to court 'had to give his name, homeland, profession, and reason for visiting, and all this information was written in a register along with a description of the person and his clothing'; this security and administrative policy probably already existed at the Achaemenid court.

Narrative accounts of audiences with the Great King form a signifi-cant corpus in Greek and Biblical writings on the Persian court (**B20**, **B21**); the same is true of satrapal audience scenes (see Xenophon, *Hellenica* 1.5.1–3; Plutarch, *Lysander* 6), but nothing remotely com-parable exists in the Achaemenid literary tradition. Instead we must turn to a rich stratum of iconography for information on the intricacies of the ceremony. Representations of the royal audience come in the form of numerous seal and gemstone images, a small painted image on a sarcophagus, and from the sculptured monumental doorjambs at Persepolis (for excellent overviews see Allen 2005b; Kaptan 2002: 31–41), although the finest surviving examples come in the form of two big stone reliefs once located at the two staircases to the Persepolis Apadana but later moved to the treasury (Tilia 1972, 1978; Abdi 2010). In the reliefs, the Great King is shown in audience in a 'frozen moment' (**F3**); he wears a court robe and crown and holds a lotus blossom and a sceptre (which he might stretch out to grant favours; Esther 4:11, 5:2, 8:4); in order to 'accentuate the immutable character of kingship' (Briant 2002: 221) he is accompanied by the crown prince, who is depicted wearing the same garb as the king, and who is also given the prerogative of holding a lotus. Also in attendance are high-ranking members of the court and the military (for a discussion of the identity of these individuals see Abdi 2010: 277–8; for a good description see also Kuhrt 2007: 536). Two incense-burners help to demarcate the royal space and accentuate its sacredness, as do the dais upon which the throne is placed (Brettler 1989: 85–6) and the baldachin which covers the scene. The relief image closely echoes a Greek description: 'The throne ... was gold, and round it stood four short golden posts studded with jewels; these supported a woven canopy of purple' (Deinon F1 = Athenaeus 12.514c). The theatrical paraphernalia of the throne room and the awesome setting of the Apadana (**F16**) were intended to instil fear and wonder in suppliants; further, the figure of the king himself, the protagonist of the courtly drama, must have been an impressive, almost overwhelming, sight. The anonymous author of the Greek version of the book of Esther brilliantly captures the scene of the terrified queen approaching the enthroned king, who is described as looking 'like a bull in the height of anger' (**B22**).

The royal throne was an icon of kingship and in the Near East both monarchs and gods were frequently portrayed enthroned (Salvesen 1998: 132; Brettler 1989: 81–5). Unsurprisingly, the expression 'sit upon the throne', indicating the practice of kingship, is found widely in Akkadian, Ugaritic, and Hebrew texts, and the close association between the throne and the ruler was widespread in ancient societies (for an excellent overview of thrones in world civilisations see Charles-Gaffiot 2011). The Achaemenid throne was high-backed and rested upon leonine feet (**F3**); Near Eastern thrones frequently employed lion or sphinx imagery (see 1 Kings 10:18–20). A rare example of sections of an actual Achaemenid-period throne (probably from a satrapal palace) was discovered near Samaria in Israel (Kuhrt 2007: 617). The unmistakable message sent by this ornate piece of furniture was obvious: the one who sat on the throne had absolute authority. It was the symbolism of the throne, not necessarily the physical artefact itself, that shifted from one king to another and the image of the throne was therefore used in the ancient Near East to describe the transfer of rule: 'as Yahweh was with my lord the king, so may he be with Solomon to make his throne even greater than the throne of my lord, king David' (1 Kings 1:37). When a king ruled with integrity and justice and courted the good-will of the gods then he had no fear of being deposed from his occupancy of the throne: 'If a king judges the poor with fairness, his throne will always be secure' (Proverbs 29:14).

The Achaemenid Great King had a footstool as well as a throne and this too was an important emblem of his kingship. Like the throne, it was loaded with ritual and symbolism. Shalmaneser III of Assyria was thus addressed as 'Valiant man who with the support of Ashur his lord has put all lands under his feet as a footstool' (*Royal Inscriptions* of *Mesopotamia, Assyrian Periods* 3.2.102–3; see further Psalm 110:1). At the Achaemenid court there was even an office associated with the footstool (**B23**) and its bearer is depicted on the north and east wings of the Apadana. Curtius Rufus' comical vignette of Alexander misappropriating a low table as a footstool (**B24**) only reconfirms the centrality of this seemingly inconspicuous piece of furniture in royal display and ideology. After all, it was a given that the Great King's feet should never touch the ground and must be protected by soft carpets (**B25**).

At the centre of the Treasury relief (**F3**) a courtier dressed in the riding habit – possibly the chiliarch – performs a ritual gesture of obeisance to the monarch. It was one of the principal roles of the chiliarch to present individuals or delegations to the king (Nepos, *Conon* 3.2–3; Plutarch, *Themistocles* 27.2–7), so his presence in the scene makes sense. He stoops forward and raises his hand to his mouth and makes a gesture that is similar the *sala'am*, or formal greeting, used in later Muslim courts. Any society that requires such codes of respectful behaviour towards categories of high-ranking individuals is likely to have autocratic political organisation, characterised by the coercive power of a king. In the ancient Near East the pattern of cosmic kingship was so deeply entrenched in the governmental systems that its codified apparatus of power manifested itself in multiple displays of non-verbal communication, and particularly in the act of showing reverence to the monarch (or his representative). Much has been written on the nature of non-verbal communication in ancient Near Eastern civilisations (see especially Gruber 1980, who provides a full bibliography), although a particular debate centres on the Greek understanding of Persian non-verbal customs and Persian displays of affection, friendliness, loyalty, and, most importantly, reverence. Unspontaneous, semi-ritualised gestures were a hallmark of Persian social communication, at least according to Herodotus (1.134), who describes in some detail a series of greeting gestures used in daily life. These same gestures were, it would seem, ritualised at the Persian court. Common rules of respectful deference are often multiplied and formalised where a strict protocol of codified gesture is required, and the Persians seem to have transformed the gestures of *la vie quotidienne* into a rarefied form of court etiquette.

Known to the Greeks as *proskynesis*, the exact nature of the ceremonial obeisance to a Persian monarch is debated (Frye 1972; Fredricksmeyer 2000). Etymologically, *proskynesis* incorporates the idea of a kiss (Greek, *pros* 'towards'; *kyneo* 'to kiss'), but when Herodotus says that one should perform *proskynesis* to a superior while prostrating oneself or bowing down, the term must describe an act performed once one is bowed or prostrate, which is, as on the Treasury relief, kissing from the hands. Importantly, for the Greeks the gesture was a religious act and suitable for performance only before a god, so that for a Greek to do it before a man undermined the very concept of *eleutheria*, or 'freedom' (Xenophon, *Hellenica* 4.1.35). Classical authors note that performing *proskynesis* before the Great King was a non-negotiable rule for an audience (Frye 1972; Fredricksmeyer 2000) and this is clearly what the chiliarch Artabanus intended to convey to Themistocles when he briefed the Greek about the ceremony (**B26**). Likewise, the chiliarch Tithraustes advised Conon that any man who appeared before the Great King must render to him 'a rite of adoration (Latin, *venerai*)', a term specifically defined by Nepos as *proskynesis* (*Conon* 3.3; see also Aelian, *Historical Miscellany* 1.21). The misunderstanding of the Persian act of *proskynesis* as a veneration of divine monarchy (a claim never made by the Achaemenid kings themselves, nor understood that way by the Persians) accounts for several Greek tales which take the distaste for this act of social submission as their theme. Herodotus (7.136) tells how the Spartans Bulis and Sperchis refused to prostrate themselves before Xerxes in a royal audience at Susa, even though the royal guards thrust their heads to the ground; and Aelian (*Historical Miscellany* 1.29) describes the Theban Ismenias as 'ingenious and typically Hellenic' in his ruse to dodge paying the required homage to the Great King (compare Plutarch, *Artaxerxes* 22.8). Notoriously, it was with this background of misunderstanding that, in the summer of 327 BCE, Alexander provoked unrest among his Macedonian followers when he introduced *proskynesis* to his court and army (Taylor 1927).

In a Near Eastern context, the Persian practice of bowing and kissing as a sign of submission and respect looks very much at home. Kowtowing, prostration, kissing the ground, or even kissing the hem of a garment or the feet of the monarch were familiar gestures in Assyrian court protocol, and some Near Eastern texts record an elaborate and flowery language of bodily self-debasement utilised to render homage to the monarch (**B27**), while other sources suggest that the relative status of monarch and subjects was carefully negotiated through different gestures of respect (2 Samuel 14:33; 1 Kings 1:15, 31).

Concluding thought

This chapter has touched on the importance of palace architecture, dress, bodily display, and court ceremonial in the creation and promotion of Achaemenid monarchy. Set within the theatre-like structure of the royal residence, court ceremony gave meaning to life in the household of the king and formalised rules for 'doing the right thing' allowed both nobles and royalty to place themselves within the structure of the court. This was augmented by the king's inaccessibility, which was fundamentally important to the Achaemenid concept of kingship. Through his 'invisibility' the monarch was able to control his courtiers, since by honouring them with access to his person, and even speaking to them face to face, he was able to activate rivalries which kept the nobility preoccupied with their social positions and which amplified the central role of the good-looking, symbolically robed Great King himself.

CHAPTER 3

The Great King in His Empire: The Movable Court

A vast motorcade of gleaming limousines ferried the entourage of King Abdullah of Saudi Arabia to Buckingham Palace for the state banquet at the start of his official three-day tour. Five jumbo jets kitted out to the height of luxury were used to airlift the King's entourage to Britain. In addition to his 23-strong group of all-male personal advisers, which includes 13 members of the Saudi royal family, there were 30 officials ranging from cabinet ministers to economists and specialists in British affairs. The octogenarian King was also believed to have brought a handful of wives and 100 servants to attend to his personal needs, including a 'travelling clinic'. (Colin Brown, *The Independent*, October 2007)

Monarchs like to travel. When they travel, they do so in style – a perk of the job, surely. But why do monarchs travel at all when they have comfortable and secure palaces to meet both their daily requirements and the needs of state? Monarchs travel because they must. They travel to meet fellow kings or leaders and to play their role on the international stage; they travel in order to witness the internal workings of their kingdom and to play an equally important role in the dramas of domestic policy; they travel to show themselves to their subjects as manifestations of power and control or to boost their popularity. Many modern heads of state even go so far as to 'press the flesh' of their admirers – shaking hands and offering pleasantries – in a convivial manner that would have been alien to the majority of absolute rulers of past societies.

In the Achaemenid period, the Persian Great Kings travelled extensively to fulfil the needs of national and international diplomacy, to fulfil religious or cultural duties, to lead armies into battle, and to participate in the lives of their subjects (Briant 1988). They were usually accompanied on their journeys by the majority of the court as well as by a huge military force. In effect, when the Great King journeyed across the Empire, the state itself was in transit: 'as goes the royal house, so goes the Empire' (Briant 2002: 415; see also Thucydides 1.129).

Greek treatises on the Persians often refer to 'the land of the king'. That is how the Greeks conceived of the Persian Empire. This chapter elaborates on that notion and explores the Great King's relationship with his lands. It will examine his journeys around the Empire and it will explore his symbolic rapport with, and practical use of, nature. The chapter will also look at the way in which the royal court *en masse* was integrated into the lands of the Empire and the way in which tribal identity and nomadic migration patterns remained embedded within royal systems of governance. In addition it will ask about the practicalities of moving the court around the Empire. How did it travel? Where was it accommodated and how was it fed?

The king's lands

Made up of twenty-three lands (although the numbering varies slightly according to the source; Briant 2002: 173), the Achaemenid Empire stretched from Libya to India and from southern Russia to the Indian Ocean, making it, at its height, the biggest Empire the ancient world had seen. However, it is fair to suggest that, in fact, there was never *one* Persian Empire but multiple Persian Empires, since throughout its 230-year history the Achaemenid Empire was in a constant state of flux, expanding and contracting and sometimes expanding again as provinces and peoples were added to the central government by force or coercion and were lost from Persian control through wars and rebellions (Egypt, for example, was lost from the Empire for almost sixty years before being reconquered). After the reign of Xerxes, however, it is fair to say that there was no significant territorial expansion, though there were still numerous national or localised revolts. The royal rhetoric recorded in the Old Persian cuneiform inscriptions and disseminated widely across the Empire in multiple languages emphasised that all conquered nations were united in service to the Great King, whose laws they were required to obey and whose majesty they were obliged to uphold.

It was Darius I, a truly outstanding bureaucrat, who first (allegedly) divided the Empire's territories into administrative satrapies in order to maintain the levy of tribute required from each region (Herodotus 3.98) and his Bisitun inscription provides the oldest extant list of the constituents of the Empire (**C1**). It begins with two core lands, Persia and Elam, and then the order roughly follows the map of the Empire in a clockwise fashion, first referring to the western provinces or satrapies, then those in the northern part, followed by the lands in the east of the Empire. The ordering of the provinces is interesting, since lands lying closest to the imperial centre (Elam, Media, Babylonia, Armenia) are privileged in the text over those at the periphery of the Empire (Ionia, Maka), suggesting an Achaemenid ideology of ethnic hierarchy. Proximity to Persia signified a higher level of civilisation (an ideology also understood and articulated by Herodotus 1.134). Royal texts constantly emphasise the size and the ethnic diversity of the Empire but always privilege Persia at its heart (**C2**, **C3**; see further Briant 2002: 178–81; Kuhrt 2002: 19–22). There are six surviving so-called Old Persian 'Empire lists' which project this world order (DB, DPe, DSe, DNa, DSaa, and XPh; see Briant 2002: 173) and there is little doubt that this official vision of the Empire was widely circulated throughout the king's lands; it is therefore little wonder that Greek sources routinely reiterate this dominant Achaemenid rhetoric (Herodotus 3.97; Xenophon, *Cyropaedia* 8.8.1; Xenophon, *Anabasis* 1.7.6; Strabo 11.11.4).

Any attempts to estimate the demographic parameters of the Persian Empire are fraught with contradictions and frustrations, mainly because the sources for such a study are highly controversial. Classical texts on Persia tend to overemphasise numbers (the size of the Achaemenid military, for instance; see Herodotus 3.89), while Iranian bureaucratic texts from Persepolis or the Babylonian Murašu Archive give only narrow demographic snapshots of a particular period and locale. Therefore estimates of the size of the Empire's population range from a conservative 17,000,000 to a more extravagant 35,000,000 (Wiesehöfer 2009: 77). The people of the wider Empire certainly mattered to the Achaemenid centre and in royal rhetoric the Empire is envisaged *through* its people, so that in official Achaemenid art the structure of the Empire (as well as its ethnic diversity) is given physical form through the representation of the peoples who inhabited the king's lands. We have already noted the depictions of foreign gift-bearers on the great Apadana staircases at Persepolis and the collaborative role they might have played in state ceremonials (at Nowruz for instance), but other representations of foreign peoples exist too, as we have seen, on doorjambs at Persepolis (F12) and on the facades of the royal tombs at Naqš-i Rustam (**F17**) and Persepolis, as throne-bearers who, together, lift high the image of the Great King who rules over them (see Chapter 2); Root (1979: 47–61) calls this the 'Atlas pose' (see also Schmidt 1970: 108–19 and plate 66). This might be interpreted as a joyous act of reciprocal collaboration – the peoples of the Empire exalting their monarch – but it is more probable that the emphasis is not so much on willing togetherness but on political subjugation. An inscription accompanying such a scene on the tomb of Darius I (DNa §4) invites the viewer to contemplate the meaning of the relief and suggests this domineering agenda:

> If you shall now think, 'How many are the lands which king Darius held?', then look at the sculptures of those who bear [i.e. carry] the throne, and then you shall know, then will it become known to you: the spear of a Persian man has gone far; then shall it become known to you: a Persian man has delivered battle far indeed from Persia.

Royal titulature re-emphasises the centrality of Persia over its world Empire and the role of the monarch in the space of the conquered peoples. Darius is therefore not only 'Great King' and 'King of Kings' (see Chapter 1) but also 'King of countries containing all kinds of men' (DNa) and the 'King of many countries' (DPe), as well as 'King in this great earth far and wide' (DNa). In Elamite and Old Persian terminology Darius is the king of 'this land' (*dahyu/xšaça* = Persia) and of all lands of the Empire (*dahyāva/būmi*). Did this mean that the king truly thought of these lands as his own property? On the surface it looks that way (Wiesehöfer 2009: 81). But the sources do not necessarily support such a view and it can be argued that in the Achaemenid period 'there did not exist a theory of supreme property of the land' (Dandamayev and Lukonin 1989: 133). Of course the king was master of the Empire and thus the conquered lands *ipso facto* came under his authority (the Old Persian word for 'land', *būmi*, has the implication of 'land under royal right') and as such the king demanded payment of tribute and taxes from his subject peoples. These fiscal obligations to the throne, 'the king's share', were called *bāji* (Old Persian) and *baziš* (Elamite; see Sancisi-Weerdenburg 1998: 33; Briant 2002: 398, 439) and were made up from a portion of produce from lands under the king's jurisdiction. The people of Parsa (Fars), as the 'insiders' of the Empire, had a unique relationship with their king and although they nonetheless honoured him with gifts of local produce (see below), they did not come under the same 'taxation bracket' as peoples of the provinces, who were, on an annual basis, additionally taxed in the form of weighed silver or in local produce or sometimes specialised produce – or what Briant has labelled 'over and above the tribute'. Egypt was thus obliged to send the king fish, flour, and corn, Cappadocia sent horses, mules, and sheep, while Babylonia (as we have noted) was required to send to Persia 500 castrated boys, bound for the royal court (for a discussion of this system see Briant 2002: 403–5). Generally, payments of foodstuffs were stored in centrally administrated granaries and warehouses, to be distributed later to courtiers, administrators, workers, and military personnel. It is worth citing Allen (2005a: 120), who sensibly notes that 'the terminology distinguishing gifts from tribute . . . may have been the result of diplomatic rhetoric. . . . The boundaries between the concepts of land-obligations, tithes, tribute, and gifts were likely to be very fluid.'

By and large Achaemenid kings were not completely free to dispense with conquered lands as they wished but territories taken from rulers and peoples who did not willingly submit to Persian rule (perhaps following a revolt) did pass into hereditary ownership and could be gifted to members of the royal family, courtiers, and favoured individuals (i.e. those on what might today be called a civil list). Free from taxation, such estates were expected to provide troops when called upon by the throne (Xenophon, *Cyropaedia* 8.8.20; see Wiesehöfer 2009: 82; Briant 2002: 419). Babylonian texts refer to these royal lands as *uzbarra*, but what strictly constituted 'royal land' is ambiguous, leading Briant to suggest that, 'in the politico-ideological sense of the term, "royal land" merged with tribute land – that is, with the Empire in its entirety', although in reality the monarch's actual ownership of land was more curtailed. Briant (2002: 421) therefore uses the term 'crown lands' to demarcate the Great King's actual lands from his ideological domain. Of course, the king, as we have seen, was the ruler of his own house and household (*viθ*; *oikos*) but Babylonian texts employ the term *bītu* and Elamite documents use *ulhi* (literally, 'house'; the Aramaic equivalent is *bēt*) to refer to estates belonging to the ruler and the royal family. We should not think of these estates as physical walled spaces or manor houses but, rather, as the monarch's general *uzbarra*, productive lands (or farmsteads) with teams of workers which were administered by estate stewards (Briant 2002: 461–2). This type of royal property generated income and rent for the king, affording him, in turn, the opportunity to be generous to others in the gifts he doled out. In all reality, the king's personal lands operated like those of any other Achaemenid noble but on a more substantial scale (on the royal *ulhi* see Henkelman 2010a).

Briant (2002: 470) is therefore able to note that 'the king was not only a master of the Empire, but he also had a separate life as a private person or, rather, the head of a house (*ulhi*)'. To emphasise the point, Briant draws attention to a well known Fortification text from Persepolis (D10) in which Darius I instructs Parnaka to charge his 'personal account' for the 100 sheep he gave to Queen Irtašduna or, in other words, to take sheep *not* from a communal resource but from his own *ulhi* and to give them to his wife's estate. This text demonstrates also that a high-ranking courtier like Parnaka served the king as both a state official and as a private manager, simultaneously tending to the king's two spheres of operation. At one and the same time the king was master of two lands – his Empire (*dahyu; dahyāva; būmi*) and his house (*viθ; ulhi; oikos*).

The Great King's road trip

The smooth running of the Empire was facilitated by an excellent infrastructure. While first-rate roads connected all of the main satrapal centres with the imperial core, the most important of these highways was undoubtedly the Royal Road, which connected Sardis to Persepolis via Susa and Babylon; an eastern branch led first to Ecbatana and thence onwards to Bactra and Pashwar, while another road (principally noticeable in the correspondence of the Egyptian satrap Aršama) connected Persepolis to Egypt via Damascus and Jerusalem. The roads were measured in six-kilometre intervals (*parasangs*) and road stations were set up around every twenty-eight kilometres of the route to accommodate the quick change of fresh horses for any imperial messenger carrying official documents (see Potts 2008). Herodotus (5.53) estimated that the distance from Susa to Sardis, 450 *parasangs*, could be covered in ninety days. Administrative documents from Persepolis, especially those classified as pertaining to 'travel rations', attest to the systematic criss-crossing of vast swathes of the Empire by men and women on state business (delivering messages, money, or goods) or conducting private affairs (honouring work contacts or attending religious ceremonies) and record the food rations they received for the journeys (**C4**; Aramaic documents from the Aršama dossier are particularly interesting in this regard: see **C5** and Lindenberger 2003: 90–1). The Persepolis texts record around 750 place names – cities, towns, and villages, provinces, districts, and lands, with the route between Susa and Persepolis being particularly conspicuous (Arfaee 2008). In addition to the main imperial roads, ancient caravan tracks, rough and unpaved but nevertheless wide enough to transport armies and merchant trains, ran across the entire landscape (Herodotus 8.83; Xenophon, *Cyropaedia* 6.2.165; Diodorus 18.26; Aristophanes, *Acharnians* 68–71; see Wiesehöfer 1996: 77).

The Great King and his court used these routes to traverse the realm not just for pragmatic reasons of state, but also to satisfy a deep-set instinct in the Persian psyche, for the Achaemenids were essentially nomads, and thus the regular progression of the royal court around and across the Empire should be regarded as a migration on a par with the relocation patterns typical of nomadic peoples generally. Nomadism has a deep antiquity in Iranian culture (Assyrian inscriptions are the first written sources to mention Iranian tribes that frequently descended from the Zagros mountains to attack urban centres in Mesopotamia; see Briant 1982) and even in Iran today some mountain tribes are nomadic. For 'tribe' we might draw on the elegant definition coined by Albert Hourani (1991: 10–11), albeit for a seventh-century Arabian context: '[Nomadic peoples were] led by chiefs belonging to families around which there gathered more or less lasting groups of supporters, expressing their cohesion and loyalty in the idiom of common ancestry; such groups are usually called "tribes"'. Following Hourani's definition, we might argue that the Achaemenid king was actually the chief of a tribe which we conventionally call a 'court'. This would not have been a great mental leap for the ancient Persians to make for, after all, their society was traditionally made up of tribes and clans. According to Herodotus, the Achaemenids were the dominant clan of the Parsagade tribe – Cyrus II's own tribe – and one of eleven clans (Herodotus 1.125; see also Xenophon, *Cyropaedia* 1.2.5, who mentions twelve clans, but Strabo's clan list at 15.3 is altogether different), but he notes that besides the members of the royal family there were also members of an Achaemenid 'phratry' who never became kings (like Hystaspes, Darius' father; see also Herodotus 1.209, 3.65, and 3.75); Wiesehöfer (1996: 35) attempts to find Old Persian equivalents for Herodotus' classifications.

In Iran the traditional migrational movements of nomadic groups (each with their own deep-set tribal and family affiliations) have always been connected with clearly defined routes and destinations where the nomads spend defined periods of the year with the ultimate goal of pursuing economic activities (trade or barter) and ensuring the productiveness of their livelihood through the welfare of their herds of sheep and goats. The temporal structure of their lifestyle can be reduced to very simple ubiquitous patterns:

- spring (mid-March to early May), migration from winter pastures to summer pastures
- summer (May to late August), settlement in summer pastures
- autumn (September to November), migration from summer pastures to winter pastures
- winter (November to mid-March), settlement in winter pastures.

Table 1. Greek sources on the migrations of the Persian court

Time of Year	Xenophon (**C6**)	Plutarch (**C7, C8**)	Dio Chrysostom (**C9**)	Athenaeus (**C10**)	Aelian (**C11**)
Spring	Susa	Susa	–	Babylon	–
Summer	Ecbatana	Media	Ecbatana	Ecbatana	Ecbatana
Autumn	–	–	–	Persepolis	–
Winter	Babylon	Babylon	Babylon, Susa, Bactra	Susa	Susa

This regular pattern of movement–settlement–movement–settlement can also be seen in the peripatetic practices of the Great King's court, and although the movements of animal herds was not the *raison d'être* behind the royal migration pattern, nonetheless it is important to note that changes in the season were an important factor in the court's movement, at least if we follow the Greek explanation, where the sources state that the king was constantly chasing an eternal springtime and settling his court in parts of the Empire which enjoyed the most hospitable weather conditions. And it was to the royal capitals of the Empire that the court regularly relocated.

The Greeks texts are in agreement with that, although there is little consensus among the Greeks on the detail of exactly *which* capital was used or *when*. The Greek sources have been vigorously analysed by Christopher Tuplin (1998b), who sets them against the Persepolitan evidence for court migrations, and can be summarised as in Table 1. The Greeks unanimously agree on a residency in Media (the cool north of Iran) for the court during the summer months – a logical place to be, far from the scorching heat of southern Iran (and especially around Susa if we follow Strabo 15.3.10 and Diodorus 19.28.1–2, 19.39.1) – but beyond that it is impossible to work out the reality of the royal seasonal migration as presented in the Greek sources, so that there can be 'no compelling evidence to prefer one variant to another' (Tuplin 1998b: 72).

While Aelian (*On Animals* 3.13) was able to compare the Great King's annual relocations to the practical migration practices of birds and fish, most Greek authors display more bafflement and derision than approbation for the nature of the royal progress (Xenophon, *Agesilaus* 9.5). Given the Hippocratic theory of the humours, the monarch's desire to enjoy the warmth and dryness of an eternal springtime was, for the Greeks, an expression of his natural effeminising dissoluteness and part of the bigger picture of Persian dissipation. The most

perverse expression of the Greek obsession with both Persian decadence and court nomadism, however, is given voice by Aristophanes,
who conjured up an absurd fantasy wherein the Persian state *en masse*
moved with the monarch merely to satisfy the king's desire to empty
his bowels; the comic playwright pictures the ruler surrounded by his
entire entourage defecating in the privacy of the mountains before
returning to the royal place (**C12**). Aristophanes wryly notes that the
Great King's road trip toilet break took no less than eight months.

A court on horseback: the practicalities of travel

The logistics of the court shifting locations required enormous organisation and colossal resources, since many thousands of people would
have been affected by, or responsible for, the move. We must recall that
members of the royal family might travel independently of the king,
taking with them their own miniature courts or households and that
here too precision planning would have been paramount. Peripatetic
courts have been a feature of many royal societies across the ages,
including in medieval and early modern Europe, but perhaps the
closest we can get to understanding how Achaemenid court nomadism functioned is to note how the Mughal emperors crossed their
empire. This Indian royal dynasty – descendants of true Persian stock
– traversed vast territories as well. As Abraham Eraly notes:

> The Mughal imperial [court] was a movable city. Virtually the whole royal
> establishment, household as well as official, shifted with the emperor, with
> staff, records and treasury. His harem moved with him, so did his artists
> and artisans, musicians and dancers, even his menagerie and library. The
> entire court and the central armed forces moved with him, along with all
> those who depended on the court and the army, with countless women and
> servants, camp-followers several times as numerous as the army, artisans
> and traders and hangers-on with their women and children and all their
> belongings, and an immense number and variety of animals and carts.
> (Eraly 1997: 55; see further Lal 1988: 60–7; Schimmel 2000: 77–80; Lal
> 2005; for court migration under the Chinese Qing dynasty see Chang 2007;
> Gabbiani 2009)

Eraly's vivid account of Mughal court nomadism is best matched by
a description of the Achaemenid peripatetic court preserved by the
Roman historian Curtius Rufus (**C13**), who probably reiterates earlier
Greek observations on the royal procession (Xenophon, *Cyropaedia*
8.3.15–20, 33–4). The accounts describe how the king travelled with his

insignia of power – religious banners, fire altars, and an entourage of Magi – and with a vast military force of bodyguards and other armed men. There were also multitudes of royal servants and kinsmen bringing the king's personal goods as well as the treasury porters guarding the king's wealth (Curtius Rufus 3.13.7; see Briant 2002: 428–9). The women of the court travelled at the rear of the vast convoy of people. The presence of the court *en masse* was *de rigour* (although, no doubt with the monarch's permission, royalty could travel independently of the king, escorted by their own entourage; see Chapter 4). Failing to join the royal cortège could rouse the royal wrath, as Pythios of Lydia realised when he pleaded with Xerxes to release his eldest son from the army. Xerxes refused, insisting that 'You [too] . . . should be following me with your entire household, including your wife, while I myself am marching along with my own sons, brothers, servants and friends' (Herodotus 7.39).

Animals facilitated the Achaemenid court's migrations by pulling wagons, chariots, and carriages and by carrying people and commodities on their backs. Mughal sources tell of 100,000 horses and 200,000 other animals, including mules, oxen, camels, and elephants (Eraly 1997: 55) and it is feasible that similar numbers were used by the Persians. The horse was the main mode of court transport, although it is probable that other sorts of pack animals were also employed for the gargantuan task of shifting the court (Tuplin 2010b: 131, 132 n.131; unlike the Mughals, there is no evidence of the Achaemenids using elephants).

For a nomadic people like the Persians, the horse had a significant practical and symbolic purpose (see generally Chamberlin 2006; Kelekna 2009; Walker 2010) and the importance of horses among the Iranian nobility is evidenced by the fact that many of them bore names compounded with the Old Persian word *aspa*, 'horse'. Several of Darius I's inscriptions note that Persia was a land containing both good men and good horses (DZe §1; DPd §2) and Herodotus (1.136) famously states that Persian fathers were intent on teaching their sons 'to ride, to draw the bow, and to speak the truth' (see also Strabo 15.3.18). The premium Persian horses were bred in the alfalfa-rich plains of Media and it was here that the main royal stud farms were located (Polybius 10.70). Most prized of all were those steeds bred on the plains of Nisaea, near Ecbatana, and Bisitun, and Nisaean horses became celebrated for their magnificence, fine proportions, and swiftness (Herodotus 3.106, 7.40; Aristotle, *History of Animals* 9.50.30). Nisaea is said to have sustained 160,000 horses (Diodorus 17.110), although stiff competition came from Media and Armenia, which were also used for breeding good steeds (Strabo 11.13.7, 8, 11.14.9), as were the provinces of Babylonia (where one satrap possessed 800 stallions and 16,000 mares; Herodotus 1.192), Cilicia (which provided an annual tribute of 360 white horses; Herodotus 3.90), Chorasmia, Bactria, Sogdiana, and lands of the Saka, which provided the Empire with its cavalry (for a full discussion see Tuplin 2010b). The Persepolis texts often speak of horses (as well as mules and donkeys), usually in the context of their food provisions and maintenance (**C14**) but also as property of the king or members of his family (PF 1668–9, 1675, 1793; PFa 24, 29; see Briant 2002: 464). The texts (PF1942, PF1943, PF1947, PF1948) also name individuals who safeguarded the welfare of the royal horses as well as groups of court officials serving as masters of the horse, as it were, and show that these men operated within a hierarchical system and could be paid well beyond the average ration rate and could enjoy a diet of regular meat (Tuplin 2010b: 132–3). This suggests a high rank at court for masters of the horse.

While there are no surviving monumental artistic representations of horses and riders in Achaemenid art, textual evidence suggests that equine statues of horses with riders were commissioned for and by royalty and nobility (**C15**; Herodotus 3.88). Small-scale representations of horses and cavalry figures survive in terracotta and metallic figurines, and on gems, coins, and textiles (see Curtis and Tallis 2005: 218–27; Rudenko 1970; Rubinson 1990; Tuplin 2010b: 106–20 provides an excellent catalogue and discussion of the visual evidence). The Persepolis reliefs show riderless horses regularly: of the twenty-three tribute delegations appearing on the Apadana staircases, seven present horses as part of their gifts (Medes, Armenians, Cappadocians, two groups of Sakas, Sagartians, and Thracians) and there are also depictions of horse-drawn chariots conveyed by Syrians and Libyans. In addition, the Great King's personal Nisaean mounts are depicted along with his chariot and the chariot belonging to the crown prince (see Sánchez 2006: 234–7; generally on chariots, see Cottrell 2004). In the royal chariot the Great King obviously took on a majestic appearance, 'outstanding amongst the rest' (Curtius Rufus 4.1.1), but, as Briant (2002: 224) makes clear, 'the royal horses and chariot do not appear on the Persepolis reliefs simply for decoration. The royal chariot obviously carried ideological weight and the vehicle was clearly part of the "royal insignia"'; indeed, the coinage of Sidon demonstrates the monarch's use of the chariot as 'insignia' perfectly (see Jidejian 2006: 122–3; Jigoulov 2010: 86–9).

As an obvious symbol of status and wealth, horses were closely connected to royal and courtly ideology and to the warrior image (**C16**; Herodotus 9.20, 22; Diodorus 17.59.2; Ctesias F19 §1); as a mark of conspicuous leisure horses played a dominant role in the aristocratic pastimes of hunting and racing (Xenophon, *Cyropaedia* 8.3.25, 33; see further Herodotus 7.196). Favourite horses could lead a pampered existence (Herodotus 9.70). A companion in life, the horse also played its role in the ceremonies of death. With the passing of a king or noble, his horse was included in the mourning procession with its mane cropped short (Herodotus 9.24; Curtius Rufus 10.5.17). The horse played a noteworthy role in Achaemenid rituals and beliefs and just as kings were mounted high on horse-drawn chariots, so Ahuramazda and other deities had similar modes of transportation (Herodotus 7.40; Arrian, *Anabasis* 2.11, 3.15; Xenophon, *Cyropaedia* 8.3.12). Moreover, just as the finest present to give a Persian was a horse (Xenophon, *Anabasis* 1.2.27), so were the gods honoured with equine gifts, such as the white horses which were sacrificed to the sun and to the waters (Herodotus 1.189, 216, 7.113; Xenophon, *Cyropaedia* 8.3.11–12; *Anabasis* 4.5.35; Pausanias 3.20.4; Strabo 11.13.7, 8, 14.9), these rituals being widely practised among Indo-European peoples (Clutton-Brock 1992; Kelekna 2009). As founder of the Empire, Cyrus II was honoured with a horse sacrificed to his memory every month (**C17**; see Henkelman 2003a: 152; for seal images of sacrifice see Garrison 2012). Moreover, the infamous tale recounted by Herodotus (3.85) of how Darius I acquired his kingdom through a trick involving the neighing of his horse is, in all probability, a Greek misunderstanding of the Iranian practice of hippomancy, or divination through the behaviour of horses (see also Ctesias F13 §17; Briant 2002: 109; Tuplin 2010b: 143), demonstrating the deep-set importance of the horse as a hallowed species in the Iranian consciousness.

Camels do not figure quite so prominently in the sources but they are nonetheless attested often enough to prove their worth to the Persians (see further Bulliet 1975; Irwin 2010) and, in fact, the Old Persian word for camel, *uša* or *uštra*, often occurs as a component in personal names (most markedly Zarathuštra, 'he who manages camels'). Images of Bactrian camels are unmistakable and copious, for they are included in the representations of several delegations from north-eastern Iran at Persepolis, whereas the swifter single-humped dromedaries are depicted only with the Arab delegation. Dromedary camels were important sources of meat, milk, and hair and while they were used as pack animals (Herodotus 1.80) they were not engaged in heavy hauling. In fact, none of the Persepolis camels are portrayed as draft animals, but post-Achaemenid-period sources give explicit references to camel-drawn carts (Strabo 15.1.43) and one Achaemenid seal image shows the Great King in a chariot pulled by a team of dromedaries (see Rehm 2006: 135). Both species of camel were used by the Persian cavalry and we know that Darius I employed camel troops (*ušabari*) in his campaign against the rebellious Babylonians (DB I §18; see Sekunda and Chew 1992: 51). Large herds of camels belonging to the king are described in the Persepolis texts being driven back and forth between Persepolis and Susa (**C18**; for a discussion of the nuances of this text see Briant 2002: 464) and Greek artists sometimes depict the Great King riding a camel (Sánchez 2009: 314). One small seal shows the Great King spearing a lion while seated on a dromedary, suggesting that camels could be used in the hunt too (Collon 1987: 156–7, fig. 700). Occasionally a much-loved camel is mentioned in the sources – like the lucky one stabled at Gaugamela by Darius I (Strabo 16.1.3).

Even with all these animals, the vast royal cortège moved slowly. Lindsay Allen (2005a: 119) proposes that the journey between Susa and Ecbatana could take over five weeks, which fits neatly with estimates of the daily distance travelled by the Mughal court, at a maximum of ten kilometres (taking some seven or eight hours) (Lal 1988: 62). The Persian Great King spent the journey doing a variety of activities: he might greet the populace as he passed by villages and hamlets (see below), or he might busy himself with the official paperwork of state – the administration of the Empire continued uninterrupted as the court trekked on. One charming Greek vignette, however, depicts the somewhat bored monarch sitting in his slow-moving chariot whittling a piece of wood to help pass the long hours (Aelian, *Historical Miscellany* 14.14).

Many such stories of the Great King on the move are to be found in the works of Classical authors, who seem to have a fascination for the notion of the peripatetic court and what it meant for Persian identity. Some anecdotes tell of the enormous efforts undertaken to ensure that the ruler's passage was both safe and smooth (**C19**), while others take an unexpected turn and depict the Great King as a kind and gentle recipient of humble gifts presented by the poorest people of the Empire. In particular, a character portrait of Artaxerxes II emerges in which his humility and natural ease with the peasantry are stressed through his willingness to accept very simple presents – dates, fresh water, or a pomegranate – with deep gratitude (**C20**; Plutarch,

Artaxerxes 4.5–5.1, 12.4–6; *Moralia* 174a; see also **D4** for the easy relationship between Artaxerxes' wife and the common folk; see further Binder 2008: 136–44; Briant 2002: 192). In return, of course, Great Kings bestowed largess upon the populace as they journeyed around their lands (**C21**; Plutarch, *Alexander* 69.1).

Of course, gift-giving could also take on a more overt political dimension. When the Achaemenid court traversed certain parts of Iran, especially around the Zagros, it came into contact with ancient peoples like the Uxians, whose tribal lands covered part of the strategically important route linking Susa to Fars. The Achaemenid rulers (and later Alexander) therefore had to negotiate safe passage for the court through Uxian territory and this was done through the mutual exchange of gifts, as the Uxians provided the kings with *baziš* (probably small livestock – that is, sheep and goats – such those recorded in **C22**, as well as men to serve as troops; see also Arrian, *Anabasis* 3.17), thus satisfying royal honour, and, in a reciprocal gesture, the Great Kings loaded the tribesmen with gifts far outweighing the value of those presented by the Uxians themselves. Why was this gift exchange necessary? Briant explains: 'The bestowal of royal "gifts"… created a link between the receiver and the giver. Through this ceremony, the Uxians . . . committed their loyalty to the king . . . and [he] received the submission of the Uxians . . . without investment of military resources' (Briant 2002: 731; see also Briant 1988: 255–6, 271; Kuhrt 2007: 826–7).

Gift-giving also played a key role whenever the travelling court approached a major city, where, greeted with celebration, it prepared to make its formal 'royal entry' (which, to all intents and purposes, was still being practised by the monarchies of Renaissance Europe; see Briant 2002: 189–90, 193–4; Knecht 2008: 99–112; Briant 2009). But before the court entered through a city's gate, envoys from the city's governor or the province's satrap sent lavish gifts of welcome to the king so as to pay respects and pledge allegiance and submission to the monarch (**C23**). Refusal to present gifts was taken by the king as proof of insubordination.

It was an obligation of the satraps to send the best produce of their regions to the Great King and by taking possession of these symbolic gifts the monarch reconfirmed his dominion over the Empire (Xenophon, *Cyropaedia* 8.6.6, 23). Perhaps the most symbolic of all these gifts given to – or demanded by – the king was that of earth and water, which played a role 'in initiating a relationship of ruler/subject and appears to have been a prime strategy used by the Persian king to attach himself to areas without resorting to military tactics' (Kuhrt

1988: 94; see further Herodotus 7.32; Strabo 15.3.22). The gifting of earth and water (probably presented to the monarch in *physical* form – a silver jar of water, and a golden dish of earth, for instance) therefore represented a country's unconditional surrender to Persia and placed the Achaemenid king in the role of life-giver to his new subjects, as he controlled the elements that sustained existence. That the king himself always travelled with his own drinking water, which had been sourced from a Persian river, is a reflection of the same process (Herodotus 1.188; Athenaeus 12.515a); the water of the Choaspes River near Susa linked the king with his homeland no matter where he might be in the Empire and, at the same time, imbued him with the qualities of kingship itself (see Briant 2002: 242). If we are prepared to believe our Greek sources (and Deinon, our main source for this, should be credited for knowing a thing or two about Persia) then the offering or partaking of certain foods and drinks became emblematic of imperial expansion policies (**C24**; Plutarch, *Moralia* 173e; Ctesias F53/Deinon F23a = Athenaeus 2.67a–b; Deinon F23b = Plutarch, *Alexander* 36.4), although Herodotus notes that the nature symbolism employed by the Persians to elucidate their expansionist strategy could have a serious lash-back (Herodotus 4.131–2; see also Athenaeus 8.332).

A court under canvas

In the open landscape, after a day's travelling, the imperial procession came to a halt and set up camp. Immediately tents were erected and a royal city of cloth, leather, and wood sprang up (**C25**). Herodotus (7.119) records that the Persian troops marching with Xerxes had the task of dismantling, transporting, and reassembling the royal tent when they reached a new camp and we should imagine that the tents of the other royals and nobles were erected by teams of servants at the same time. Systematically arranged to reflect hierarchical and defensive concerns, the royal camp was constructed with the Great King's tent at the centre of the complex, facing towards the east and decorated with distinguishing devices (Curtius Rufus 3.8.7). Standing at the epicentre of the camp, the king's tent became the symbol of royal authority itself (Plutarch, *Eumenes* 13) and inside the tent the king carried out the same rituals and duties that he followed inside the palaces. Cyrus is depicted listening to the trial of a traitor (and condemning him to death) inside his tent, although the subsequent execution takes place elsewhere (Xenophon, *Anabasis* 1.6.5–11). As a mark of honour and as a display of royal largess, the Great King might gift a favoured courtier (even a foreigner) a splendid tent, often richly furnished with couches, textiles, gold plate, and slaves (**C26**). Some fine tents were even considered heirlooms (Xenophon, *Cyropaedia* 5.5.1–2). The tent was a visible emblem of imperial authority – so much so that the enemy capture of a royal tent and its rich accoutrements was a symbol of the collapse of monarchic authority itself – as Alexander came to fully appreciate once he had moved into the tent which had previously belonged to Darius III (**C27**).

The royal tent was a colossal structure made from colourfully woven textiles and leather panels, supported by a framework of pillars; in all respects, the king's tent was a collapsible version of a palace throne hall and it is reasonable to think of the Apadana at Persepolis or Susa as stone versions of the royal tent. Several descriptions survive of a series of state tents utilised by Alexander after his conquest of Persia (**C28, C29**; Aelian, *Historical Miscellany* 9.3) and it is clear that the Macedonian monarch was making use of Achaemenid tents, possibly captured after the defeat of Darius III at Issus in 333 BCE (Miller 1997: 51; Spawforth 2007a: 94–7, 112–20). Alexander's tents are described as truly colossal, with the textile roof supported by fifty golden pillars and enough space to hold 100 couches. While it is difficult to pronounce firmly on the shape of the royal tents, it has been proposed that they were rectangular and with a circular canopy at the centre – this helps make sense of Greek texts that specifically speak of an *Ouranos* ('heaven'): 'in Persia the royal tents and courts [have] circular ceilings, (like) skies' (Photius, *Lexicon s.v. ouranos*; see Spawforth 2007: 120). The Greeks knew about Persian state tents because several had been taken as war booty during the period of the Persian war and its aftermath; they were clearly a staggering sight in the eyes of the Greeks (Herodotus 9.82–3; Xenophon, *Anabasis* 4.21) and consequently they left their imprint in the later Greek imagination (a description of a tent in Euripides' play *Ion* (121–48), of c. 413, was probably inspired by a Persian tent stored in a treasury at Delphi). Should we doubt the scale and grandeur of Persian state tents, then Margaret Miller reminds us that Ottoman-period Turkish imperial tents still survive which testify to the luxury of their Achaemenid ancestors (Miller 1997: 50–1). Moreover, reports of tented accommodation in Mughal sources equate closely with the descriptions we have of Persian tents, confirming the centrality of the tent in the presentation of monarchy in the east (Lal 1988: 64–6; Andrews 1999; on tents in the ancient Near East see Homan 2002).

Once the tents had been erected, the work began of feeding the court and the camp – an immense and costly undertaking (**C30, C31**). We have already noted how food produce from all over the Empire was brought to the table of the Great King, but it is clear that as he travelled throughout his realm – sometimes to its far edges in pursuit of war – then cities, towns, and villages were required to meet the needs of the army and court at the encampment (**C32**). Like a swarm of locusts, the court could easily strip the surrounding countryside of its produce; a royal visit was both a blessing and a curse (Herodotus 7.118–19; see also Athenaeus 4.146a–b and Joel 2).

While occasionally we read that the nomadic court was affected by local food shortages (Plutarch, *Artaxerxes* 24.3), by and large the image we receive is that, even while on the move, the Great King's table (and by extension that of the royal household) was served daily with abundance, magnificence, efficiency, and order. But what food was served to the king and court?

We know little of the recipes concocted by the royal chefs but one text is useful in providing us with knowledge about the ingredients which were used (**C33**): the *Stratagems* of Polyaenus records an inscribed inventory, purportedly found by Alexander, of the foodstuffs brought before the Great King and his household on a daily basis – enough produce to feed no less than 15,000 people, if we accept the words of Ctesias and Deinon (Ctesias F39/Deinon F24 = Athenaeus 4.146c–d; the origin of Polyaenus' text might in fact lie in the *Persica* of Heraclides or, more likely, Ctesias). The sheer volume of food and drink recorded by Polyaenus might lead us to suspect that he is merely indulging himself in the familiar Greek trope of imagining fantastical Persian excess (*tryphē*; see Herodotus 1.133; Sancisi-Weerdenburg 1995; Lenfant 2007b) but, given that he carefully estimates the amount of produce in terms of Greek measurements and that he distinguishes the apportionment of food according to the court's location (Babylon, Susa, Ecbatana, and Persepolis), the text can be accorded some reliability ('all of the information *feels* right', says Briant 2002: 288) and can, in fact, be augmented by evidence provided by Heraclides of Cyme (**C34**), who similarly lists huge quantities of food served at court. Heraclides carefully notes how the produce was distributed from the king to his entourage (including men and women of the royal family) and how it was subsequently distributed by the royals and their courtiers to their own respective households. Therefore the Great King's table was the locus of food distribution to many people of varying social rank. Xenophon (*Cyropaedia* 8.3–4) understood the essence of this practice, but he linked it to the monarch's display of beneficence to chosen individuals.

Wouter Henkelman (2010a) has demonstrated how the Greek conception of the king's dinner is accurately reflected in the Persepolis Fortification archive (and other Achaemenid-period documents) and he has brilliantly analysed how the intricate royal food distribution system operated – with livestock and foodstuffs flowing into and out of the royal household (see also Stevenson 1997: 144–52). Known as the J Texts, these Elamite tablets listing products 'delivered to the king' seem to confirm Polyaenus' inventory and they show that when the king or a member of the royal family relocated (not necessarily as part of the main court migration) they received provisions from the central administration (royal individuals included in the J Texts include Darius' wife, Irtašduna (or Irtaštuna), in PF 730–2, his son Aršama in PF 733–4, 2035, and his brother-in-law/father-in-law Gobryas in PF 688). Briant (2002: 290) notes though that the J Texts can often merge with the so-called Category Q Texts, relating to travel rations (see also comments by Janković 2008; Potts 2008). Henkelman concludes that 'the crown's internal hierarchy included officials responsible for provisioning the royal table who travelled with the court' and that the 'redistribution of commodities within the court society was a matter of the court administration. . . . The Elamite and Greek sources both (implicitly) understand the Table of the King as a complex organization with its own rules, hierarchy, and bureaucracy' (Henkelman 2010a: 732).

It has been suggested that the preparation of a royal dinner is depicted on the staircase of the *taçara* of Darius I at Persepolis: men in riding habit hold wine skins, bowls, and pots and carry live lambs and kids (Brosius 2007: 44, following Sancisi-Weerdenburg 1989). However, doubts have been raised about this interpretation – are these scenes more properly related to religious rituals (Razmjou 2004), or do they narrate the presentation of local *baziš* (Sancisi-Weerdenburg 1998)? Interestingly, similar scenes have been found on the fragmentary staircase of the palace of Artaxerxes I, and one particularly interesting fragment shows a stretcher bearing four lambs being carried towards the palace (for an image see Jacobs 2010: 408). Sancisi-Weerdenburg (1998: 29) argues that 'it is unlikely that the living animals carried by these persons were to serve as ingredients for the royal banquet in the palace where they decorated the entrances. A barbecue within the ceremonial halls is difficult to imagine.' She makes a valid point. However, it should not be supposed that the preparation of the meat took place within the king's dining room itself; after all, the (messy) slaughtering, skinning, butchering, cooking, and dressing of even a small lamb or kid takes considerable time and requires the skills of professional staff; meat dishes must have been prepared in kitchens (indoor or outdoor varieties). Living animals are depicted on the staircase relief to emphasise the freshness of the meat being offered to the king and the lambs simply represent the notion of fresh meat. These are not images of living lambs *per se*; similar artistic conventions are found in Egyptian art (see Wilkinson 1992: 95; Desroches Noblecourt 2007: 60–9).

The king of nature

Recent archaeological investigations in central and southern Iran have unearthed evidence for numerous royal 'pavilion sites' dotted across the landscape (Arfa'i 1999). These pavilions were small but elegant palace lodges, often located away from the main highways in protected and secluded areas, suggesting that these structures were utilised by the royal family as they traversed the kingdom – this is certainly the case for the best-excavated of these pavilions, at Jenjān in Fars, where elite architecture (fine stone column bases and doorjambs) and high-quality finds strongly imply the site was visited by members of the royal party travelling between the seasonal capitals (Potts 2008). The pavilions stood as symbols of royal and administrative power at a local level and they must have been sustained by estate produce; they might also have been surrounded by gardens, parks, arable land, and even game reserves – the celebrated Persian *paradeisoi* (**C35**; Xenophon, *Anabasis* 1.2.7; Plutarch, *Artaxerxes* 25.1; Briant 2002: 427).

These *paradeisoi* (Median, **paridaiza* from **pari*, 'around' and **daiza*, 'wall'; Old Persian, **paridaida*; Hebrew, *pardes* – for example Nehemiah 2:8; Song of Songs 4:13; whence the English *paradise*) were an essential part of Achaemenid cultural expression and throughout the Empire these carefully cultivated gardens, forests, and estates were living symbols of Persian dominance. Xenophon regularly encountered them as he trekked the western half of the realm and the astonishing beauty of various *paradeisoi* clearly left a mark on him (**C36**). The earliest reference to a Persian-style park and garden comes in the form of a Babylonian text dating to regnal year 5 of Cyrus II which speaks of a *pardēsu* (**C37**; Bremmer 2008: 37; Dandamayev 1984a), but it is during the reign of Darius I that more regular references to *paradeisoi* are found in the Persepolis texts, which enable us to speculate more fully on their maintenance and use (PT 59; for a full exploration of Persian *paradeisoi* see Tuplin 1996: 80–181; Brown 2001: 119–37; Lincoln 2012: 5–9, 18–19, 59–85). In addition to textual sources, archaeological evidence of Achaemenid gardens exists at Pasargade, Persepolis, Susa, and other royal and satrapal sites throughout the Empire.

It is clear that the parks and woodlands were well stocked with all sorts of wild animals and that the hunting of both smaller animals and big game chiefly took place in the safety of these vast game reserves (Curtius Rufus 7.2.22, 8.1.11; see Chapter 5 for hunting practices) but beyond the thrill of the hunt and the obvious sensual hedonism offered by royal gardens, the *paradeisoi* were encoded with a rich political and religious symbolism. The royal parks were an Empire in miniature and flora and fauna from every area of the king's dominion were resettled and replanted within their confines (Uchitel 1997; Bremmer 2008: 38). This was a longstanding Near Eastern tradition and Egyptian pharaohs and Mesopotamian kings had boasted of cultivating their gardens with foreign plants, wherein they flourished. The Assyrian king Tiglath-pileser I bragged how 'I took cedar . . . [and] oak from the lands which I had dominion . . . and planted [them] in the orchards of my land' (*Assyrian Royal Inscriptions* 2.290), thereby emphasising that an exotic garden symbolised the monarch's control of a huge territory. Most famously, according to the Greco-Babylonian priest-cum-historian Berossus (F8 §141), Nebuchadnezzar of Babylon built high stone ter-races 'and planted them with trees of every kind . . . and completed the so-called "hanging *paradeisos*", because his wife, who had been born and raised in Media, longed for mountain scenery'.

In the Persian era we hear of Achaemenid monarchs enriching their *paradeisoi* with foreign shrubs and fruit trees (PPA31) and there is even mention of royal vine-cutters (or grafters) who are charged with carefully pruning precious grape vines from Lebanon and transport-ing and replanting them in Persian soil (PF-NN1564). The idea of the king creating a fertile garden – displaying both symmetry and order – constituted a powerful statement of monarchic authority, fertility, legitimacy, and divine favour (even gods were portrayed as gardeners: see Psalm 80:11; Psalm 104:16; Homer, *Iliad* 5.693), so much so in fact that, as a potent symbol of resistance to Persian rule, the rebellious citizens of Sardis completely destroyed the royal park 'in which Persian kings took their relaxation' (Diodorus 16.41).

Near Eastern monarchs prided themselves on the meticulous atten-tion they provided for the cultivation, care, and nourishment of their lands. Thus in Assyria a cylinder text commemorating the founding of Dur-Šarrukin, Sargon's capital city, enthusiastically praises the king for the care he shows the city's surrounding acreage:

The sagacious king, full of kindness, who gave his thought to . . . bringing fields under cultivation, to the planting of orchards, who set his mind on raising crops on steep slopes whereon no vegetation had grown since days of old; whose heart moved him to set out plants in waste areas where the plough was unknown in the former days of kings, to make these regions ring with the sound of jubilation, to cause the springs of the plain to gush forth, to open ditches, to cause waters of abundance to rise high . . . like the waves of the sea. (Tomes 2005: 76–7)

An Achaemenid-period text from the Hebrew Bible, Ecclesiastes, has a Persian-style prince proclaim his royal prowess through his botanical accomplishments:

I made great works:
I built houses and planted vineyards for myself;
I made myself gardens and parks,
and planted in them all kinds of trees.
I made myself pools
from which to water the forest of growing trees.
(Ecclesiastes 2:4–6)

This demonstrates that an effective ruler was not just a warrior and sportsman but a gardener king too, a cultivator who personally tended to agricultural matters to ensure the prosperity of his realm and in this light the Great King ordered his satraps to create and maintain *parade-isoi* in their provinces (Xenophon, *Cyropaedia* 8.6.12). Xenophon was both flabbergasted by and full of admiration for Cyrus the Younger's vigorous and sophisticated gardening skills (*Oeconomicus* 4.8–13, 21–5) and the Latin Vulgate version of Esther (1:5) stresses that the royal garden at Susa 'was planted by the care and the hand of the king'. The idea of the gardener king is given further emphasis by the appearance of the monarch in a series of seal and coin images in which he actively ploughs the land and sows it with seed (see Briant 2003).

Of all the plants cultivated in royal gardens, Near Eastern kings were traditionally identified with (or even *as*) fine trees. The Sumerian monarch Šulgi for instance was at one and the same time 'a date palm planted by a water ditch' and 'a cedar planted by water' (Widengren 1951: 42) and famously the kings of Israel were depicted as both a 'shoot' and a 'branch' of the Davidic house (Isaiah 11:1). Assyrian kings were frequently represented standing next to the so-called 'Tree of Life' – an important cult symbol in the Near East generally. This special relationship between kings and trees lies behind the infamous

Herodotean story of Xerxes' infatuation with a plane tree (Herodotus 7.31), which Briant (2002: 235) suggests shows evidence for the existence of a Persian tree cult (see further Aelian, *Historical Miscellany* 2.14). Several seal images support this idea: one inscribed with Xerxes' name (SXe; Kuhrt 2007: fig. 7.1) shows the monarch about to decorate a tree with jewellery, an exact visual parallel to the Greek account, while other seals show the monarch in close proximity to date palms (note the location of Darius' chariot between a pair of palm trees on his name seal in **F18**).

The Great King was equally associated with the grape vine as a symbol of fecundity and strength. According to Herodotus (1.108) the king of Media dreamed that a vine emerged from the genitalia of his daughter, thereby predicting that Media would be overthrown by his daughter's unborn son (the future Cyrus II). This may well have its origins in a Persian story about Cyrus' birth and might help explain the symbolism of the golden jewel-encrusted vine which supposedly decorated either the royal bed chamber or the audience chamber (Athenaeus 12.514f–15a, 539d).

Royal power was also expressed in the king's relationship to the bigger cycles of nature, particularly the weather. Ctesias records several stories (**C38, C39**) which may encode within them genuine Iranian traditions about the monarch's ability to evoke wind, rain, and thunder through apotropaic rituals and these vignettes can therefore be linked to his important cultic role in religious rites of state. Moreover, as we have already noted that the monarch drank only water taken from Persian rivers, it is worth considering his wider relationship with waters, which he channelled and controlled by ordering the construction of canals, sluices, and qanats (Herodotus 3.117; Briant 2002: 415–19).

Concluding thought

The Achaemenid monarch was undeniably the master of all lands. He dominated all countries. The king symbolically demanded gifts of earth and water and saw any refusal to present this tribute as an act tantamount to treason. Like a splendid migratory bird, he traversed his realm in seasonal journeys and fed off the fat of the land. He was a superior horseman and he bonded closely with this ideologically important animal. He tamed the countryside by enclosing it in royal parks and, as the ultimate earthly representative of the divine, communed with storms and brought forth rain. In all ways the King of Many Lands was also the king of nature and of life itself.

CHAPTER 4

Harem: Royal Women and the Court

Fifty years ago, King George VI died and suddenly Elizabeth became Queen. The immediate transfer of power caused tensions between the Queen and her newly bereaved mother ... because there was absolutely no formal, constitutional role that the Queen Mother could adopt as her own. 'The Queen Mother minded so much she became unapproachable,' recalled the daughter of one of her attendants, 'and she also resented and was horribly jealous of her daughter becoming Queen'. . . . The new Queen made every effort not to upstage her mother in public. . . . When the Queen gave her mother the use of Sandringham, for example, she was highly sensitive to any suspicion that she could be thought to be usurping her mother's position as hostess. 'She would leap away from the teapot which she had been about to pour when she saw the Queen Mother approaching,' a courtier remembers. (Andrew Roberts, *BBC News Online*, 6 February 2002)

This chapter explores the role of royal women at the Achaemenid court and examines the evidence relating to queens (kings' wives and mothers), princesses, and concubines within the rigid hierarchical system of the Great King's household. The chapter will question the parts they played in power-politicking at court and assess their familial functions as the mothers, wives, daughters, siblings, and sexual partners of the monarch. As we will see, the women of the Achaemenid dynasty were part of a specific and potentially authoritative unit within the inner court, for they constituted the make-up of the royal harem itself.

Perhaps no other aspect of Achaemenid court society has attracted more controversy than the issue of the royal harem. The very use of the word 'harem' has caused dissent and rancour among modern scholars, some of whom are willing to embrace the employment of the word as a legitimate term to describe an important aspect of the court, while others baulk at its use in any context. This chapter will explore the validity of using the term 'harem' and go on to survey the evidence for the lives of royal women at the Persian court and the integral roles they played in Achaemenid court society.

'Harem': moving beyond the cliché

'Harem': a word that conjures up the popular image of a closely guarded pleasure palace filled with scantily clad nubile courtesans idling away their days in languid preparation for nights of sexual adventure in a sultan's bed. It is a world of scatter cushions, jewels in the bellybutton, and fluttering eyelashes set above gauzy yashmaks. These clichés find their most vivid expression in nineteenth-century Orientalist paintings and literature, and in popular Hollywood movies of the last 100 years (see Llewellyn-Jones 2009b). Unsurprisingly, this vision of Oriental sensual excess has often led scholarship to dismiss the notion of the harem as a western fabrication, an *open sesame* to an Arabian Nights fantasy world, and little more than that.

If we want to utilise the word 'harem' in its correct context and use it to consolidate some facts about royal women in the Persian Empire, we must dispense with the Orientalist clichés entirely. Let us start by expanding our awareness of what a harem really is.

While a harem can be a physical space, an identifiable area of a palace or house which is used by women – and by children, eunuchs, and privileged men for that matter – a harem can also simply refer to women and their blood kin grouped together; a harem does not necessarily need a defining space. 'Harem' has at its core the Arabic *ha'ram*, meaning 'forbidden' or 'taboo'. By implication it means a space into which general access is prohibited (or limited) and in which the presence of certain individuals or certain types of behaviour are forbidden (see Peirce 1993: 3; Marmon 1995; Schick 2010). The fact that the private quarters in a domestic residence, and by extension its female occupants, are also referred to as a 'harem' comes from the Islamic practice of restricting access to these quarters, especially to males unrelated by blood kinship to the resident females. The word 'harem' is therefore a term of respect, evoking religious purity and personal honour and, as Hugh Kennedy has stressed, in Middle Eastern royal practice a ruler would use 'harem' to refer to his women and to all other individuals under his immediate protection – children, siblings, courtiers, and slaves – in other words, the personages who made up his inner court (Kennedy 2004: 160–99). Is this the way to think about using the term in its ancient Persian context? The lack of documentary and archaeological evidence makes it difficult to establish who made up the Great King's harem, let alone speculate on how and where its members were housed and hierarchically structured, but perhaps Kennedy's observation might work here also. But there can be no denying that the study of any royal 'harem' must include (perhaps even privilege) women.

It is difficult to know how the ancient Persians actually referred to a harem – either in its physical or in its ideological form – although it has been suggested that the Old Persian *xšapā.stāna*, meaning 'place where one spends the night', might have been employed (Shahbazi 2003) but it is hard to substantiate this. As we have seen, the Old Persian term *viθ* as used by Darius I in his inscriptions seems to carry with it the triple sense of 'dynasty', 'house' ('palace'), and 'household', so *viθ* might have been used to describe the harem in its double meaning of a (flexible) space and a group of people, but it is impossible to say so with any certainty. Another candidate for 'harem' is the Old Persian word *taçara*, 'suite of rooms', but this, while attractive, is far from certain and the word does not have a double meaning to incorporate the people who might inhabit those rooms.

We have already seen how the Achaemenids cultivated a separation between the public and private spheres, between visibility and invisibility, in terms of palace structure, court ceremonial, and monarchic ideology, yet this was not a system in which *seclusion* was endorsed but one in which *separation* was desired. Separation was not exclusive to women, given that the Great King himself consciously played with the notion of his separation from his subjects, nor (as we shall see) did the ideology of royal separation exclude royal women from active participation in the affairs of the dynasty, or from economic transactions, or from independent travel, or even from the owning and maintenance of personal estates of land.

Separation is the central issue of the spatial and representational divide of traditional palace and elite house structures in the Middle Eastern world and indeed the modern Farsi word *andarūnī*, a term used by Iranians for the private family quarters and for the people who inhabit them, literally means 'the inside'. It is used in opposition to *birun* – the public space and sphere of a household used for welcoming and entertaining guests of both sexes. In contemporary Iran the *andarūnī* consists of all the males of a family and their wives, mothers, and grandmothers, and a whole array of male and female offspring ranging from babies to adolescents. Like *andarūnī*, the Arabic-root 'harem' also refers to a distinct group of people who inhabit a permeable but hierarchically bound space which is separated but not secluded from the wider social space.

The ideology of the harem is a hallmark of almost all ancient Near Eastern monarchies and it makes little sense that in the long history

Table 2. The known ancient words used for 'harem'

Ancient court	'Harem' word	Literal translation
Assyria	*bitat*	interior
Assyria	*bit sinnišati*	women's house
Assyria	*sikru*	enclosure
Israel and Judah	*penima*	inside
Mari	*tabqum*	corner/inside corner
Egypt	*hnrt*	place of seclusion

of royal harems this important institution should be absent from the Achaemenid royal court. Moreover, spatial polarity is often highlighted in the known ancient words used for 'harem' (Table 2), stressing over and again its removal (in the physical and abstract forms) from the outer court.

Despite the interesting and illuminating work recently undertaken on ancient Near Eastern royal harems (Marsman 2003; Solvang 2003), studies of the ancient Persian court by and large either underplay the place and role of the harem or totally deny its presence. Kuhrt, for instance, generally questions the practice of royal polygamy in Near Eastern civilisations and is reluctant to acknowledge the institution of the harem in any Near Eastern society, arguing that historians rely too heavily on its existence to explain or concoct a ranking system for royal women (Kuhrt 1995: 149, 526), although a hierarchical structure among court women is of fundamental importance to the maintenance of dynastic order (see below). Briant (2002: 283) likewise speaks of 'the myth of the harem' and in this he follows Heleen Sancisi-Weerdenburg, who argued that generally the pernicious roles attributed by the Greeks to harems and queens were nothing more than a widespread literary cliché (Sancisi-Weerdenburg 1987a: 43, 38). Certainly, Plato's representation of the imperial harem as the route of royal degeneracy and the inevitable decline of empire (**D1**) or the problematic epilogue of Xenophon's *Cyropaedia* with its diatribe against Persian effeminacy (and probably not by Xenophon at all) are representative of the wider Greek paranoia about, and misunderstanding of, the part played by Persian women – but it would be hard to maintain that this pejorative view of Persian royal women pervades every Greek source (Llewellyn-Jones and Robson 2010: 66–8, 82–7; see further pertinent comments by Harrison 2011: 64–8). Nonetheless, for Briant the word 'harem' conjures up so effectively the misguided stereotypes promulgated by Orientalist art, literature, and cinema that he seems unable to move beyond the fantasy. He reluctantly, and obliquely, concedes that 'although the term *harem* must be retained for convenience, the usual meaning cannot be applied to any women other than the royal concubines' (2002: 285). This gets us nowhere.

More puzzling still is Maria Brosius' methodical exclusion of the harem from her important study *Women in Ancient Persia* (1996). While she notes the wide array of royal females found at the Achaemenid court, and correctly observes that there was a distinct hierarchy of women, ranging in importance from the king's mother and the king's wives (of Persian stock) to the non-Persian concubines and, ultimately, slaves, she does not attempt to describe these women as a specific unit within the court. This does not make sense, given that in any developed court system the presence of women of specific social status would have called for a codified hierarchical structure which must have been reflected in such issues as court protocol and even designated (if not permanent) social and living spaces. Brosius is correct to refute the idea of female seclusion, noting that 'It is clear . . . that there is no truth in suggestions that women lived in seclusion and were confined to the palace' (Brosius 1996: 188) but her belief in a 'Greek notion that women lived in the seclusion of the palace, hidden away from the outside world' (Brosius 2006: 43) needs dissecting. It is not satisfactory to accept at face value that *all* Greeks advanced an image of 'Oriental seclusion' onto their construction of court women; in fact, the Greek texts rarely say as much. Persian women's confinement is *not* an issue ever envisaged by Classical Greek authors of the fifth or fourth centuries BCE and, in fact, key writers contemporaneous with the Achaemenids like Herodotus, Xenophon, Plato, Isocrates, Aristotle, and even Ctesias (the most maligned of Greeks when it comes to 'women's matters') show royal women operating in a wide array of public spheres: travelling the country, having economic autonomy and political agency, and even hunting in the open countryside. There is no Greek text of the Achaemenid period which specifically talks about female seclusion or the hidden or carefully guarded lives of women. On the contrary, Plato states that the Persian king had no need to keep his queen in seclusion or to have her guarded because her own sense of social superiority kept her self-vigilance in operation (**D2**).

It is later Greek authors, like Plutarch, who over-dramatise the Persian fixation on the rigorous policing of their wives and concubines (**D3**). It must be recognised, though, that Plutarch was writing during the first century CE, when the romantic stereotype of the secluded Persian woman had become a stock image in Greek fictional literature.

It was the Greek-speaking authors of the newly emerged genre of the novel who first gave rise to a vogue for romantic adventure stories set within the palaces of Achaemenid kings and their romantic tales deliberately played with the tensions associated with viewing women in the harems of eastern monarchs. The Greek novelists, working from the fourth-century BCE *Persica* of Ctesias, Deinon and Heraclides of Cumae, concocted their stories long after the fall of the Persian Empire. While they recognised the historical truth that royal Achaemenid women had been part of a regulated court society in which the harem played a key role, the stories which they composed were intended to arouse the passions of (male) readers through an erotic voyeurism. Chariton's novel *Callirhoe*, written at some time between 25 BCE and CE 50, is generally regarded as the earliest extant piece of Greek prose fiction and tells the story of a beautiful Greek girl, Callirhoe, who is forced into concubinage in the harem of Artaxerxes II. By locating his story in old romantic Persia, and within the harem of his imagination, Chariton allows a distinct form of Orientalism to permeate his narrative. In fact *Callirhoe* can be seen as a formative contributor to a long line of beautiful, if deeply misunderstood and precarious, Orientalist clichés that permeate later Greek works of literature. Edward Saïd in his seminal study of 1978 regarded Aeschylus as the first proponent of Orientalism, while Sancisi-Weerdenburg (1987a) regards Ctesias as the culprit; in fact it is Chariton, working some 200 years after Aeschylus, who is responsible for a particularly passé visualisation of the east, which might be termed the 'the jewel in the bellybutton' school of Orientalism (see further Llewellyn-Jones 2009b).

By the first century CE the romantic 'harem motif' had embedded itself so firmly within the popular imagination of Greek and Roman readers that historians like Plutarch and, later, Aelian were using the stereotypical image of the secluded Oriental harem as factual content in the construction of their eastern biographies and histories (for a full discussion of this process see Llewellyn-Jones forthcoming a). It is also vital to recall that in writing his Greek *Lives* Plutarch had a particularly virulent anti-Persian prejudice (see Llewellyn-Jones and Robson 2010: 40–3). Plutarch's *Life of Themistocles* has a definite agenda and his *Boys' Own*-style adventure story of the Greek statesman's flight from Persia in a curtained carriage, travelling disguised as a woman, necessitates Plutarch's exaggeration and gives him a vehicle to express his opinion that the despotic Persians exercised extreme control over their women. However, in his *Life of Artaxerxes*, which revolves around the workings of the inner court in some detail, and is derived in large part from Ctesias' and Deinon's observations of court life, nothing of this strict barbaric 'Oriental seclusion' is suggested (for the unreliability of Plutarch on the Themistocles matter see Nashat 2003: 21, 23).

Moreover, misunderstandings regarding the 'Oriental seclusion' of Persian women arise in part from cavalier translations of the Greek spatial term *gynaikaion* or *gynaikonitis* as 'women's quarters'. Janett Morgan (2007, 2010) has revealed that this translation is widely off the mark and that a better rendering of these Greek terms would simply be 'the place where the women are', suggesting *any* temporary space utilised by women and by family. In the ancient Greek understanding, *gynaikaion* is never a fixed, let alone secluded, female-only space, so that to read Persian court structures through an imperfect understanding of the Greek terminology is futile and to think of 'harem' in terms of a secluded female-only space or as a form of oppressive purdah is a crucial misconception of the nature of the term and the institution.

Brosius (2007: 25) asserts that the strong economic status of royal women 'provides a clue to palace organisation' but unfortunately she offers no further exploration of this potentially important statement. Despite recognising the Great King's immediate family as the most important group of the inner court and acknowledging the presence of several groups of women ('female royalty and noblewomen', including mother, wives, heir, other children, and royal siblings, 'attendants', 'royal concubines, and administrative personnel') she cannot find a 'place' for them at court, and her reading of 'harem' (which might be rooted still in a Saïdian reading of Orientalism, although she does not explicitly state this) inhibits her from drawing them into a collective institution (Brosius 2007: 31–3). In contrast, Jack Balcer (1993: 273–317) and Tony Spawforth (2007a: 93, 97, 100) both see the logic of a female court hierarchy and thus employ 'harem' as the simplest and most effective way to talk about the women and personnel of the Persian inner court without any pejorative associations.

There is no reason to abandon using 'harem'. We can use the term safely, without an Orientalist gloss and free of misconceptions or preconceptions. Scholarship needs to rise above and beyond the harem cliché and recognise that, in the light of not having an Old Persian term which survives, 'harem' is the most appropriate term to use to describe the domestic make-up and the gender ideology of the Persian inner court.

Honour and visibility

Marc van de Mieroop (2004: 149–51) has suggested that because stereotypical harem images have not been sufficiently interrogated by scholarship, it is too often assumed that any indigenous evidence for harems in ancient societies reflects the oppressed status automatically expected of women in these cultures. While there is no compulsion to abandon the term 'harem', we do need to readdress our perception of it as an oppressive sphere. Because popular conceptions of the harem (from Chariton on) always feature a lack of freedom for women and their imprisonment within the gilded cage of the royal palace, harem women are usually perceived as sad, lonely, sometimes desperate individuals. Take, for instance, an emotive description of the harem women at the Siamese royal palace written by Anna Leonowens (later of *The King and I* fame) in 1873:

> [The women] have the appearance of being slightly blighted. Nobody is too much in earnest, or too much alive, or too happy. The general atmosphere is that of depression. They are bound to have no thought of the world they have quitted, however pleasant it may have been; to ignore all ties and affections; to have no care but for one individual alone, and that the master. But if you become acquainted with some of these very women . . . you might gather recollections of the outer world, of earlier life and strong affections, of hearts scarred and disfigured and broken, of suppressed sighs and unuttered sobs. (Leonowens 1873: 40)

These are intense words, emotional rather than rational, involved rather than detached, perhaps even melodramatic. And that is part of the difficulty in trying to get to grips with the idea of the harem, since the word arouses emotions – and in Leonowens' case 'harem' denotes a depressing lack of freedom. But the idea that 'freedom' must be linked to 'visibility' is a construction of the modern (i.e. post-industrial) west and has been given even greater emphasis in our own age, in which a cult of celebrity has distorted all rules of public and private in the most alarming ways.

'Freedom' in the modern sense of the word does not equate with ancient concepts of public visibility. In Near Eastern antiquity, as in ancient Greece, a high-ranking woman felt no honour in being put before the public view (Llewellyn-Jones 2002: 155–214) so that true authority and prestige lay in a woman's removal from the overt public view and in her separation from the public gaze. This was certainly the case among high-status women, for whom numerous social conventions (including veiling and the demarcation of space) ensured their public invisibility and thereby boosted their sense of honour and, simultaneously, the honour and status of their male kin. In Persia it was important for the status and honour of Achaemenid royal women that their public invisibility was publicly demonstrated. The Hebrew book of Esther opens with the story of Queen Vashti (an ostensibly fictional character operating in a historically viable space), who is holding a feast for the court ladies in the harem of the palace at Susa while the king and his nobles dine outdoors in the garden (Esther 1:9). The drunken Great King commands Vashti to appear before his male guests but, shocked and reviled by the suggestion of appearing before non-blood-kin males, Vashti refuses and her rebuff of the king's orders brings about her swift downfall. This story, reminiscent in many ways of the themes in the Herodotean tale of Gyges and Candaules' wife (Herodotus 1.8), finds further reflection in the Greek sources, which confirm that the royal women of Persia did not drink with their husbands and that the appearance of such high-ranking women in male company would be thought improper (Plutarch, *Artaxerxes* 5.3; *Moralia* 140b).

The play on visibility and honour and shame would help explain the complete absence of the human female form in the official palace art of the Empire; indeed, women are rarely depicted at all in Achaemenid art and then are represented only in small-scale works, although sometimes of precious and semi-precious materials (Brosius 2010a; Llewellyn-Jones 2010a, 2010b). Women were not readily looked upon in real life so as to augment and ensure their social honour and they were not viewed in large-scale artworks for the same reason. The high social rank of royal females, like that of the Great King himself, was stressed by their conspicuous invisibility (again, not to be confused with seclusion). While we should not necessarily believe Plutarch's exaggeration that Persian women were locked away behind doors, his reports (and those of other Greeks) of women travelling in curtained carriages (*harmamaxae*) is certainly believable and gives us a sense of how the Persians conceived of elite women's public life.

The *harmamaxa* was a deluxe four-wheeled 'chariot wagon' composed of an enclosed box, long enough to recline in, which was richly upholstered and decorated with hangings. It was a vehicle supremely suited to transporting women and it was used by Persians for 'shuttling their harem about' (Oost 1977/8: 228; see also **C13**) and perhaps it was this type of vehicle that was provided for a group of women called *dukšišbe . . . puhu Mišdašba pakbe*, 'royal ladies . . . girls, daughters of

Hystaspes', who are recorded travelling from Media to Persepolis in PFa 31 (Brosius 1996: 93). When the king travelled with his court and set up camp, the *harmamaxae* could be placed together to produce a harem wing on wheels (as suggested by Herodotus 9.76; see Miller 1997: 51). That Artaxerxes II's wife, Stateira, had a *harmamaxa* which often appeared with its curtains open, in order that the young queen might greet the women of the Empire, is highly unusual (**D4**; Plutarch, *Moralia* 173f, says that Artaxerxes encouraged his wife to do this). Certainly her imperious mother-in-law, Parysatis, regarded Stateira's eccentricity as a breach of court protocol and an affront to decorum; in this respect, the king's mother is probably more in accord with orthodox royal conceptions of female visibility. Interestingly, royal concubines operated in this sphere of high-status invisibility as well (**D5**). Xenophon (*Hellenica* 3.1.10) recalls that Mania, the extraordinary female governor of Dardanus, a dependant of the satrap Pharnabazus, watched and even commanded battles from the protection of her curtained wagon. This demonstrates best of all the way in which women participated very actively in society while retaining a sense of harem.

The same can be made of Greek tales of royal women hunting (Ctesias F15 §55; Athenaeus 12.514b). The hunt could be enjoyed without breaching rules of segregation by controlled access to game parks or even the erection of screens behind which the royal women could sport freely; both these measures were adopted for Mughal harem women (Lal 1988: 60, 129, 185–6, 201).

The royal women of Achaemenid Persia did not live in an oppressive purdah, nor did they inhabit a world of sultry sensuality, but they certainly formed part of a strict hierarchical court structure which moved in close proximity to the king. As a component of his harem (in the true sense of the word), they followed in the peripatetic lifestyle of the court. There can be little doubt that their honour and chastity were carefully (self-)guarded, but this does not mean that royal women were dislocated from interaction with wider court society or that they lacked autonomy. But it is logical to recognise the royal harem as a vital component of Persian court culture and to recognise its political importance in the maintenance of dynastic power: women gave birth to future heirs and vigilantly – sometimes ferociously – guarded their and their offspring's positions within the ever-changing structure of court hierarchy (see Chapter 5). The Achaemenid dynasty was essentially a family-run business and at the heart of the operation was the harem. For the women of the royal family, prestige and access to power lay in their separation from the public gaze and in their intimate proximity to the king, whether as his mother, wife, daughter, sister, concubine, mistress, or even slave. But restricted visibility did not mean lack of freedom.

Is there an archaeology of the harem?

There can be little doubt that royal women had their own apartments (Briant 2002: 283–4) either in tents, wagons, or palaces; Herodotus (3.68–9, 7.2–3) certainly thought as much when he described the physical layout of the inner court of Smerdis and the book of Esther (2:13, 16) also envisages separate living spaces for women. When the Greek doctor Democedes arrived at court he was escorted by a eunuch to meet the king's wives (Herodotus 3.130) and we also hear that 'before the age of five a boy lives with the women and never sees his father' (Herodotus 1.136) – although this is no doubt something of an exaggeration, in line with other Greek texts on the harmfulness of a 'harem rearing' (**D1**).

What can be done with these observations? In his *History of the Persian Empire*, Olmstead paints an atmospheric picture of an L-shaped building at the southern edge of Persepolis (**F19**) which Herzfeld (1941) and Schmidt (1953) identified as the harem:

> Surrounded by the guardrooms of the watchful eunuchs was a tier of six apartments to house the royal ladies. Each tier consisted of a tiny hall whose roof was upheld by only four columns and a bedroom so minute that even with a single occupant the atmosphere must have been stifling. (Olmstead 1948: 285)

Such a description makes it unsurprising that many scholars have found it difficult to accept this section of the terrace as the space occupied by the Empire's foremost women, certainly when compared with the Greek and Hebrew texts, although few scholars have analysed the physical remains of the structures in any detail. Brosius (2007: 33) dismisses Herzfeld's and Schmidt's designation of the area out of hand: 'so far no structure has been identified at Persepolis which could have served as the women's quarters'. Indeed, the building has often been classified as an overflow storeroom of the nearby treasury (Wilber 1969: 73).

The position of the L-shaped building towards the back of the terrace provides strong support for it being a (temporary) residential area of part of the harem. Add to this a number of uniform apartments within the complex, each consisting of a main room connected with one smaller room or two such subsidiary chambers, and it would appear that the argument for a living space is enhanced. These were certainly the principal criteria for the structure's initial identification as the harem (Schmidt 1953: 255; supported by Shahbazi 2004: 163), although doubts have been cast on Herzfeld's initial motives in identifying the remains as such. Allen notes that at the time of the first publication of its discovery in the 1930s, Herzfeld was in the process of negotiating funds for the excavations and that the potential recovery of a harem was held to be propitious because of the hope (unfulfilled) of finding precious artefacts within the remains (Allen 2007: 329).

Let us reconsider the location of the harem on the terrace. It lies well inside the area of the platform defined as private. In fact, Herzfeld argued for the strict separation of this area from those accessible to the public, on the model of similar layouts of the majority of other ancient Near Eastern palaces (Herzfeld 1941: 226; Allen 2007: 328). A glance at the plan of Persepolis and other Near Eastern residential palace quarters (at, for instance, Babylon and Nimrud) reveals that these buildings contain individual rooms of modest scale, certainly in comparison with the monumental grandeur of the areas intended for public display. At Persepolis the protection of these structures by the thick southern fortification wall immediately behind the harem contributes to the function proposed here for the building, as one would expect to find accommodation used by the king and the royal family to be best protected; indeed, the presence of guard reliefs at major entrances to the compound suggest that security was paramount (Root 1979: 10) (the figures of soldiers carved into the connecting wall between the upper terrace and the harem are usually overlooked by scholars). Crucially then, this space at the terrace rear, which was allocated as living quarters for at least some of the royal family, was hidden by high fortifications and was well guarded by the military. It was secure and private.

The harem is grouped with other palatial residential structures both on and off the platform and it is actually integral to the building immediately above it – identified as Xerxes' palace and private residence. Xerxes' palace is connected to the harem by two grand, well worked flights of stairs, which must have been utilised by the king or his courtiers when they required direct access to the rooms below (**F19**; Schmidt 1953: 244). They could move between the two parts of the palace without having to traverse any public space. Schmidt's excavations found that the lower flights of steps were formerly enclosed, while the upper section was open, and that the more monumental, well dressed, and polished western stairway also contained one of the few physically evidenced (well worked) doors in the area. Schmidt also identified a direct access route, via the stairways, connecting the harem with the Council Hall and the Hall of a Hundred Columns, allowing the king and the royal family to move conveniently and directly from their private apartments to the public areas without breaching security (Schmidt 1953: 255).

As to the apartments themselves, they are laid out in two rows, all interconnected by long narrow corridors. From archaeology (**F19**) one can identify a maximum of twenty-two apartments, each consisting of a large hypostyle room with one or more adjoined chambers (Herzfeld 1941: 229; Schmidt 1953: 137, 260). The main rooms are well decorated with niches and plastered walls and elegant stone door lintels and column bases, which are so well crafted that the general execution of the stonework is just as fine as that on the palaces of the kings (Wilber 1969: 94). The average apartment measures approximately ten by ten metres – and while in no way a negligible living space, it would be hard to imagine royal personages passing their days perpetually in a room this size. This alone helps to negate the image of royal women living in strictly guarded confinement – the claustrophobia would have been cruel – and Briant rightly voices his concern that it is not at all clear 'that the royal princesses lived cloistered in their apartments' (Briant 2002: 285). It is better to think of each chamber as perhaps a separate (and temporary) domestic quarter (for sleeping?) or as an antechamber or storage area but not as a room used by a single occupant all of the time.

A big courtyard in the harem's main wing and the large room attached to it are therefore best interpreted as a communal space for the harem rather than for a grand individual's private use (as Schmidt proposed), since it lacks the domestic quarter/antechamber units which accompany the main halls of Darius' and Xerxes' palaces. In view of the regulated control of movement to this area, both from within and outside the harem, it could have functioned as an audience chamber for royal women or princes or perhaps even the king when he chose to remain there. Interestingly, what appears to be a female audience is depicted on a cylinder seal (**F20**). The parallel with the motif of the king's audience (**F3**) is explicit and is proof of the high regard in which royal women – possibly in this instance the king's mother – were held (Brosius 1996: 86; Brosius 2010a; Lerner 2010). It is very likely that in this large hall a space was set aside for other activities, including communal eating and entertainment, as well as the collective rearing of younger children; we must certainly be rid of any notion of women shut up all day in cramped, isolated cells. The cluster of defined 'apartments' certainly accords with Diodorus' description of residences on the terrace (7.70–1): 'Scattered about the royal terrace were apartments of the kings and members of the royal family as well as quarters for the great nobles'. Variations within the standard model of the chambers may provide a convenient indicator of some hierarchy among the inhabitants, although this assumes that greater living space is an indicator of status. More sub-chambers could also reflect the presence of a larger number of attendants.

Finally, of course, as we have had occasion to note, the whole court could not have resided in the limited terrace area and within the harem itself space was at a premium. It is tempting to conclude that the mass ranks of the court generally resided in tents and covered wagons strewn about on the plain below and (those of highest rank perhaps) within the mud-brick and stone buildings on the plain, while the permanent stone buildings of the terrace, including the harem, were reserved for a privileged few of the inner royal family, with perhaps favoured wives and royal mothers the most likely to have their own apartments and, consequently, command the most intimate access to the king (Walthall 2008: 19).

A harem who's who

Who made up the royal harem? It is difficult to be precise, but it seems likely that the Achaemenid harem, operating within the highly sophisticated Persian court system, was just as complex as the harem structures in other court societies. In most historical periods the harem was headed by a chief queen, usually the king's mother or, in her absence, the most favoured (or influential) wife, who gathered about her the other royal and noble women – secondary wives, royal sisters, royal daughters, and others. Beneath those favoured women ranked the concubines, the female administrative personnel, and, at the lowest level, the female slaves. This might work as a model for thinking about the structure of the Achaemenid harem also, although in reality the harem hierarchy must have been in a state of continual flux as, for instance, wives gave birth to sons rather than daughters and thereby gained some hierarchical cachet or a concubine suddenly became a favoured companion of the Great King. All that can be said with some certainty is that, according to the Persepolis

Table 3. Elamite court titles for women, deriving from Assyrian and Babylonian
prototypes

Elamite title	Assyrian/Babylonian title	Translation
*sunki ammari	*ummi šarri*	The king's mother
*sunki irtiri	*aššat šarri*	The king's wife
*sunki pakri	*mārat šarri*	The king's daughter

tablets, high-ranking women of the royal house were honoured with the title *duxθrī (literally, 'daughter'), which has been preserved in Elamite transcription as *dukšiš* (pl. *dukšišbe*), which can be generically translated as 'princess' or 'royal lady' (for instance PF 1795; PF 823). *Dukšišbe* was used collectively for Achaemenid royal women but their individual status was determined by their relationship to the king. Thus, the Persepolis texts record Elamite court titles, deriving from Assyrian and Babylonian prototypes, which give us an indication of how royal women were addressed (some examples are presented in Table 3). Achaemenid sources from Babylonia also refer to a woman belonging to the royal household as a 'woman of the palace' (*ša ekalli*). However, the Greek term *basileia* ('queen'), which is used to identify a specific royal female of high status (usually the king's mother or wife) in Greek texts, cannot be justified when set alongside *bona fide* Persian evidence; Brosius therefore argues compellingly for a translation of *basileia* simply as 'royal woman' (see Brosius 1996: 20, 27–8; Brosius 2006: 41).

Although they might have been called *ša ekalli*, it is not certain whether royal concubines enjoyed the title *dukšiš* too, although it is unlikely. Deinon's *Persica* gives an interesting glimpse of some kind of formalised hierarchical court etiquette among royal women which carefully demarcated concubines from more superior royal ladies (**D6**; on concubines, see below). Some sort of hierarchical structure seems to be reflected in the all-female audience scene on the cylinder seal we explored earlier (**F20**) (similar models are found in Neo-Elamite and archaic Greek contexts too; see Brosius 2010a; Lerner 2010). A woollen tapestry saddle cloth found at Pazyryk in the Crimea has another intriguing (and rare) scene showing Achaemenid royal women standing at an incense burner (see Lerner 2010: 160; Brosius 1996: 86). Hierarchy here is augmented both through scale and (as in the cylinder seal) through dress: all women wear crowns but in each case the higher-status woman wears a long veil draped over the rear of her crown.

Let us explore the harem ranks a little more, and observe three of the categories in more detail: the king's mother, the wives of the king, and the royal concubines.

The king's mother

While a king might have many wives, he could have only one biological mother, so it is not hard to grasp the notion that the king's mother held the highest place of authority among the court ladies (**D7**). This is true in successive eastern and western civilisations (on the title 'king's mother' in its Near Eastern context see Brosius 1996: 22–4). Of equal prestige to her position as the monarch's birth mother was her role in connecting two generations of rulers. In Persia, and the Near East generally, while the king's mother was not expected to exercise official power, she might gain political clout through the careful maintenance of her son's favour (by using flattery according to Plutarch, *Moralia* 174b) as a consequence of her own ambitions and personal skill. In other words, the king's mother's power was indirect. Nonetheless, she could influence her son in his policy-making. For instance, Amestris, the mother of Artaxerxes I, regularly intervened (not always for the best) in the bitter dynastic conflict between the king and her son-in-law, Megabyzus (**D8**). Nevertheless, the actual power that the king's mother could wield was limited and she acted only with the consent of the king, although strictly within the domestic sphere she may have been given *carte blanche* to take decisions on her own. Ctesias implies that the king's mother had control over behaviour within the harem, policing its mores and punishing the treasonous crimes of family, eunuchs, court doctors, and other harem personnel (**D9**; see further Ctesias F15 §54; Llewellyn-Jones 2002: 38–9). However, a king's mother sometimes acted without the consent of her son and her actions could even be treasonous (Ctesias F17 = Plutarch, *Artaxerxes* 2.3–3.6) but she suffered the consequences. Parysatis, Artaxerxes II's mother, infamously pursued a vendetta against her daughter-in-law, Stateira, to its bitter end, when she poisoned her at a private dinner and for this unorthodox behaviour Parysatis was exiled to her estates in Babylonia (**E16**; see a discussion in Chapter 5).

That the king's mother could own private estates is significant in itself because it speaks of the land wealth an influential royal woman could amass as personal property, gifted by the crown (Plato *Alcibiades* 1.123b). Parysatis' affluence became proverbial in the Greek-speaking world (Plutarch, *Artaxerxes* 4.1, 19.6; Xenophon, *Anabasis* 1.4.9,

2.4.27; Aelian, *Historical Miscellany* 12.1) and her wealth is also confirmed by numerous texts in the Babylonian Murašu archive, where detailed documents record some of the financial affairs of Parysatis' estates in Mesopotamia and their careful administration by her estate managers and financial middle men; they provide clear evidence of this powerful woman's economic independence and acumen (Stolper 1985).

Recent work on the Persepolis texts has identified a woman long known to scholars as the wealthy landowner Irdabama to be – in all probability – the mother of Darius I, a woman descended from a family of local Elamite dynasts (Henkelman 2010a: 693–7; Henkelman 2011a: 613). Economically active, and with the authority to issue commands to the administrative hierarchy at Persepolis, Irdabama is well attested in the texts overseeing her vast personal estates, receiving and distributing food supplies and commanding an entourage of *puhu* ('servants', 'pages') and *kurtaš* ('workers') at Tirazziš (near Shiraz) and elsewhere (PFa 27, PF 737, PF 739). Irdabama is attested at the ceremonial cities of Persepolis and Susa, and even as far away from the Persian heartland as Borsippa in Babylonia (Brosius 1996: 130–41; Henkelman 2010a: 693–7). She clearly travelled widely around central Iran and Mesopotamia with her own courtly entourage and she and her court are often attested travelling independently of the Great King's court; in this, the behaviour of the king's mother shadows that of her son, who, as we have seen, toured the countryside as an element of his royal duty (see Chapter 3; Briant 2002: 191). As part of her personal progress through the Empire's heartland, Irdabama (and no doubt other important royal ladies as well – see below) could deputise for the king in his absence. Interestingly, European monarchies of the middle ages and early modern periods employed much the same tradition and European queens and queen mothers frequently travelled with their own households, setting up courts in places often far from the king, but always rejoining the monarch's court for religious festivals, state ceremonies, or family events (see, for instance, Starkey 2008: 39–58). Of more surprise, perhaps, is the fact that some of the highest-ranking women of the Mughal imperial harem operated the same system and traversed northern India in curtained palanquins surrounded by armies of courtiers – and all without breaching the very strictest form of Muslim purdah demanded by Mughal royal society (Lal 2005).

One of Irdabama's servants, a man named Rašda, is well attested in the Persepolis texts (e.g. PF 800, 849); he was probably an important royal commissioner whose jobs included taking care of Irdabama's work-force. His personal seal, an Elamite heirloom (PFS 77*; Lerner 2010: 157 fig. 14.5), represents an audience scene before an enthroned female protagonist – no coincidence perhaps, given the evident importance of Irdabama – and it is reasonable to envisage her holding audience ceremonies to mirror those of the Great King himself. As Henkelman postulates, 'One may wonder whether Rašda purposely chose or was given this particular seal. Regardless of that question, however, the image is a powerful reminder that court protocol need not have been confined to the king and his satraps' (Henkelman 2010a: 694). Irdabama's conspicuous presence in the Persepolis texts and her obvious economic agency make a stark contrast to Atossa (Old Persian, Udusana), the wife of Darius and mother of Xerxes, who plays such an important role in Herodotus' *Histories*, and whom he envisages as a significant political motivator. Atossa barely makes an appearance in the tablets (only twice in fact – PF 0162 and 0163) and in light of the Persepolis evidence we should perhaps modify the way we use Herodotus.

The Persepolis Fortification texts, their archival cognates, and their seal images are clearly of vital significance in expanding our knowledge of the duties, privileges, and powers of Achaemenid royal women and they suggest that those of the highest ranks enjoyed exceptional autonomy (Brosius 1996: 123–46), although we should not postulate this level of independence for all categories harem women. Spending power may have accrued political power, but access to high levels of wealth was nonetheless limited. Despite their ability to travel independently of the king, this in no way negates king's mothers and other high-ranking royal females being part of the central harem: the structure of the royal hierarchy was maintained with or without their physical presence, and the wealthy women followed the principles of social and spatial separation no matter where they were.

The king's wives

Kings' wives could accrue wealth and status through landowning and the management of workforces. The *dukšiš* Irtašduna (known in Greek sources as Artystone) was, allegedly, the favourite of Darius I's wives (Herodotus 7.69), an idea which does seem to be borne out from her prominence in the Persepolis archives (see for instance **D10**). Like Irdabama, Irtašduna held at least three estates, managed by stewards and maintained by workforces, and she too can be located travelling around the Empire's core, sometimes with Irdabama (PFa 14a) and sometimes in the company of her son, Prince Aršama (Greek, Arsames; PF 733, PF 734). Her elaborate personal heirloom seal (PFS 0038; see Garrison and Root 2001: 83–5) is found on eight letter orders and nine documents listing foodstuffs 'consumed before Irtašduna' (Henkelman 2010a: 698–703).

Achaemenid kings were polygamous, although it appears that they took only Persian women as wives. It is difficult to know if the king picked out a 'chief' wife – on par with the pharaonic Egyptian tradition of appointing a 'great royal wife' (*hmt nsw wrt*), who ranked higher than the other royal wives (*hmt nsw*; Robins 1993) or whether precedence in the harem pecking order was negotiated on a more *ad hoc* basis. There does not seem to have been an official Persian title for a 'chief' wife, which suggests that it was not a recognised court position.

Our knowledge of the names of Achaemenid royal wives is largely confined to Greek sources and they usually name just one wife for each king – Amestris (I) is the only known wife of Xerxes I, and Damaspia is the only named wife of Artaxerxes I. This is probably the result of the Greek preoccupation with the 'norm' of monogamy and their inability to put themselves comfortably into a different cultural mind-set; it is highly likely that, in reality, all Great Kings took multiple wives so that they could beget numerous heirs. Near Eastern literature often stresses the significance of multiple offspring – especially sons – to a man's social position (Budin 2011: 334–46). A New Kingdom Egyptian didactic text known as the 'Instructions of Any' starts with an injunction for a man to marry a wife and beget children:

> Take a wife while you are young,
> That she make a son for you . . .
> Happy the man whose peoples are many,
> He is saluted on account of his progeny.
> (Trans. Lichtheim 2003: 11)

And Sumerian proverbs (1: 146–7) call on the blessings of the gods for healthy issue from a buxom wife:

> May Inanna make you a hot-limbed wife to lie by you!
> May she bestow on you broad-armed sons!
> May she seek out for you a place of happiness. . . .
> Marrying is human.
> Getting children is divine.
> (Alster 1997: 29–30)

The pressure felt by kings to father many children was essential to their success and reputation as mighty monarchs, and heartfelt royal pleas to the gods – such as one addressed to Shamash in the Mesopotamian tale of King Etana – are telling: 'Take away my shame [and] give me an heir', he begs the god. Likewise, Kirta, the childless king of Ugarit, pours forth an anguished cry to his gods (column II: 1–5) to grant him heirs:

> What to me is silver, or even yellow gold,
> Together with its land, and slaves forever mine?
> A triad of chariot horses
> From the stable of a slavewoman's son?
> Let me procreate sons!
> Let me produce a brood!'
> (Trans. Parker 1997: 13–14)

Although Kirta had seven wives, they all either died in childbirth or of disease or else had deserted him, and Kirta had no surviving children. His mother had borne eight sons, although Kirta himself was the only one of his brothers to survive childhood and now he had no family members to succeed him and he saw that his dynasty's demise was inevitable. To prevent this catastrophe, the wives of Near Eastern monarchs were expected to be fertile sexual partners and those of the Persian Great Kings were responsible for the Achaemenid dynasty's promulgation; as Briant (2002: 778) puts it, 'royal power was transmitted through the womb of the family'.

Some women clearly performed particularly important political roles in dynastic continuity. In the early Achaemenid period, for instance, the possession of a royal predecessor's wives ensured the successor's hold on the throne, and the control of the harem gave a new ruler the potential to legitimise his reign through the physical possession of a former monarch's household. Darius I had capitalised on this when in his bid for power he had married all the available royal women of the line of Cyrus II – the former wives and sisters and daughters of Cambyses II and Bardiya – whereupon he incorporated them into his harem and established them as the most high ranking of all his existing wives. He quickly fathered children by his new acquisitions and promoted his sons born 'in the purple' above those born before his accession (Brosius 1996: 47–64; see also Ogden 1999: 45). In this Darius I was following a common Near Eastern practice: Ramses II of Egypt, for instance, inherited the women belonging to the harem of his father Seti I as a demonstration of dynastic longevity (Leblanc 1999);

upon his military victory and subsequent accession to the throne of Israel, David claimed the females of the harem of Saul (2 Samuel 12:8) and Solomon inherited his father's harem of women and servants (de Vaux 1961: 115).

While diplomatic marriages are attested early on in the dynasty's history, the Achaemenid kings made more of a habit of forming marriage alliances with great Persian noble families or marrying within the family itself by taking cousins, nieces, and half-sisters as wives. The only fully incestuous marriage known to have taken place was that of Artaxerxes II to his daughters Atossa (II) and Amestris (II) (Plutarch, *Artaxerxes* 23.5); the accusation of Cambyses' incest with his sisters should be treated very carefully, as it is probably founded in Egyptian propaganda (Herodotus 3.31).

Royal concubines

According to Herodotus, 'every [Persian] has a number of wives, a much greater number of concubines' (1.135), an image also later presented by Strabo (15.3.17): 'They marry many wives and also maintain a number of concubines for the sake of having many children'. While this scenario of empire-wide polygyny should not be taken at face value, it may well be representative of the elite of Persian society in the Achaemenid period, since Persian nobles, and certainly satraps, imitated royal polygyny and as a mirror image of the royal court they housed numerous concubines within the satrapal palaces. Pharnabazus, the satrap of Phrygia, kept a court full of concubines, and Mania, his female governor, is recorded as soliciting the goodwill of the satrap through the presents and compliments she pays to his concubines (Xenophon, *Hellenica* 3.1.10 provides us with excellent evidence for harem networking).

Historically, at least in the Greek (and Hebrew) sources, Persian royal concubines (Greek, *pallakai*; Hebrew, *pilgeš*; Aramaic, *lehena*) were generally considered to be beautiful girls who could be bought as slaves or received as gifts and tribute from different parts of the vast Empire (**D11, D12**; Aelian, *Historical Miscellany* 12.1). Concubines could also be regularly acquired as war booty or were captured from rebellious subjects. The childless King Kirta of Ugarit supposed that a brood of sons would follow on from his acquisition of aristocratic war-captured concubines and with that goal in mind he raised an army to march on the kingdom of Udum, demanding of its King Pubala (column VI: 22–8, 33–4):

What is not in my house you must give me:
You must give me Lady Huraya,
The fair-one, your firstborn child
Who is as fair as the goddess Anat,
Who is as comely as Astarte . . .
Who will bear a child for Kirta . . .
(Trans. Parker 1997: 23)

Herodotus confirms that after quelling the Ionian uprising, 'the most beautiful girls were dragged from their homes and sent to Darius' court' (6.32; see also Herodotus 4.19, 9.76; Plutarch, *Moralia* 339e) and the Persian practice of taking concubines as war booty is corroborated by a report in a Babylonian chronicle that, following the Persian sack of Sidon in 345 BCE, Artaxerxes III transferred to his Babylonian palace large numbers of women (**D13**). Of course, the Greeks too acquired Persian concubines as war prizes: for instance, 329 royal concubines of Darius III were part of Alexander's post-Issus plunder (**D14**).

Brosius (1996: 32) suggests that many of the captive foreign women who entered the places as royal concubines came from families of high social status, and King Kirta's demand for Princess Huraya of Udum appears to suggest this, although it is difficult to verify that this was always the case – after all, the Egyptian king refused to send his daughter to Cambyses' harem, fearing that she would be destined for concubinage and not marriage (**D15**). The Biblical story of Esther does not necessarily suggest a high social status for the heroine before her entry into the royal harem as a concubine (Esther 2:5–7) and this is certainly the case in later (Muslim) harem institutions, where girls were routinely collected from poor families (Peirce 1993). Briant (2002: 279) makes the important point, however, that not all captive women were bound for the privileges of the royal harem at all and that most of them would have disappeared into the huge regiment of domestic staff who worked throughout the places as *arad šari* ('royal slaves') and *arad ekalli* ('palace slaves'). The book of Esther further notes that the more fortunate young women chosen for the harem were instructed for a year in courtly arts and etiquette before being considered eligible for congress with the monarch. After that event, however, the novice graduated to a higher level of harem society and she could then be summoned by the king as his inclination dictated (**D12**).

The Greeks generally referred to concubines (both Greek and non-Greek) as *pallakai*, a term denoting low-class females, perhaps of the *demi-monde*, but the term's application cannot be justified for what we know about the status of Persian concubinage. Certainly the concubines of Persian kings should not be classed as even reputable disreputable women and in no way should these women be confused with courtesans, prostitutes, or mistresses. Artaxerxes I fathered at least eighteen sons with his concubines and Artaxerxes II had 150 sons by his (**D16**; Plutarch, *Artaxerxes* 26; Justin 9.1). While the official take was that children born to concubines were regarded as inferior to any child born to a royal wife (and the Greeks routinely – but inaccurately – called them *nothoi*, 'bastards'), 'the history of the succession of Achaemenid kings tells another story' (Brosius 1996: 33). As a result of wars, epidemics, the high infant mortality rate, or succession struggles within the royal household, an opportunity sometimes arose for the son of a concubine to ascend to the throne. Darius II was crowned king despite being the son of a Babylonian concubine named Cosmartidene, a fact which suggests that concubinage was not necessarily a dormant institution and that concubines could gain high status and even become the mothers of kings. In the harem status system the child of a concubine always outranked his or her mother, since the child took eminence (and the blood royal) from the father, but the reality of the harem was that circumstance or personal ambition could change the hierarchy, and with it the course of dynastic politics. Antagonism between wives and concubines is often recorded in the Hebrew Bible (see for instance Genesis 22:24, 25:6, 35:22, 36:12), which is paralleled by texts from similar court cultures (such as the epic Japanese *Tale of Genji* or the Qing novel *A Dream of Red Mansions*; see Zhou 2010), and it is probable that the same tensions permeated the Achaemenid court. However, the majority of concubines must have passed their lives as nameless nonentities in a court full of competitive women (Brosius 2011: 71). Concubinage was not necessarily a satisfying state of existence.

Several essentially historiographic texts afford an insight into the Greek preoccupation with the sex life of the Persian monarch (**D17**, **D18**, **D19**; see also Ctesias F13 §16; Athenaeus 12.514b). But what must we make of these ostensibly 'historical' reports? In some respects they resemble images of concubines found in later popular Greek literature, especially the Greek novels which drew on fashionable clichés of Persian concubinage and exploited the historical figure of the captive concubine for dramatic effect (Llewellyn-Jones forthcoming a). The allure of the fantastical seraglio proved to be irresistible to post-Achaemenid-period Greek authors, although perhaps most familiar is Aelian's (semi-fictional) account of Aspasia, the Greek-born concubine of Artaxerxes II (not to be confused with Pericles' celebrated *pallakē*) who is passed around the Persian court from brother (Cyrus the Younger) to brother (Artaxerxes II) and then to son (Crown Prince Darius). Aspasia's story is a highly romanticised and eroticised treatment of the royal concubine image (Aelian, *Historical Miscellany* 12.1).

But what of the number of concubines suggested in the 'historiography'? Were there 300, 329, or 360 royal concubines? Briant argues, with feasibility, that we are dealing here with symbolic numbers directly or indirectly relating to the Persian calendar in the context of sun worship; by settling on these numbers the image of the Great King as a man above men was confirmed because of 'a perfect proportionality between his own rhythm and cultic time' and it stressed the sacred character of the Achaemenid monarch (Briant 2002: 281). Briant therefore suggests that the ranks of the royal concubines were fixed at 360 and that the Greek evidence for this goes straight back to the Persian court. We should be less inclined to see a fixed number, since Greek, Hebrew, and even Babylonian reports imply a continual traffic in concubines and female slaves entering the harem (for example when 'stocks' were depleted; see **D11**, **D12**, **D13** and Scheidel 2009: 257). Certainly later harem systems had no fixed quota of royal concubines (Peirce 1993: 31). Briant's claim that 360 is a symbolically loaded number is no doubt correct but the exactness of the figure says more (or at least as much) about the Greek need for order and emblematic regulation than it necessarily does about the Persian desire for symbolic harmony.

While it is possible that Greek readers saw in these reports of the royal concubines images of eastern erotica, it is more likely that they perceived something else besides: a wonderment at the Great King's ability to amass, house, support, not to say sexually exploit, so many women (note Herodotus' comment at 7.187 on the 'numberless' concubines at court). The accumulation of females on this scale speaks for the king's virility as well as his wealth because while the concubines were there to provide for his bodily comforts and needs, their bodies were symbols of his dominance – not simply of man over women or of master over slaves, but of monarch over Empire. Like the diverse food served at the royal table, the precious stones and timbers brought to the workshops at Susa, or the rare flora planted in the royal gardens, the women who had been collected together and sent to the Great King from all parts of the Empire were physical manifestations of the Persian realm itself. Through their fertility the monarch populated his court and his realm.

The political harem

Within this hierarchy of peoples, contradictions arose as to the function of the harem's role in creating political stability and continuity. As in other Near Eastern courts, personal intrigues within the harem generated significant power politics. The manoeuvrings of Atossa, the wife of kings Cambyses, Bardiya, and Darius, and Amestris, the wife of Xerxes, Parysatis the sister-wife of Darius II, and Stateira the first (known) wife of Artaxerxes II are not simply acts of casual vindictiveness conjured up for the titillation of a Greek audience but genuine political power struggles in which rival wives and mothers pushed their favoured sons forward to gain the position of crown prince or Great King. These reports of amphimetric conflicts (the sons of the same father by different mothers can be termed *amphimetores*) demonstrates the importance of the harem as a political institution. This particular strain of courtly tension has been well argued for by Daniel Ogden (1999) in relation to the courts of the Hellenistic world and by Elizabeth Carney (2000) for the early Macedonian court, but has generally been overlooked or ostracised from Achaemenid studies. Yet in a court where polygyny was practised on a grand scale, but where there was no role for an official 'queen' or *first* wife, 'royal wives hated each other; the various groups of paternal half-siblings hated each other; but the most intense hatred of all was reserved for the relationship between children and their stepmothers' (Ogden 1999: x). To confuse matters further, as we have seen, primogeniture was not employed by the Persian monarchy. Moreover, in a policy such as that of the Achaemenids, where the Empire was considered to be the personal domain of the royal family, it was natural that the important women within the royal family would assume legitimate roles of authority. Brosius (1996: 105) has stressed that royal mothers took it upon themselves to guard the safety of the throne and the son who occupied it. Parysatis, for example, became entangled in the deaths of the pretender Sogdianus who threatened Darius II's accession to the throne, and of the eunuch Artoxares, the Paphlagonian who later tried to overthrow him (Ctesias F15 §40, §54).

But harem politics went beyond the royal women's roles as 'dynastic guard dogs'. Sometimes personal squabbles or bitter vendettas were played out in the harem, with royal women jealously guarding their personal status as much as the dynastic well-being (see Chapter 5). A Neo-Assyrian text aptly demonstrates this fact. It is a letter of complaint from a king's daughter, Šerua-eterat, a princess of the blood, to her sister-in-law Libbali-šarrat, who had married into the royal family and was therefore outranked by the blood princess (see further Novotny and Singletary 2009: 172–3). And Šerua-eterat's grievance? That Libbali-šarrat had not shown her the respect due to a royal noblewoman of her rank:

> Why do you not write me letters, why do you not send me any message by word-of-mouth? Isn't it because, in all honesty, people might say: 'That one (i.e. Šerua-eterat) is higher in rank than she'? After all, I, Šerua-eterat, am the eldest daughter born in the official residence to Esarhaddon the great and legitimate king, king of the world, king of Assyria, while you are only a daughter-in-law, the lady of the house of Ashurbanipal, the eldest son of the king born in the official residence of Esarhaddon, king of Assyria. (Oppenheim 1967: 158)

There is no record of a reply, although it is interesting to speculate on how this tense relationship developed, especially following Esarhaddon's death and Ashurbanipal's accession to the throne – and Libbali-šarrat's elevation to queen. As such, Libbali-šarrat then outranked Šerua-eterat – although it is impossible to know if Esarhaddon's haughty daughter ever changed her attitude towards the new queen and treated *her* with due deference.

However, while the royal harem was often a particular centre of intrigue, rebellion, and even assassination, it also served the important role of binding the throne close to the cooperating noble families, and to bind together the Achaemenids themselves as a dynasty. As kings and nobles married each other's sisters, daughters, and cousins, the process of marriages kept Achaemenid royalty and Persian nobility within a confined group, strengthening and re-strengthening its dynastic rule through its offspring – although the dynasty also lay itself open to the genetic problems of consanguinity and incest.

Achaemenid royal polygyny also served a major political purpose in tying the Empire together, for the harem women produced ranks of children: sons to serve as satraps and to implement and assist the king's rule or to serve in his military forces; and royal daughters to marry high-ranking courtiers and local dynasts and thus create political alliances and allegiances through marriage and through childbirth. Throughout the Empire provincial rulers and nobles became bound to the royal house through a complex network of marriages as territories were enmeshed into the greater imperial infrastructure. The harem was therefore an institution fundamental to the integral policy of the Achaemenid Empire as it helped to centralise sovereignty in the figure of the Great King over the Persian courtiers and other imperial nobles, and was used to maintain the political power of the dominant ethno-class, the Achaemenid dynasty.

Concluding thought

Leslie Peirce, in her excellent study *The Imperial Harem. Women and Sovereignty in the Ottoman Empire* (1993: 3), makes a vital observation on the nature of absolute monarchy and the intimate relationship with its royal women:

> Sex for . . . any monarch in a hereditary dynasty, could never be purely pleasure, for it had significant political meaning. Its consequences – the production of offspring – affected the succession to the throne, indeed the very survival of the dynasty. It was not a random activity. . . . Sexual relations between the [ruler] and chosen women of the harem were embedded in a complex politics of dynastic reproduction.

Taking this logical idea very seriously, it is clear that any trivialisation of the Achaemenid royal harem as a brothel-like pleasure palace fails to do justice to its central role in the political milieu of the court and, indeed, of the Empire at large. Dismissing the existence of the harem or seeing it only as an invention of the Greek imagination or of the overheated fantasies of western archaeologists damages our quest to understand the nature and functioning of the Achaemenid king and his court. This alone justifies a fuller study of the royal harem.

CHAPTER 5

The Pleasures and Perils of Court Life

Lady Diana, Princess of Wales, reported a plot to assassinate her. Diana documented her concerns in a letter that she entrusted to the former Royal Butler, Mr Paul Burrell. She identified the man behind the plot. Diana was warned about a conspiracy against her by a sympathetic insider. A member of the Royal Family warned the princess: 'You need to be discreet, even in your own home, because "they" are listening all the time.' (*Daily Mirror*, 20 October 2003)

The Persian court was the locale of intrigue, subterfuge, cruelty, and danger as Achaemenid kings and queens plotted against their opponents and murdered their rivals, or else were out-manoeuvred and assassinated first. And yet the court was also a place of sophistication, culture, pleasure, and delight – although for the royalty and nobility who inhabited this rarefied world, the pleasures of court were a serious business too – as the Greeks well understood:

Tyrants and kings, being in control of the good things of life, and having had experience of them all, put pleasure in the first place, since pleasure makes men's natures more kingly. All persons, at any rate, who pay court to pleasure and choose a life of luxury are lordly and magnificent, like the Persians and the Medes. For more than any other men in the world they seek pleasure and luxury, yet they are the bravest and most noble barbarians. Indeed, to have pleasure and luxury is a mark of the freeborn; it eases their minds and exalts them. (Athenaeus 12.512a–b)

The unknown Achaemenid-style Israelite prince who, allegedly, and at some point in the Persian period, composed the Hebrew Biblical book now familiarly called Ecclesiastes, reflected on the meaning of princely pleasure and his musings give us an insight into what Achaemenid royalty thought, and valued as, pleasurable:

I did great things. I built residences for myself and I planted my vineyards ..., gardens, and parks. ... I acquired slaves, both male and female, and I had servants who were born to the house. I also had a flock of cattle and sheep, more than all who were before me in Jerusalem. I gathered for myself silver and gold, the wealth of kings and provinces. I had for myself singers, male and female, and the delights of mankind: many women . . . nothing that my eyes desired did I keep from them; I did not refuse my heart any joy. (Ecclesiastes 2:4–6)

Building and planting projects, the accumulation of animals, slaves, and women, and the display of conspicuous leisure through hunting, feasting, drinking, and celebrating had a major part to play in defining and consolidating royal identity. Kings and nobles were united by the refinements of court arts, the thrill of the chase, and the delights of the banqueting table, while codes of hierarchy and the demands of self-worth simultaneously pressurised courtiers to demand of one another recognition of the intimate favour they enjoyed with the king as individuals. At the Achaemenid court pleasure had a political significance.

Court arts

Traditionally royal courts have been centres of art and culture, and monarchs who have understood the importance of the arts in creating the spectacle of a theatre state have benefited greatly from the patronage they bestowed on painters and sculptors, musicians, poets, playwrights, and theatrical impresarios. Louis XIV made Versailles the hub of European artistic expression and his rich patronage of the greatest artists of the day meant that they devotedly created for him a flattering artistic language (which we might call 'propaganda') by lauding the king as God's anointed and thus an undisputed ruler (Burke 1994). The arts have always played a crucial role in the projection of monarchy and court culture expressed itself through the court arts, which were expressions of a monarchic ideology, and patronage of the arts was a means by which rulers demonstrated power, good taste, and munificence. As yet, however, there has been no systematic study of the patronage of the court arts by the Achaemenid monarchs (as noted by Kuhrt 2010). This is perhaps a result of the scarcity of source materials which speak in any meaningful way of the interaction between the Great King, his court, and the artists who served him, although occasional references emerge showing kings and nobles commissioning works of art, like an equine statue custom-made for Aršama, the satrap of Egypt (Driver 1956: no. 9), or a bespoke statuette of beaten-gold representing Artystone/Irtašduna, which was commissioned by her husband, Darius I (Herodotus 7.69). In Assyria we know that monarchs could be very active in promoting and commissioning royal art and a letter sent by a craftsman asks King Sargon to review some preparatory sketches for a new statue which had been ordered:

> We have caused to bring an image of the king; in outline I have drawn [it]. An image of the king of another sort they have prepared. May the king see (them) and whatever is pleasing before the king, we shall make instead. May the king give attention to the hands, the elbows, and the dress. (Waterman 1930: vol. II, p. 233)

There is no reason to doubt that the Achaemenid kings did not have a similar hold on the manufacture of the royal image as they had over the ideological texts created for them and in the Persepolis archives we do occasionally hear of specialist craftsmen serving the monarch's needs at the heart of Empire (PF 872–4, 1049) – one is even mentioned by name: 'Addarnuriš the Assyrian who [carves] cedar (?) (wood) (at) Persepolis' (PF 1799). A distinct artistic repertoire of motifs (the Persian hero with animals or monsters, sphinxes, human-headed winged bulls) can be found in large-scale three-dimensional sculpture and wall reliefs from Iran and other areas of the central Empire, as well as in cylinder and stamp seals dispersed throughout (predominantly) Asia Minor. These are unified in style and manufacture; that style has been termed the 'court style' because the artefacts comprise a carefully constructed artistic programme that flourished at the royal artistic centres and was then disseminated across the realm (Boardman 1970: 305–9; Kaptan 2002: vol. I, pp. 107–32).

The world of the performing arts was also part of Achaemenid court culture and, given Persia's long and noble history of producing fine poetry and song, it is no surprise that the tradition can be traced back to at least the Achaemenid period. In fact we know of a court tradition for stories told through music from passing references to singers at the court (**E1**) and songs about the heroic deeds of Cyrus the Great seem to have been especially popular (**E2, E3**). In the sources, royal concubines are expressly noted for their musical skills: 'During dinner (the king's) concubines sing and play the harp, one of them taking the lead as the others sing in chorus' and we learn that, 'at night they sing and play on harps continually while the lamps burn' (Heraclides F1 and 2; also E1), which feasibly suggests a 'complex and developed form of musical entertainment' (Kuhrt 2010: 907). Perhaps their musical repertoire went beyond heroic tales about Cyrus, to include love songs and tragic romances like the doomed love affair of Stryangaeus and Zarinaea recorded by Ctesias (F7, F8a–c; Llewellyn-Jones and Robson 2010: 36–9) which was almost certainly based on an Iranian poetic tradition and the story of Zariadres and Odatis, preserved in précis by Chares of Mytilene (**E4**), who ascertains that it was 'very well-known among the barbarians . . . and . . . [was] exceedingly popular'.

Where there was music, there must have been dance, and we learn that the court was not only entertained by professional dancers like Zenon of Crete, 'who was, by far, Artaxerxes [II's] preferred performer' (Ctesias F31 = Athenaeus 1.22c), but by the Great King himself, who, during the feast of Mithra, was encouraged to drink and then dance the so-called *persica*, a war dance, by 'clashing shields together, crouching down on one knee and springing up again from earth . . . in measured time to the sound of the flute' (Xenophon, *Anabasis* 6.1.10). Dance it seems was both a courtly art and an expression of manliness, 'for the Persians learn to dance as they learn to ride and they consider dance movements related to riding and very suitable for getting exercise and increasing fitness' (Athenaeus 10.434e), although combat sports proper were also enjoyed as a court entertainment. A royal command performance was given before Darius II by the famous Greek panc-ratist Poulydamas and an appreciative court of spectators thrilled to the foreigner's feat of wrestling (and killing) three Immortals (**E5**; see Llewellyn-Jones 2012: 343–5, with fig. 17.4).

It is also worth noting, in the context of dance, the importance of codified movement and gestures – what can be called 'correct deport-ment' – generally practised by elites as part of the visual display of court culture. In most court societies this form of outward behaviour – correct bodily carriage and facial countenance, specific hand move-ments and feet positions – was an expression of the inner being and Elias was keen to study these aspects of the 'presentational self' in the European courts. He believed that court arts such as painting and sculpture recorded 'actual gestures and movements that have grown strange to us, [but were once] embodiments of a different mental and emotional structure' (Elias 1994: 49). Achaemenid art might indeed record similar attitudes of courtly carriage, such as the so-called 'hand over wrist' gesture, which can be seen employed by elite men (and even women) and which might denote respect or even prayer (Root 1979: 272–6), while in the audience scene (**F3**) the challi-arch's gesture of raising his fingers to his lips could be interpreted as an act of reverence, greeting, or even subordination (and contrasts with Xenophon's description that hands were hidden within long sleeves when in the presence of the monarch; *Cyropaedia* 8.3.12; *Hellenica* 2.1.8). At Persepolis courtiers are depicted performing a series of gestures (like hand-holding and delicate touching) which emphasise their intimate and sociable interactions.

Cup-bearers who served the Great King with his wine (see below) had to be adroit at the art of handing the silver receptacles to their users and the elegant skill of presentation was highly regarded, as becomes clear from Xenophon's description of the act: 'Now the cup-bearers of those [Persian] kings have an exquisite way of serving the wine: they pour it without spilling a drop and they present the cup with three fingers; they proffer the cup on the tips of their fingers and offer it in the most convenient position for the drinker to take hold of it' (*Cyropaedia* 1.3.8). This is, to use Elias' term, an expression of *civilité*, a cultured behaviour expected of a courtier, and there can be little doubt that other examples of this mode of behaviour were present in the sophisticated court culture of Persia. Moreover, the mores of the royal court spread out to the provinces as well because, as Xenophon would have it, Cyrus the Great 'commanded all those who were being sent out as satraps to imitate him in everything they had seen . . . [and to] educate their children at court' (*Cyropaedia* 8.6.10). Ideals of courtly deportment, etiquette, as well as ceremonials and the pleasures of court society thus systematically spread throughout the wider Empire.

The table and the chase: banqueting and hunting

We have already noted the immense amount of food which constituted the king's table and how it was distributed to his elite retinue, who, in turn, used it to feed their own households (Chapter 3) and it is clear that lavish meals served on costly table settings of precious metals were a hallmark of court life (on tableware see Allen 2005a: 88–92). We know something of the eating habits of the Persian elite, if not much about the recipes they created, and although Kuhrt (2007: 578) notes that 'the ingredients of the meals were not particularly exotic or expensive and were put together in accordance with ideas about maintaining health', the reality is that we have no way of knowing how the raw ingredients were combined or what kind of rich dishes might have been enjoyed. Perhaps Kuhrt says more about current thoughts and trends in eating habits than authentic Achaemenid customs and the fact that Herodotus notes that the Persians had a particular penchant for syrupy or milky deserts (confirmed by the ingredients listed by Polyaenus; **C33**) suggests that something other than health food was desired. Moreover, Herodotus (1.133) says that the Persians 'eat only a few main dishes, but they frequently consume an assortment of nibbles – but these are not served together at one time but are distributed randomly throughout the course of the meal' and Xenophon confirms (*Cyropaedia* 1.3.3) this Persian fondness for 'fancy side dishes and all sorts of sauces and meats' (see also Athenaeus 14.640f; for the appropriate translation 'nibbles' see Sancisi-Weerdenburg 1997: 341). Taking the Greek reports as her starting point, Sancisi-Weerdenburg (1997: 339) argues for a 'presence at court of specialist cuisiniers, producing not so much dishes as works of art' and she suggests that 'even if we cannot sketch more than its outlines, there is every reason to qualify cooking at the Persian court as *haute cuisine*'.

Like all other aspects of his official life, the ideology of invisibility governed the Great King's dining habits and according to Heraclides (**E6**) the sovereign tended to dine alone and hidden from view in a chamber (or some other specified space) and his selected guests sat outside to eat, 'in full sight of anyone who wishes to look on', although the most highly honoured guests were served by the royal butlers in a hall close to the king's dining room. The two spaces were separated by a screen or hanging that permitted the king to view his guests but kept him obscured from their sight. However, as the dinner drew to a close a few of the guests were called by name by a eunuch and were summoned to drink in the king's company; this was a mark of exceptional distinction because it was during these drinking bouts that important matters of state were discussed and personal ambitions might be realised (Herodotus 1.133; Strabo 15.3.20; Athenaeus 4.144b, 5.102c). A courtier specifically honoured with a regular place at the king's table was known as a *homotrapezus* ('messmate'), a title held by such high-ranking nobles as Megabyzus, Darius I's brother (Ctesias F14 §43), although even foreigners could be awarded this auspicious title (Herodotus 3.131, 5.24).

Beyond the daily consumption of food, which even for the court might have been repetitive, better pleasure could be had in eating and drinking in the festive atmosphere of a royal banquet, such as an almost legendary one thrown by King Ashurnasirpal of Assyria for 69,574 guests over a period of ten days (Pritchard 1969: 558–60) or that thrown by Xerxes in the third year of his reign when he gave a state feast for all his administrators, ministers, and satraps, and for all the women of the court (**E7**). Xerxes' banquet lasted a full 180 days. The importance of dining in this extravagant fashion is examined and explained by Jean Bottéro (2004: 99):

A banquet represented something more than the simple provision of daily bread, it gave eating and drinking their full meaning. . . . A banquet broke with the ordinary, occasioned as it most often was by fortunate circumstances in life that were outside the daily routine and thus naturally joyful.

The royal banquet *par excellence* was that held on the Great King's birthday (Old Persian, *tykta*, 'perfect'; Herodotus 9.110), a time of great rejoicing amid the court but also one of ritual importance as well, since the royal birthday might have served as the setting for an annual ceremonial renewal of royal power, as seems to have been the case in the Seleucid period (Bickerman 1938: 246; Sancisi-Weerdenburg 1989: 132–3). This type of royal banquet is depicted by Xenophon (*Cyropaedia* 8.4.1–5) but it is Herodotus who shows the most interest in the event and several of his stories are set during this important annual court festivity. Thus we learn that the birthday celebration 'is the one time of the year when the king anoints his head and bestows gifts on the Persians' and that 'the law of the Royal Supper stated that on that day no one should be refused a request' (Herodotus 9.109–10); he notes also that the Persian nobility followed the royal example because 'of all days in the year a Persian most distinguished his birthday and celebrated it with a dinner of special magnificence'; on that day they have 'an ox or a horse or a camel or a donkey baked whole in the oven' (Herodotus 1.133). With such a surplus of food, and the rule for the drinking being 'No restrictions!' (Esther 1:5; **E7**), dining at a royal banquet might be regarded as a form of extreme sport, and one on a par with another Achaemenid courtly passion: hunting.

Bizarrely, in its own way hunting was less of a sport *per se* than an art form; it was not simply a matter of killing animals. A successful hunt had to end in an animal's death but it had to be a specific type of animal that was killed, and in a particular way; it must have been free to flee its predator or to turn and attack the hunter but it also must have been killed deliberately – and with violence (there could be no use of traps, poisoned baits, or nets). But more than anything else, the hunter's prey had to be a *wild* animal (even if temporarily captured) with every chance of being hostile to the hunter and it could not be thought to have been tame or docile around humans. There was no sport in hunting dairy cows, for example. As Matt Cartmill (1995: 773) explains, 'hunting is by definition an armed confrontation between the human world and the untamed wilderness, between culture and nature and it has been defined and praised and attacked in those terms throughout history'. For the elites of successive courts and noble houses, the hunt became an elaborate ritual encrusted with jargon and ceremonial which served to validate the aristocratic credentials of the hunters, for the court hunt had nothing to do with providing for economic necessity – it was predominantly a political and ideological activity (Allsen 2006) and the countless depictions of the hunt on Achaemenid seals demonstrate the centrality of the image in Persian thought.

The frequency and duration of royal hunts reflect the nexus between hunting and governance, as do the amount of resources invested in the hunt, and while it is difficult to get precise data about the number of hours the Persian king spent in the saddle, Classical texts suggest that he was at least conceived of *à la chase* for considerable amounts of his time. By way of comparison, and by his own testimony, the Mughal emperor Jahangir hunted almost daily (Allsen 2006: 20; Jackson 2010: 156–7), as did Louis XV of France. He was a particularly enthusiastic huntsman and during the thirty years of his prime he killed a staggering 210 stags a year, in addition to countless boars, wolves, and wildfowl, and it has been estimated that in one year's hunting he covered 8,100 miles on horseback (Mitford 2001: 23). Monarchs have always laid stress on their ability in the hunt and it was in this display of chivalric bravery that the Great King was able to demonstrate his manhood, for hunting was set on a par with warfare, as the same skills were necessary for both and thus monarchs had to be 'leaders in war and hunting' (Pseudo-Aristotle, *De Mundo* 398a).

Hunts took place in *paradeisoi* or in the open field (see Chapter 3). Xenophon suggests that the best thrill could be had when hunting game in the wild (**E8**) and this may well have been the case, because game-park hunting meant chasing prey which had been captured and brought into the locale specifically to be killed. An event of this kind may have lacked the frisson of danger of hunting in the open terrain but, nonetheless, it was the symbolic execution of the hunted creature that was the most important part of the hunt and in many cases this simply led to the time-saving method of pre-capturing animals to be executed by the monarch later, as is often seen in Neo-Assyrian palace reliefs. This in turn confirmed the centrality of game parks, where captured animals were brought and released, or else an area was fenced off and designated a hunting ground.

Every royal hunt was meticulously planned and was under the charge of court officials who were responsible for procuring wild animals (if in a *paradeisos*) and training and caring for the huge mastiff dogs which accompanied the hunting party. Grooms and stable-hands were needed for the horses (Chapter 3) and bodyguards were ever present because, after all, on a hunt the Great King's life was particularly vulnerable (as noted by Herodotus 3.30 and Aelian, *Historical Miscellany* 6.14). Courtiers tasked with organising the hunt had every chance of elevation to the highest court offices. Ottoman court records from 1478 CE attest to the high-profile presence of hunting officials, for the names of forty-eight keepers of the royal hounds, fifty-eight keepers of hunting birds, and nine falconers of the Sultan are preserved in the archives, which means that 115 of the 530 permanent staff of the Ottoman palace were related to the running of the royal hunt (Murphey 2008: 159). These positions served as stepping stones to the highest level of government and there is every possibility that Achaemenid courtiers benefited from a similar system.

Successful royal hunts also required military personnel to be involved as 'beaters' to flush out the prey. Monarchs tended to participate in the so-called 'ring hunt', a formation which involved a massive number of people, since it eliminated the problem of chasing the prey; cornered by a diminishing circle of hunters, the prey tended to flounder and the monarch could then enter the ring to symbolically eliminate the animal. A refinement of this was the idea of 'fencing', where large nets might be employed by a section of the military to literally fence off an area, such as an entire mountainside, to force the prey to confront the king and his courtiers. Whatever methods were involved, accompanied by a large escort of nobles, servants, and even concubines, the Great King must have looked an impressive sight in the saddle (**E9**; on concubines attending the hunt see Heraclides F1 = Athenaeus 12.514c; concubines also accompanied the Mughal royal hunt – see Lal 1988).

The greatest sport was to be had in hunting lions. This was royal sport *par excellence* and in fact from very ancient times lion hunting was the strict preserve of royalty: 'To finish the lion with the weapon was my own privilege' affirms one Old Babylonian ruler (*Šulgi Hymn B*; Watanabe 2002: 83). A series of fascinating letters sent by one Yaqqim-Addu to the king of Mari reports how a lioness was captured in the region of Bit-Akkaka and how for five days Yaqqim-Addu tried to keep it alive and healthy so that it might be delivered to the monarch, who might then take his royal pleasure (and prerogative) in its slaughter. The last of Yaqqim-Addu's letters tells a sorry tale of administrative bungling:

Speak to my lord, thus (says) Yaqqim-Addu, your servant.
A lioness was captured during the night in a barn (at) Bit-Akkaka. The next

morning I was told the news and I left. In order that no one killed the lion, I stayed all day at Bit-Akkaka, saying to myself, 'I must get it (the lioness) alive to my lord'. I threw (it) a [dog] and a pig; it killed them, left them, and did not want to eat them at all. I sent a message to Bidakha that a cage should be brought. (But) the day after, before the cage reached me, the lion died. I examined this lioness; she was old and ill. My lord may say, 'Someone must have killed that lion'. If anyone has touched this lion, (I should be treated) as if (I had broken) the taboo of my lord. Now because this lion is dead, I had its skin flayed and gave its flesh to be eaten. The lion was old, and it is (because) of (its) weakness that it died. (Watanabe 2002: 85)

Yaqqim-Addu's discomfort at reporting the death of the lioness to the king is palpable and it is the worry of being found guilty of having broken 'the taboo of my lord' (that is, being accused of killing the animal himself) which is clearly at the root of his anxiety.

Egyptian pharaohs and Assyrian rulers boasted of their prowess in slaying countless lions (**E10, E11**). King Ashurbanipal, for example, delighted in representing himself in the act of ritual slaughter, grasping a lion by the throat and stabbing it in the belly as it stood facing him (this feat was possible given that the now locally extinct Asiatic lion was smaller than its African counterpart; Reade 1988: 72–9; Jackson 2010: 158–61). On his personal name seal (SDa), Darius I is depicted shooting arrows at a rearing lion while the carcass of another slayed feline lies beneath his chariot's wheels (**F18**; see further Herodotus 3.129; Diodorus 15.10.3; Polybius F133). The use of chariots in hunting seems to have developed in Egypt and Assyria, where they were used extensively in both war and the hunt as indicators of prestige, so closely associated were they with kings and the nobility, although in fact chariots were far from ideal hunting platforms, as they were fragile and liable to break on unsuitable terrain. While one way round this was to change to horseback if the prey fled into a forest or marsh, teams of troops were also sometimes used to stop the animal fleeing from the flat plains. Whatever the reality of the royal lion hunt, the motif of the king as slayer of lions is repeated on Persian coinage (Briant 2002: 715) and in seals and reliefs, where the lion sometimes morphs into a mythical hybrid creature and is dispatched by the king in his guise as 'Persian hero' (Root 1979: 300–11; Briant 2002: 232; **F7**).

Persians hunted by 'throwing spears from horseback and with bows and slings' (Strabo 15.3.18) but protocol strictly governed this aspect of the royal lion hunt and prerogatives were given to the king so that it was his right alone to cast the first spear at the prey (Xenophon, *Cyropaedia* 1.4.14; Plutarch, *Moralia* 173d). Ctesias' account of Megabyzus' fall from favour illustrates the intricacies of this court custom (**D8**). By spearing a lion, Megabyzus not only defiled the courtly protocol which gave the king alone the right to kill a lion, but seemed to question Artaxerxes' ability as a hunter and – by extension – his fitness to rule (the same theme reappears in a story of one of Alexander III's hunts; **E12**). It appears that in a later court edict Artaxerxes I revised the protocol of the lion hunt (**E13**) but nonetheless, as Briant (2002: 231) points out, 'during royal hunts . . . courtiers had to be circumspect. While someone who came to the aid of the king could be richly rewarded . . . the example of Megabyzus indicates that it was not a good idea to appear to be a rival'.

Intrigue, faction, rebellion

Rivalry was endemic at court and palaces were dangerous places to be. A Neo-Assyrian text labels the royal court, with its antagonistic (sometimes vicious) inhabitants, as 'the lion pit'. A set of Sumerian proverbs also explore this theme:

> A palace is a huge river; its interior is a goring ox. . . . A palace is a slippery place where one slithers; If you say, 'Let me go home!', just watch your step. . . . A palace . . . is a wasteland. [As] a freeborn man cannot avoid corvée work, a princess cannot avoid th[is] whorehouse. (Alster 1997: vol. I, p. 147)

The hub of dynastic and political life, the Achaemenid court was a dangerous place, a stage on which games of intrigue, faction, and revenge were played out with astonishing regularity (see Wiesehöfer 2010: 521–3). The tension of court politicking permeated every aspect of the royal household and few individuals were untouched by some form of intrigue. Court nobility was highly susceptible to political machinations and personal rivalries and the book of Esther demonstrates this clearly, based as it is on a story of destructive intrigue. Esther reveals that while courtiers were committed to holding office, the fact that 'every court job was temporary and could be transferred from one day to the next' (Briant 2002: 258) meant that they feared for their cherished posts, which could be revoked at any moment, leaving them marooned within the competitive structure of the court. Of course, none of this was unique to Persia, for court societies of all periods have suffered from the strain of imposing and then maintaining power, as David Lewis (1977: 21–2) reminds us:

I am myself disposed to take seriously stories of the irrational caprice and wanton cruelty of [Persian] monarchs. Nothing is reported of Periander, tyrant of Corinth, which does not find ready parallels in well-attested information about Ali Pasha of Iannina at the beginning of the nineteenth century, and, allowing for some differences of institutions, the Persian court will be subject to the same kind of pressures which have afflicted the courts of absolute monarchs down to the time of Stalin.

Among the courtiers, powerful clans and political cliques confronted one another openly, especially during periods of intense change in the government, such as times of royal accession, when power might become divided among competitive court factions (Herodotus 7.1). It is not clear whether at every change of reign the great nobles and dignitaries had to surrender their court offices together with all the perks that the jobs brought with them (as certainly happened under the Sargonid kings of Assyria; van de Mieroop 2004: 258–9; Melville 2006). It is possible that every new Achaemenid king would decide whether to restore them to office or appoint new incumbents. In his narrative of Persian court history Ctesias routinely records the names of the most important eunuchs to serve under successive monarchs (see Chapter 1) and on occasion he stresses that two generations of servants served two generations of rulers: 'Darius' son, Xerxes, became king and Artapanus, son of Artasyras, was influential with him, just has his father had been with Xerxes' father' (Ctesias F13 §24). He further mentions that some high-ranking courtiers also spanned the generations ('Mardonius the Old was influential, too') but, even so, it is difficult to know whether at the death of the king his eunuchs and ministers were officially required to step down from office only to be placed again in the same position by the successor.

Holding on to high office might have been challenging, for it was all too easy to be slandered by a rival, as Datames came to know to his great cost (Nepos, *Datames* 5). Royal favour was easily lost – the dramatic careers of Megabyzus and Tiribazus show that this was unmistakably the case (Briant 2002: 320–322; Bremmer 2008: 553–7). Tiribazus, who had held the august title 'friend of the king' (see Chapter 1), nevertheless ended up revolting against Artaxerxes II but, given his chequered career, it is easy to understand why: at one time imprisoned by the king, on two other occasions Tiribazus was honoured with pledges of marriage to two of Artaxerxes' daughters, Amestris (II) and Atossa (II). But when Artaxerxes reneged on both pledges, the 'friend of the king' could no longer suffer the humiliation and incited Artaxerxes' crown prince, Darius, to join him in a plot against the king's life (on conspiracies against the Achaemenid kings see below).

As part of their education young courtiers were required to pay attention to a very basic fact of life: some nobles were honoured by the king while others were disgraced by him (Xenophon, *Anabasis* 1.9.3; Plutarch, *Moralia* 174b) – and disgrace could be devastating. So when Orontes, Atraxerxes II's son-in-law, fell from grace due to the machinations of Tiribazus, the king 'excluded him from the company of his friends and showered him with humiliation' (Diodorus 15.11.12). Ostracism from the circle of 'friends' coupled with no official court position meant political death for any disgraced grandee or, worse still, it could mean expulsion from the court itself. Twice in his colourful career Megabyzus found himself banished from court (Ctesias F14 §40–3) and even a king's mother was not exempt from expulsion from the inner sanctum of power (Plutarch, *Artaxerxes* 19). This demonstrates that all courtiers – even members of the royal family – had their individual destinies bound up in the Great King's favour and that promotions and rewards were granted only as a result of merit being recognised by the throne. Success at court was directly related to the devotion displayed by a courtier to the ruler on a personal basis.

But it was at the top of the hierarchical ladder that court factionalism had its most devastating effect. Rivalry, treachery, and vendetta were ever present, even within the inner circle of the royal family itself, as succession issues plagued the political heart of the dynasty. Throughout its history the Achaemenid family's inability or inertia in establishing any rules of primogeniture led to chaotic family discord, tumultuous political upheaval, and bitter personal power-plays, so that succession issues became a perennial crisis for the Achaemenids, who exacerbated the matter with poisons, plots, and murder. Polygamy may have helped consolidate the Empire-wide grip of the dynasty on its subject peoples but it gave new meaning to sibling rivalries and at the close of the reign of Darius II a particularly violent sibling-made upheaval occurred at court which threatened the survival of the Persian governmental system.

Darius' influential sister-wife, Parysatis, had more than fulfilled her dynastic duty and had produced numerous healthy sons and daughters for the royal nursery but the two eldest sons, Prince Arses and Prince Cyrus (named after his illustrious ancestor and known to history, therefore, as Cyrus the Younger), got the bulk of the parental attention. Parysatis had a particular fondness for Cyrus but King Darius favoured Arses and began to train him for the throne (on the family of Darius II see Briant 2002: 612–20). Deciding to keep Arses close to him at court for training in kingship, Darius sent Cyrus to Ionia to act as the royal overseer of the troublesome and powerful satraps Tissaphernes and Pharnabazus. Once established in the west, Cyrus attracted the friendship of Lysander of Sparta and bought the services of Greek mercenary soldiers, many of whom were subsequently garrisoned in the Persian-controlled cities of Ionia.

In the autumn of 405 BCE Darius II became ill and summoned Prince Cyrus to rejoin the court at Babylon but when Cyrus arrived he brought with him a bodyguard of 300 mercenary hoplites as a show of his new-found military prestige. Upon Darius' death the throne passed to his eldest son, Arses, who took the throne name of Artaxerxes II, but the court was immediately plunged into chaos when Tissaphernes took the opportunity of the old king's death to inform the new monarch that his younger brother, Cyrus, was plotting to usurp the throne. Artaxerxes, determined to establish himself as unrivalled monarch and to brook no challenge from any family member, immediately had his brother arrested and imprisoned.

Parysatis quickly intervened, however, and begged Artaxerxes for Cyrus' life and, persuaded of his innocence, the new king sent Cyrus back to Ionia to take up his duties once more. Safely ensconced in his palace on the western frontier, Cyrus began to muse seriously on recent events and quickly came to realise that his safety lay in ousting Artaxerxes from the throne once and for all and becoming Great King himself. Therefore in February 401 BCE the impetuous twenty-three-year-old Cyrus assembled his troops in order to march on Babylon and in August the armies of the two brothers met at the tiny hamlet of Cunaxa, just north of modern Baghdad, where, in the midst of a ferocious battle, Cyrus made a bold but foolhardy charge against Artaxerxes and was mortally wounded and died. His decapitated head was sent to Babylon to be displayed to the court.

Some historians have suggested that the cyclic stories of intrigues, factions, and insurgences at the Persian court are more literary motifs than authentic records of actual events (Briant 2002: 322) but it is more likely that the conservative nature of the court itself truly engendered repetitive actions on the part of frustrated courtiers. As Keaveney (2003: 128) astutely notes:

> Monarch after monarch was surrounded by thrusting officials and relatives. Given that this circumstance did not change we need not . . . wonder if, in reign after reign, they led to the same . . . consequences. It is the

unchanging nature of court life over a long period rather than a 'reprise de motifs littéraires' which led to the repetitious nature of the tales.

'Hell hath no fury'

We must accept that intrigue was a reality of court existence and that court conspiracies could quickly escalate into rebellion and open warfare. The Achaemenid court was after all a violent place, as Robert Rollinger's detailed investigations have shown (Rollinger 2004, 2010). In Rollinger's studies of the Greek historiographic depiction of violence at the Persian court it transpires that many of the most memorable acts of cruelty are perpetrated by the women of the Achaemenid royal house. This might be read as a literary trope; however, it is important to set the rivalries, intrigues, double-dealings, murders, and executions explored by the Greek authors in the context of dynastic politics. Persia was controlled by an absolute ruler – that is not Orientalist cliché, it is a fact. Absolute monarchies are open to a particular form of political tension which focuses on the royal family and on the noble families which surround the king, and within such institutions the women of the ruling family often rise to positions of political agency, not through any formal route to power, but by other, less recognised means (for cross-cultural comparisons on this theme see Morris 1979; Wan 1988; Anderson 1990; Holdsworth and Courtauld 1995; Rawski 1998; McDermott 1999; Zega 2002; Nelso 2003).

As Michael Fowler and John Marincola have stressed (2002: 292), it is wrong to see Persian royal women merely as literary 'types' created by Greek authors. While a connection between the barbarian milieu and violence seems to be essential to the Herodotean view of the world, Ctesias is more than likely to have recorded the real actions of court women, as reflected in other court histories of the same period: the Davidic court history's depiction of Bathsheba, a principal wife of king David of Israel and the mother of Solomon, shows her to be a power-ful guardian of the throne (1 Kings 1; Marsman 2003; Solvang 2003) and the Assyrian royal annals record how Naqia held onto the reins of power and established a sense of concord at court as her grandson Ashurbanipal ascended the throne (Melville 1999). In Persia, Atossa manoeuvred her son Xerxes onto Darius' throne because she had the power and ability to do so, or at least this was how Herodotus (7.3–4) interpreted Xerxes' relatively smooth accession to the Persian kingship (on royal women and succession issues see further de Vaux 1961; Bailey 1990; Novotny 2001; Dodson and Hilton 2005; see also Chapter 1).

Particularly intense in its narrative and detail is Herodotus' story of Xerxes' wife Amestris and her bitter struggle with his mistress Artaÿnte (who simultaneously was Xerxes' niece – being the daughter of his brother Masistes – and daughter-in-law – being married to Crown Prince Darius). (Incidentally, Hazewindus [2004: 102] is wrong to call Artaÿnte Xerxes' 'concubine', as she is clearly his unofficial lover.) This masterful Herodotean novella (**E14**) is probably based on a Persian oral tradition (after all, Herodotus certainly does not provide an eyewitness account) but it must have had a historical background insofar as we know that some kind of dispute between Xerxes and his brother ended in the downfall of Masistes and his family. Sancisi-Weerdenburg (1983) argued that the tale was based on an indigenous Persian tradition in which Masistes tried to usurp his brother's throne and it is certainly true that elements of Herodotus' account have a special meaning when read in a specifically Iranian context. For instance, Artaÿnte's desire to possess a beautiful garment made by Amestris is best interpreted when we acknowledge that it was the king's own robe which she cherished. As we have seen, the royal robe was a powerful symbol of legitimate kingship (Chapter 2) and by demanding this symbolic vestment Artaÿnte laid claim to sovereignty, not for herself of course, for that was impossible in the Persian tradition, but for her already powerful family (and it is possible that the name of her father, Masistes, derives from the Old Persian *maθišta* – 'the greatest'– giving an added historical dimension to the Herodotean tale of court intrigue). In the story, when Amestris hears of Artaÿnte's request, she bides her time (for a year, Herodotus says) until the occasion is right, but then she acts swiftly, bloodily, and with chilling finality. Amestris is intent on securing the succession of her son Darius and she reads Artaÿnte's request for the robe as the treacherous act it is, yet her wrath does not focus on Artaÿnte herself (because she is Prince Darius' wife and therefore the possible mother of a future Achaemenid heir), but on Artaÿnte's (unnamed) mother – Amestris' equal in dynastic terms. The imperial matriarch turns on a rival dynastic matron and Amestris puts a halt to Masistes' family ambitions in a demonstrably emblematic way: his wife's breasts – symbolising her motherhood and dynastic fecundity – are cut off and thrown to the dogs. Since dogs were thought of as dirty scavengers and eaters of refuse and corpses (Proverbs 26:11; 1 Kings 16:4, 21:19; Homer, *Odyssey* 18.87), their presence at the *dénouement* of Herodotus' story is particularly telling and can be compared to an episode in the Hebrew Bible where palace dogs are left to eat the corpse of the hated queen Jezebel (2 Kings 9:36–7; on female mutilation in the Near East see further Amos 4:2–3; 2 Kings 8:11–12, 15:16; Hosea 14:1).

Ancient Iranians would have understood the details of this grisly story well, for there was a long tradition of treating the bodies of vanquished foes with acts of demonstrative cruelty. Images of a 'Persian peace' propagated by the Achaemenid kings on the reliefs at Persepolis belie the fact that, as the heirs of the great Neo-Assyrian Empire, the Persians readily inherited many kinds of savage punishment documented in Assyrian and later Neo-Babylonian chronicles, such as impaling, decapitation, burning, whipping, strangling, stoning, castration, blinding, cutting of a living body in two, cutting off nose, ears, lips, hands, arms, snipping out the tongue, branding, flaying, crucifixion, and skinning alive. So the punishment Masistes' wife received at the hands of the vengeful Amestris was consistent with that doled out to other victims in the Near East, and the sex of the victim was not a reason for lighter chastisement.

In spite of these scenes of high drama, it is important to realise that the powerful court women of Herodotus and Ctesias do not dominate men in order to deceive them; nor do they subdue them for their own access to power. In fact, in the Greek sources no royal woman is ever recorded conspiring to treason with over-ambitious eunuchs or courtiers but instead they work within the confines of the court system to vigilantly protect the dynastic bloodline. So it was, for instance, that Parysatis became implicated in the death of the pretender Sogdianus, who threatened Darius II's accession to the throne (Ctesias F15 §50), and any treasonable activities from eunuchs could lead to their torture or death – which was always ordered at the express command of the king's women (the king rarely doled out their fates; see Llewellyn-Jones 2002). Artoxares the Paphlagonian 'king-maker', the most powerful of Darius II's eunuchs, met his end on the direct orders of Queen Parysatis (Ctesias F15 §54; Brosius 1996: 100; Lewis 1977: 21) and similarly the powerful eunuch Petasakes was blinded, flayed alive, and crucified on the express commands of Amytis, the wife of Cyrus the Great (Ctesias F9 §6). The ability to take the life of powerful court eunuchs demonstrates the personal and political clout of some Achaemenid queens.

It must be conceded, however, that, on occasion, a queen became embroiled in a personal vendetta which had ostensibly nothing to do with the security of the dynasty. After Inarus of Libya failed to free Egypt from Persian rule, the rebel leader and many Greek mercenaries who had aided him were brought to Persia as prisoners but were granted amnesty and safety by Artaxerxes I. But the king's mother,

Amestris (Xerxes' widow), was embittered because another of her sons, Achaemenes, had died in the battle against Inarus. Ctesias (F14 §39) depicts her pleading with Artaxerxes for the head of the traitor and he records that 'because she kept bothering her son about it, she got her way', although it took her five years to reach her goal: 'she impaled [Inarus] on three stakes; and she beheaded as many Greeks as she was able to get hold of – fifty in all'. Ctesias categorically states that Amestris carried out this action in revenge for the death of her son, although Artarxerxes seems to have had no intention of avenging his younger brother's death since it occurred legitimately under the rules of war. Amestris' five-year-long harassment campaign finally resulted in her longed-for revenge and the restoration of (as she must have perceived it) family honour. Parysatis likewise systematically hunted down and destroyed many individuals connected to the death of Cyrus the Younger despite the fact that he also died in battle. Grief was a powerful catalyst for retribution (Ctesias F17 §66).

Ctesias (F14 §44) also records that when Amestris' daughter, Princess Amytis, lay dying of a terminal illness, having been tricked into a sexual relationship by her doctor, Apollonides of Cos (who had been commissioned to cure her disease), '[Amytis] told her mother to take revenge on Apollonides' – which is exactly what Amestris did. She imprisoned and tortured the doctor for two months before having him buried alive. Interestingly, although Amestris told King Artaxerxes the full details of his sister's disgrace, the king gave his mother *carte blanche* to deal with the situation herself. This is perhaps logical, since the disgrace of Amytis needed to be kept secret within the inner court and judgement on the nature of the doctor's crime was therefore best committed to the clandestine jurisdiction of the king's mother.

On the surface we can identify two strands to the way in which royal women used their power to gain revenge: one was to satisfy a personal slight, the other to meet a political affront, although of course the two were often intertwined. However, a third reason can be suggested for why some royal women were drawn to murder or mutilation: simple jealousy and a clash of personalities could also overwhelm dynastic politics. Peirce's important studies of harem politicking at the Ottoman court have illuminated a dark world in which intense domestic rivalries among the harem women had a direct impact upon imperial policy, as women went head to head with one another out of jealously over rank and status, or to secure their own status, or, predominantly, to solidify the status of their sons. Such revenge killings, punishments, and mutilations were commonplace (Peirce 1993: 2008) and this was much the case in the Achaemind court too.

Ctesias makes clear that an intense rivalry existed between two queens at Artaxerxes II's court – his mother, Parysatis, and his wife, Stateira – and the hostility was fuelled by each woman's desire to hold the place of honour in Artaxerxes II's affections, or at least to influence his decisions (**E15**). Parysatis detested Stateira 'because she wished to have no one as powerful as herself' (Plutarch, *Artaxerxes* 17.4) and Ctesias (F15 §56) relates the injuries that the royal family had inflicted upon Stateira's natal family, all of whom had been executed by Darius II for treason. As for Stateira, her influence as a genuine power at court can be recognised by the fact that the Egyptian pharaoh sent as a 'diplomatic gift' a beautiful young courtesan named Timosa to be her slave (Athenaeus 13.609). Being the mother of three of the king's sons afforded Stateira even greater prestige at court and she influenced Artaxerxes noticeably. The king often gave in to the repeated importuning of his wife and it was at her behest that Clearchus of Sparta was executed. This brought Stateira into direct conflict with Parysatis, who championed Clearchus' position at court.

Arguably, Ctesias' story of Stateira's poisoning (**E16**) is too complex to be made up (see also Ctesias F27 §70). Poisonings were common at the Persian court – Xenophon states that courtiers regularly died in court intrigues at the hands of skilled poisoners (**E17**) – and Parysatis certainly had a reputation for being a crafty exponent of this most deadly of courtly arts (Ctesias F16 §61). So it is significant that we know that the office of royal food-taster functioned prominently at the Persian court (**E18**). The royal cup-bearer was also a prestigious office held only by the monarch's most trusted courtiers, like Nehemiah, who performed that duty for Artaxerxes I (Nehemiah 1:11), or the son of the high-ranking Prexaspes, who served at Cambyses' court (Herodotus 3.34), for the cup-bearer was charged with managing all of the court's wine-pourers and tasters, although he alone poured the king's wine into his egg-shaped cup and tasted the monarch's drink to check that it was poison free (on the elaborate etiquette of handing the king his cup see Xenophon, *Cyropaedia* 1.3.9, 8.4.3). Fear of poison might be a reason why the Great King drank a wine unique to him – the Syrian Chalybonian wine (Athenaeus 2.28d) – and water from Susa contained in special pots (see Chapter 3). Ctesias also reports not only that the Great King and his mother had exclusive access to a special Indian poison kept within the palace for the purpose of causing a swift death but also that they also hoarded precious antidotes against even the deadliest poisons (**E19**). There was actually a specific death sentence reserved for individuals charged with poisoning: 'there is a broad stone on which they place the poisoners' heads and with another stone they pound and crush until their face and head are mashed to a pulp' (Ctesias F29b §9) and, as Briant (2002: 263) has rightly observed, 'the existence of this torture implies that the threat of poison was taken seriously'.

Ctesias' specific report of an Indian poison perhaps reflects the importance of the use of poison at the Indian royal courts, especially that of the near-contemporary ruler Chandragupta. Poison is the focus of Book I of a work called the *Arthashastra*, a treatise on statecraft, economic policy, military strategy, and court politics written by an influential courtier-philosopher named Kautilya. It includes all the precautions to take against the king being poisoned, as well as the remedies if he is. The *Arthashastra* then dictates the royal punishment for the one who has perpetrated the mischief. All efforts are made to take care of the king inside and outside his palace. The king is in general advised always to remain guarded against poisoning and to be equipped with antidotes for adverse situations (see Shamasatry 1923).

So it was that Parysatis enacted her revenge on Stateira with the aid of poison – and even though Ctesias' report looks like a plot from a fairy tale, the sharing of a common cup or dish appears to have been a standard way of conducting a poisoning in antiquity (and at later courts), drawing any suspicious attention away from the dish or drink in question (Suetonius, *Claudius* 44; Tacitus, *Annals* 13.16, 7.2.2; Levy 2011). Certainly that was Parysatis' intention, Ctesias explains, because Stateira was vigilant in watching out for assassination attempts, fearing that her mother-in-law might one day make such a move. Plutarch, however, stresses that the two women had started visiting each other's apartment and had begun to reconcile their hostilities and so, just as Stateira began to relax her guard, Parysatis struck. Not surprisingly Artaxerxes' revenge upon his mother and her intimates was swift and bloody – and typically masculine.

The works of Herodotus and Ctesias may contain literary clichés which reflect the misogynistic tone of Greek literature in which powerful women were perceived as a threat to the political world of men. But there is truth in their accounts of harem politics if we read these stories in the light of what Wiesehöfer (1996: 83) has recognised as 'a society of tribal origins [where] political marriages contracted in order to ensure loyalty were particularly important, especially since the question of the succession to the throne in the polygamous Persian royal house was liable to assume vital significance'. Revenge murders and honour killings must be seen as a significant and *bona fide* instruments in the politicking of absolute monarchies, and especially in the dynastic power plays of the inner court.

The death of kings

Taking the wise precaution of appointing a trusted courtier to pour a drink or test some food was no guarantee of a king's safety. It appears that an audacious attempt was made on the life of Darius III when the eunuch Bagoas poured poison into the king's cup, although, warned of Bagoas' plot, Darius magnanimously offered the eunuch the 'honour' of drinking from the royal goblet himself: 'the king called upon Bagoas to drink a toast to him, and handing him his own cup the king compelled him to take his own medicine' (Diodorus 17.5.6). Nevertheless, it would seem that corrupt cup-bearers had every opportunity to poison the king and even Alexander III's cup-bearer Iollas was accused of plotting this heinous crime (Arrian 7.27.2) and there is every possibility that Alexander may have died from poisoning (**E20**).

This same Bagoas had allegedly elevated Darius to the throne having already murdered Artaxerxes III (this time he had successfully poisoned the king's wine) and also his son Artaxerxes IV (**E21**). However, the Greek creation of the figure of Bagoas as a wicked eunuch king-maker has been expertly deconstructed by Briant (2002: 769–71), who has demonstrated that the idea of the wicked eunuch was used as a *topos* by the likes of Aelian and Plutarch as a device to show the alleged weaknesses of the last Achaemenid monarchs, Artaxerxes IV and Darius III, both of whom are presented as Bagoas' 'puppet kings'. An alternative Persian version of the reign of the last Achaemenid finds a reflection in Justin and Diodorus, in which Darius III justifies his rule through his personal bravery on the battlefield; neither Justin nor Diodorus makes the slightest allusion to Bagoas' machinations or to the idea of Darius' usurpation of the throne. Instead Darius III can be seen to have served faithfully within the inner court of Artaxerxes II and, as the son of an influential courtier named Arsanes, he was the cousin of Artaxerxes III and thus according to Achaemenid succession practice he was a legitimate heir to the Persian throne.

In spite of Briant's rehabilitation of Darius III within an authentic Persian record, it must be conceded that the period surrounding a ruler's death was always a time of uncertainty and violent plays for power might result from the political vacuum if an heir designate

Table 4. Nature and dates of death of the Achaemenid Great Kings

Name	Nature and date (BCE) of death
Cyrus II	Battlefield; November 530
Cambyses	Natural causes (?); after 18 April 522
Bardiya	Assassination; 29 September 522
Darius I	Natural causes; after 17 November 486
Xerxes I	Assassination; between 4 and 8 August 465
Artaxerxes I	Natural causes; after 24 December 424
Xerxes II [Sogdianus]	Assassination; early 423
Darius II	Natural causes; April 404
Artaxerxes II	Assassination; after January 358
Artaxerxes III	Assassination; after 26 August 338
Artaxerxes IV [Arses]	Assassination; summer 336
Darius III	Assassination; July 330

had not taken control of the situation. Arian (*Anabasis* 3.14.5) actually has Darius mastermind the assassination of Artaxerxes IV, with Bagoas acting as his aide, although Justin writes Artaxerxes IV out of his history altogether (he makes Darius III the direct successor of Artaxerxes III), suggesting perhaps that there was a Persian tradition of *damnatio memoriae* surrounding Artaxerxes IV, who might have been implicated in his father's death. Babylonian documents indicate that Artaxerxes IV was certainly recognised as a Great King (albeit that his occupation of the throne might have been very brief; Kuhrt 2007: 418–19) while another document from the city, known as the 'Dynastic Prophecy' (**E22**), mentions a king murdered by a eunuch (presumably a reference to Bagoas' murder of Artaxerxes IV) before referencing the seizure of the throne and five-year reign of his successor (who must therefore be Darius III). All that can be said with any certainty is that evidence for the period is both confusing and frustrating.

To read these stories of court machinations and assassinations as evidence for the decay of the Empire in its last phase is not only futile but completely wrong. Persia on the eve of its conquest by Alexander was still a vitally powerful world force and the truth of the matter is that throughout its violent history the Achaemenid dynasty had always suffered from the strains of familial rivalry and personal ambition. The murders of Artaxerxes III and Artaxerxes IV were merely part of a very long and bloody tradition. Table 4 reveals that seven of the twelve Achaemenid Great Kings met their deaths at the hands of an assassin of some sort (and only three monarchs had the luxury of a peaceful death). To this we can add the murder (or execution) of at least two crown princes: Darius, son of Xerxes I, assassinated soon after 8 August 465; and Darius, son of Artaxerxes II, executed sometime around the summer of 370.

Perhaps the most tantalising evidence concerns the murder of Xerxes I early in August 465 BCE; we know the exact date because a Babylonian astrological text refers to the assassination of the king by his son (**E23**; Stolper 1988). Diodorus (11.69.1–5), however, says the king was murdered by Artabanus, son of Artasyrus, a captain of the guard with his eye on the throne (see also Nepos, *Kings* 1). Diodorus goes on to state that Artabanus was aided and abetted by the eunuch Mithridates, who had access to the royal bed chamber, and that afterwards Artabanus set out to murder Xerxes' three sons, Darius, Hystaspes, and Artaxerxes. Ctesias depicts Artabanus (here named 'Artapanus', although clearly the same individual encountered in Diodorus, who, after all, used Ctesias as a source) deceiving Prince Artaxerxes into believing that Xerxes was murdered by Crown Prince Darius, his elder brother (**E24**). Artaxerxes killed Darius and when Artabanus swore loyalty to Hystaspes (who was satrap of Bactria), the ambitious commander was also killed. By 3 January 464 BCE Artaxerxes I was recognised as king as far away as Elephantine in southern Egypt.

Given his prominence in the Classical sources, there can be little doubt of Artabanus' implication in the regicide (Kuhrt 2007: 242–3, 308–9) but what are we to make of the Babylonian evidence that Xerxes was murdered by his son? As Kuhrt (2007: 243) suggests, 'the Greek stories smack . . . of an elaborate cover-up by Artaxerxes of his part in his father's murder'. In other words, it is highly likely that Prince Artaxerxes was one of several courtiers to rebel against Xerxes and that in the coup the prince availed himself of the opportunity to dispose of both his father and his brother in his ambitious (and successful) bid for the throne (see further Abdi 2010).

Likewise, the end of Artaxerxes II's long reign saw the court slide into corruption and chaos as tensions mounted around the soon-to-be-vacant throne. Of Artaxerxes' three known sons (Justin 10.1.1), Darius was made co-regent (and thus recognised as heir apparent) at the age of fifty, but the status of crown prince was precarious and being nominated heir designate did not necessarily eliminate sibling rivalry, and he was subsequently executed for conspiracy (**E25**, **E26**). Artaxerxes II later killed his half-brother Ariaspes at the instigation of his younger son, Prince Ochus (later Artaxerxes III; **E27**). Artaxerxes II is said to have had 115 sons by his concubines but, according to Justin (10.3.1), on becoming king around November 359 BCE Artaxerxes III did away with his brothers, sisters, and all other possible rivals to the crown – Curtius Rufus (10.5.23) claims that eighty brothers were murdered in one day; Polyaenus 7.17 states that he concealed his father's death for ten months, during which time he enacted his pogrom, so that his official reign may have begun only in 358–57 BCE (Briant 2002: 681).

Briant (2002: 564–5) sees stories of the murder of kings in the royal bedroom as suspect and little more than a repetitive series of 'scarcely credible' Greek literary motifs. But his scepticism is unwarranted. The accounts are logical and wide-ranging – ancient kings were frequently murdered in their beds (the XIIth dynasty Egyptian text *Instruction of Amenemhat* cleverly plays on this fact; see Parkinson 1999: 203–11) and Xenophon accurately narrates Cyrus' fears for his personal security, as Cyrus realises 'that men are nowhere more obvious prey to harm than when at dinner, or when drinking wine, in the bath, or asleep in bed' (*Cyropaedia* 7.5.59; see also 8.4.3). There is no doubt that the physical elimination of rivals or potential opponents as well as serial murders and wholesale massacres were part and parcel of Achaemenid court life.

At the Great King's death, the sacred fires were extinguished and life throughout the Empire went on hold as a period of mourning was observed (Diodorus 17.114.4–50) and at this time the Persians shaved their heads and lamented their loss (Herodotus 9.24 notes their 'unending lamentation'; see also Arrian 7.14.4; Plutarch, *Alexander* 72.1). The monarch's corpse was prepared by specialist morticians (perhaps even embalmers) and was then transported to Fars for burial in rock-cut tomb-chambers at Naqš-i Rustam and Persepolis (**F21**; only Cyrus II received a free-standing Ionian-style tomb, at Parsagade). As the royal hearse trundled across country in the company of a vast cortège, the Persian populace witnessed for a final time the spectacular display of that particular king's brilliance (we have, unfortunately, only the description of Alexander's cortège as it travelled from Babylon to go on, but there is no doubt that his funeral procession closely followed the Achaemenid model; see Diodorus 18.26.1–28.2). As Briant (2002: 524) notes, 'This was a sensitive period, marked by official mourning throughout the Empire. Only afterward it seems could the coronation ceremonies at Parsagadae begin.'

There is limited evidence for the observation of royal cults of dead monarchs (Ctesias F13 §23), the most tantalising of which is preserved in the Persepolis texts where, Henkelman has persuasively argued, there is a reference to a tomb of Hystaspes (the father of Darius I) in the care of high-level courtiers and receiving regular food offerings (PF-NN 1700; Henkelman 2003a). Even more importantly, PF-NN 2174 – dating to years 19–20 of Darius (503/2 BCE) – provides evidence of an official cult with monthly meat offerings for the dead king Cambyses II and for the lady Upandush (Greek, Phaidyme), the daughter of Otanes, the widow of Cambyses and Bardiya, and the wife of Darius, and thus a woman of considerable dynastic importance (in fact she may have been the highest-ranking of Darius' many wives).

Sadly, our knowledge of the rites, rituals, and traditions surrounding the death of the Great King is sparse, but perhaps a recently found Neo-Assyrian text (K 7856), composed in the Babylonian language, will offer some insight into both the feelings solicited by a monarch's death (in this case either Esarhaddon or Ashurbanipal) and the rituals his heir designate enacted for the comfort of the king in the afterlife:

> The ditches wailed, the canals respond, all trees and fruit, their faces darkened. Bir[ds] wept, that in the grass . . . nine tim[es...] I slaughtered horses and ma[res] to (the god) Šam[aš] and I gave them to be buri[ed]. . . . [Father], my begetter, I gently laid him in the midst of that tomb, a secret place, in royal oil. The stone coffin, his resting place – I sealed its opening with strong copper and secured the clay sealing. I displayed gold and silver objects, everything proper for a tomb, the emblems of his lordship, that he loved before Šamaš and I placed (them) in the tomb with my begetter. (Adapted from Kwasman 2009)

Concluding thought

The court, wherever it resided, was the cultural centre of the Empire, the dominant expression of 'Persianness'. The pleasures of court life were manifold but never devoid of meaning: the very table of the Great King's banqueting hall was an expression of his Empire, and the monarch, his family, his courtiers, and his servants enjoyed a varied cuisine, the raw materials for which were drawn from across the known world, for a significant part of the royal diet was supplied by tributary presentations (for interesting comparisons with Qing dining practices see Rawski 1998: 46–9). Eating, especially at lavish court banquets, was a political act; it was also a feat of endurance.

The Achaemenids probably prized poetry, song, and storytelling as much as they prized their horses and their hunting. Imperial skill in hunting game, especially lions, was set alongside a king's prowess in warfare or his rationality in the council chamber, and this is why in official rhetoric they were able to state that 'As a warrior, I am a good warrior. At once my intelligence holds its place, whether I see a rebel or not. Both by intelligence and by command at that time I know myself to be above panic, both when I see a rebel and [when] I do not see one. I am furious in the strength of my revenge' (DNb §2g–I; **A10**).

'Revenge' was an important concept for the Achaemenids, for with great privilege came great danger. Over the 230 years of its existence, generations of the Achaemenids routinely engaged in dynastic blood-shed, torture, and murder. As such, it was not an easy clan in which to make a mark, but if we accept the Classical sources then in the middle of the fourth century BCE, Artaxerxes III distinguished himself for ruthlessness with the annihilation of swathes of his kith and kin (in earlier decades Artaxerxes II had almost completely eliminated the noble house of Terituchmes, but failed to completely wipe it out, so Artaxerxes III must take the prize for brutality; Ctesias F15 §56). But in his turn Artaxerxes III succumbed to the machinations of ambitious courtiers. No Achaemenid king, no matter how powerful his projected image, knew a completely restful night.

Brothers waged war against brothers, sons sets themselves against fathers, and mothers, wives, sisters, and daughters likewise shared in the dangerous sport of court politics. Using sex, flattery, persuasion, bullying, and an arsenal of weaponry, most importantly poison and patience, the women of the Persian court participated in the preor-dained rituals of butchery. Most notable among the Achaemenid women was Parysatis. She clearly continued to fascinate the Greeks for many generations after her death and, following Ctesias, they constructed her as a second Semiramis (Llewellyn-Jones and Robson 2010: 76).

Yet the stories of death and destruction at court are not mere liter-ary *topoi* on the part of sensationalist Greek authors, no more than are their reports of the extravagance of the king's table or the fraught politics of the hunting field. As James Davidson (2006: 35) sensibly articulates, 'the Greeks did not invent things, but were quite happy to misunderstand, modify, or simply decontextualize some salient Persian facts, images, and representations, for, of course, it was the grains of *truth* that gave negative constructions their cogency'.

Part II

Documents

A1. The royal investiture

Ctesias F17 = Plutarch, Artaxerxes 3.1–4

Shortly after the death of Darius [II], the king [Artaxerxes II] went to Parsagade to be initiated into the royal rites (*teletē* i.e., 'mystery rite') by the Persian priests. It takes place at the shrine of a goddess of war (Anahita), whom one might liken to Athene. The initiate must enter the shrine, remove his own dress, and put on the clothes once worn by Cyrus the Elder (Cyrus II) before he had become king, eat a cake of figs, swallow terebinth and drink a bowl of sour milk. If there are other rituals, then they are not known to outsiders. When Artaxerxes was about to perform these rites, Tissaphernes came up to him bringing one of the priests who – because he had been in charge of Cyrus (the Younger's) traditional education during his childhood and had taught him to be a Magus – was, it seemed, more upset than any other Persian when Cyrus had not been made king. Because of this he was trusted when he started making accusations against Cyrus. He accused him of planning to lie in wait in the sanctuary so as to attack and kill the King when he was removing his clothes.

A2. Coronation hymn of Ashurbanipal

Akkadian cuneiform text (Livingstone 1989: 26–7)

May Shamash, king of heaven and earth, elevate you to the shepherd-ship over the four regions! May Ashur, who gave you the sceptre, lengthen your days and years! Spread your land wide at your feet! . . . May the greater speak and the lesser listen! May concord and peace be established in Assyria! Ashur is king – indeed Ashur is king! Ashurbanipal is the representative of Ashur, the creation of his hands. May the great gods make firm his reign, may they protect the life of Ashurbanipal, king of Assyria! May they give him a straight sceptre to extend the land of his peoples! May his reign be rewarded, and may they consolidate his royal throne for ever! May they bless him day by day, month by month and year by year and guard his reign! In his years may there constantly be rain from the heavens and flood from the (underground) source!

A3. The 'vassal treaty' of Esarhaddon

Akkadian cuneiform text from Nineveh (Parpola and Watanabe 1988: 188–97)

On the day that Esarhaddon, King of Assyria, your lord, passes away, (on that day) Ashurbanipal, the great Crown Prince des[ignate], (grand)son of Esarhaddon, your lord, shall be your king and your lord; he shall abase the mighty, raise up the lowly, put to death him who is worthy of death, and pardon him who deserves to be pardoned. You shall hearken to whatever he says and do whatever he commands, and you shall not seek any other king or any other lord against him.

A4. Princely education

Plato, Alcibiades *121c–22a*

When the eldest son, the heir to the throne, is born, all the subjects celebrate with a feast. . . . Then the boy is brought up, not by some no-account nurse, but by the most highly respected eunuchs in the royal household. . . . When the boys are seven years old they take up horseback riding with their tutors and begin hunting wild game. . . .

When he is fourteen, (a boy) is entrusted to people known as 'royal tutors'. These are four men of mature age who are judged to be the best in that they are the wisest, the most just, the bravest, and the most self-controlled. The first of them instructs him in the worship of the gods – the Magian lore of Zoroaster, son of Horomazes, and in what a king should understand. The most just of the men instructs him to be truthful throughout his life. The most self-controlled man teaches him not to be mastered even by a single pleasure, so that he will become accustomed to being a free man and a good king whose foremost duty is to rule himself and not become a slave to his desires. The fourth man teaches him bravery and to be undaunted, because fear makes a man a slave.

A5. Succession debates

Herodotus, Histories *7.2–3*

A violent struggle broke out among [Darius'] sons concerning the succession to the throne; for in accordance with the Persians' law the king may not march with his army until he has named a successor. For there were to Darius, even before he became king, three sons born of a previous wife, Gobryas' daughter, and, after he had become king, of

Atossa, Cyrus' child, four others. Indeed of the former, Artobazanes was the oldest and of those born afterwards Xerxes. But not being of the same mother, they were factious: Artobazanes because he was the oldest of all the offspring and on account of the fact that it was customarily held by universal norm that the oldest should have the throne, and Xerxes with the argument that he was the child of Atossa, Cyrus' daughter, and on account of the fact that Cyrus was the one who had acquired for the Persians freedom. Darius was not willing to show a judgement on this matter, but at this same time, in fact, Demaretus, Ariston's son, had gone up to Susa, bereft of his kingdom in Sparta. . . . That man, having learned by inquiry of the differences between Darius' children, went, as the report has it, to advise Xerxes to say (in addition to the things he was already saying) that he himself was born to Darius at the time he was king and had gained power over the Persians, but that Artobazanes was born when Darius was just a nobleman. Hence it was neither reasonable nor just for another (son) to have privilege over him, as was also the custom in Sparta, asserted Demaretus, (where) it was commonly held that if one was born before one's father became king and another was born afterwards to him while he was king, the one born after the succession to the kingdom should have priority. So Xerxes used Demaretus' suggestion, and Darius came to know that he had made a logical speech and appointed him king. But, as far as it seems to me, even without Demaretus' suggestion Xerxes would have been king; for Atossa had all the power.

A6. Xerxes as co-regent?

Elamite tablet from Persepolis; PF-NN1657
7 litres of flour, allocation from Mirizza, a Parthian named Tamšakama, spearbearer, sent/assigned by Xerxes, together with his three companions, sent from the King to Parthia: they received (it as) ration (for) one day. Third month, 24th year. Their ration (was) 1.5 litres, one servant received 1 litre. He (Tamšakama) carried a sealed document from the King.

A7. Co-regency

Justin, Epitome of the Philippic History of Pompeius Trogus
10.1.1–3
The Persian king Artaxerxes [II] had 115 sons by his concubines, but fathered only three by his legitimate wife (Stateira): Darius, Ariaratus,

and Ochus. In the case of Darius, Artaxerxes broke with Persian custom, among whom there is a change of king only at death. Because of his tender feelings towards Darius, the father made him king during his own lifetime, believing that nothing he bestowed on his son was lost to himself and anticipating a truer pleasure from being a father if he lived to see his son wearing the royal insignia.

A8. Greek speculations on Persian royal divinity

Plutarch, Themistocles *27.4–5*

Amongst our many excellent customs, this we account the best, to honour the king and to worship him, as the image of the preserver of all things. If then you approve of our practices, fall down before the king and revere him, you may both see him and speak to him; but if you think otherwise, you will need to use messengers to intercede for you, for it is not our national custom for the king to grant audience to any man who does not pay him obeisance.

A9. Uncompromising advice to a ruler

Akkadian version of a Babylonian text from Nineveh
(Foster 2005: vol. IV, p. 13)

If the king has no regard for due process, his people will be thrown to chaos, his land will be devastated . . . misfortunes will hound him.

If he has no regard for his princes, his lifetime will be cut short. If he has no regard for scholarly council, his land will rebel against him. If he has regard for a scoundrel, the mentality of his country will change; if he values the clever trick, the great gods will hound him in right council in the cause of justice. . . .

If he takes money from the citizens of Babylon and appropriates it . . . [or] hears a case involving Babylonians but dismisses it for a triviality, Marduk the lord of Heaven will establish his enemies over him and grant his possessions to the foe. . . .

If he calls up Sippar, Nippur, and Babylon collectively to enforce labour on those peoples, requiring of them service . . . Marduk . . . will turn his land over to the foe so that the troops of his land will do forced labour for his foe. . . .

If he grants his horses to feed on the fodder of the citizens . . . the horses that consumed the fodder will be led off to an enemy's harness. . . .

If [he] ... exhorts bribes from [the people] ... [he will be] obliterated to a wasteland ... [his] achievements will be reckoned as a puff of air.

A10. Achaemenid royal ideology

Old Persian inscription of Darius I from his tomb: DNb §2g–i; later repeated verbatim by Xerxes on his tomb: XNb

This is my ability: that my body is strong. As a warrior, I am a good warrior. At once my intelligence holds its place, whether I see a rebel or not. Both by intelligence and by command at that time I know myself to be above panic, both when I see a rebel and [when] I do not see one. I am furious in the strength of my revenge, with both hands and both feet. As a bowman I am a good bowman, both on foot and on horseback. As a spearman I am a good spearman, both on foot and on horseback. These are the skills which Ahuramazda has bestowed on me and I have had the strength to bear them.

A11. Yahweh and the command for genocide

Hebrew Bible, 2 Samuel 15:1–3

[The prophet] Samuel said to Saul, 'I am the one Yahweh sent to anoint you king over his people Israel; so listen now to the message from Yahweh. This is what the Lord Almighty says: 'I will punish the Amalekites for what they did to Israel when they waylaid them as they came up from Egypt. Now go, attack the Amalekites and totally destroy everything that belongs to them. Do not spare them; put to death men and women, children and infants, cattle and sheep, camels and donkeys.'

A12. A dream omen of Ashurbanipal

Akkadian cuneiform tablet (Pritchard 1969: 606)

The goddess Ishtar heard my anxious sighs and said, 'Fear not!' and gave me confidence [saying], 'Since you have lifted your hands in prayer and your eyes have filled with tears, I have had mercy'. During the night in which I appeared before her, a *šabrŭ* [cult attendant] lay down and had a dream. He awoke with a start and reported to me as follows: 'Ishtar who dwells in Arbela, entered. Quivers hung to the right and left of her, she held a bow in her hand and held her sharp sword unsheathed, ready to do battle. You [Ashurbanipal] stood before her, while she spoke with you like a real mother [and] addressed you. ...

"You are set on fighting. Wheresoever I wish to go, there I am on my way. . . . Stay here where you belong! Eat bread, drink sesame-beer, prepare joyful music, praise my divinity, while I go and carry out this work and let you gain your goal! Your face shall not become pale, your feet shall not falter, your strength not yield in battle!" She took you in her lovely babysling and thus protected your entire figure. In her face fire flamed, with raging anger she marched forth; against Teumman, king of Elam, with whom she is very angry, she set out'.

A13. Court propaganda: a fighting king

Plutarch, Artaxerxes 24.10–11

With his quiver at his side and his shield on his arm, [Artaxerxes II] led them on foot, dismounting from his horse, through steep and craggy passes, and the sight of his cheerfulness and unfailing strength gave wings to his soldiers, and so eased their journey that they made marches of over 200 furlongs each day.

A14. Darius III: warrior king

Diodorus, Library 17.5.3–6.3

Darius' selection for the throne was based on his known bravery, in which quality he surpassed the other Persians. Once when king Artaxerxes [III] was campaigning against the Cadusians, one of them with a wide reputation for strength and courage challenged a volunteer among the Persians to fight in single combat with him. No other dared accept, but Darius alone entered the contest and slew the challenger, being honoured in consequence by the king with rich gifts, while among the Persians he was conceded the first place in prowess. It was because of this prowess that he was thought worthy to take over the kingship. This happened about the same time as Philip died and Alexander became king. Such was the man whom fate had selected to be the antagonist of Alexander's genius, and they opposed one another in many and great struggles for the supremacy.

A15. The destruction of Sidon

Diodorus, Library 16.45

[Artaxerxes III] was very eager not to receive Sidon on the terms of a capitulation, since his aim was to overwhelm the Sidonians with a merciless disaster and to strike terror into the other cities by their punishment ... the King maintained his merciless rage. ... But the people of Sidon, before the arrival of the King, burned all their ships so that none of the townspeople should be able by sailing out secretly to gain safety for himself. But when they saw the city and the walls captured and swarming with myriads of soldiers, they shut themselves, their children, and their women up in their houses and consumed them all in flames. They say that those who were then destroyed in the fire, including the domestics, amounted to more than 40,000. After this disaster had befallen the Sidonians and the whole city together with its inhabitants had been obliterated by the fire, the King sold that funeral pyre for many talents, for as a result of the prosperity of the household-ers there was found a vast amount of silver and gold melted down by the fire. So the disasters which had overtaken Sidon had such an ending, and the rest of the cities, panic stricken, went over to the Persians.

A16. A who's who of Israelite courtiers

Hebrew Bible, 1 Chronicles 27:25–34

Azmaveth son of Adiel was in charge of the king's storehouses; Jonathan son of Uzziah was in charge of the storehouses in the field, in the cities, in the towns, and in the towers; Ezri son of Kelub was in charge of the field workers who farmed the land; Shimei the Ramathite was in charge of the vineyards; Zabdi the Shiphmite was in charge of the wine stored in the vineyards; Baal-Hanan the Gederite was in charge of the olive and sycamore trees in the lowlands; Joash was in charge of the storehouses of olive oil; Shitrai the Sharonite was in charge of the cattle grazing in Sharon; Shaphat son of Adlai was in charge of the cattle in the valleys; Obil the Ishmaelite was in charge of the camels; Jehdeiah the Meronothite was in charge of the donkeys; Jaziz the Hagrite was in charge of the sheep. All these were the officials in charge of King David's property. Jonathan, David's uncle, was a wise adviser and scribe; Jehiel son of Hacmoni cared for the king's sons. Ahithophel was the king's adviser; Hushai the Arkite was the king's confidant. Ahithophel was succeeded by Jehoiada son of Benaiah and by Abiathar. Joab was the commanding general of the king's army.

A17. Explaining the nature of the court and Empire

Pseudo-Aristotle, De Mundo 398a–b

The chief and most distinguished men all had their appointed place, some being the king's personal servants, his bodyguard and attendants,

others the guardians of each of the enclosing walls, the so-called jani-
tors and 'listeners', that the king himself, who was called their master
and god, might therefore see and hear all things. Besides these, others
were appointed as stewards of his revenues and leaders in war and
hunting, and receivers of gifts, and others charged with all the other
necessary jobs. All the Empire of Asia, bounded on the west by the
Hellespont and on the east by the Indus, was split up according to race
among generals and satraps and subject-princes of the Great King; and
there were couriers and watchmen and messengers and superintend-
ents of signal-fires. . . . It was beneath the dignity of Xerxes to administer his own Empire and to carry out his own desires and superintend
the government of his kingdom; such functions were not becoming for
a god.

A18. King and councillors

Hebrew Bible, Esther 1:13–22

Since it was customary for the king to consult experts in matters of
law and justice, he spoke with the wise men who understood the times
and were closest to the king—Karshena, Shethar, Admatha, Tarshish,
Meres, Marsena and Memukan, the seven nobles of Persia and Media
who had special access to the king and were highest in the kingdom.

'According to law, what must be done to queen Vashti?' he asked.
'She has not obeyed the command of king Xerxes that the eunuchs
have taken to her.'

Then Memukan replied in the presence of the king and the nobles,
'queen Vashti has done wrong, not only against the king but also against
all the nobles and the peoples of all the provinces of king Xerxes. For
the queen's conduct will become known to all the women, and so they
will despise their husbands and say, "king Xerxes commanded queen
Vashti to be brought before him, but she would not come." This very
day the Persian and Median women of the nobility who have heard
about the queen's conduct will respond to all the king's nobles in the
same way. There will be no end of disrespect and discord. Therefore,
if it pleases the king, let him issue a royal decree and let it be written
in the laws of Persia and Media, which cannot be repealed, that Vashti
is never again to enter the presence of king Xerxes. Also let the king
give her royal position to someone else who is better than she. Then
when the king's edict is proclaimed throughout all his vast realm, all
the women will respect their husbands, from the least to the greatest.'

The king and his nobles were pleased with this advice, so the king did as Memukan proposed. He sent dispatches to all parts of the kingdom, to each province in its own script and to each people in their own language, proclaiming that every man should be ruler over his own household, using his native tongue.

A19. Darius II issues commands through his satrap Aršama

Aramaic papyrus from Elephantine (AP 21; Lindenberger 2003: 65 no. 30a)

[To my brothers,] Yedoniah and his colleagues, the Jewish [garrison], from your brother Hananyah.

May the gods bless you my brothers [always].

This year, regnal year five of Darius (II), the king sent to Aršama [. . .] [. . .]. You should count as follows: four [. . .]. [. . .]. And from the fifteenth day to the twenty-first day [. . .].

Be pure and take care. [Do] n[ot do] work [. . .] do not drink [. . .] nor [eat] anything of leaven. [… at] sunset until day 21 of Nisan.[. . .] Bring into your chambers [. . .] and seal up during [these] days.[. . .]

[To] my brothers Yedoniah and his colleagues, the Jewish [garrison], from your brother Hananyah, son of [. . .].

A20. City walls and a plague of locusts

Aramaic document from Bactria (Shaked 2004: 28, document A4)

On behalf of Akhvamazda to Bagavant. And now concerning what you sent to me, saying:

'[A message] was sent to me on your behalf, (instructing me) with the order to build a wall and a ditch around the town of Nikhšapaya. Then I fixed the time a made the troop (of workers?) approach. Yet Spaita, the magistrates, and (certain) others of the garrison of the place came to me saying, "There are locusts in great number and in thickness and the harvest is ready for collection. If we build this wall the locusts will plague this town and will bring great harm [. . .] in the country." Me, I do not have the authority to let them go through with it and [another] affair… [And now] the troop who was needed . . . I have let go so that they may crush the locusts so that they can collect the harvest. When the time comes they will build the wall and the ditch.

Daizaka the scribe knows this order.'

To Bagavant who is at Khulmi. 3 day Sivan [regnal year] 7 of Artaxerxes. The subject of Akhvamazda. You bring this letter.

B1. Rituals of dining

Heraclides F2 = Athenaeus, Dinner of the Sophists *4.145a*
Heraclides of Cumae, the author of the *Persica*, says in Book 2 of the work called *Preparations*: When the Persian kings dine, all their servants bathe and wear fine clothing while they attend them, and they spend almost half the day preparing the dinner. Some of those who eat with the king dine outside, and anyone who wishes can see them, while others eat with the king inside. But even they do not eat in his direct company: instead there are two rooms placed opposite one another and the king eats in one and his guests in another. The king sees them through a veil which hangs over the door, but they cannot see him.

B2. Seating etiquette

Xenophon, Cyropaedia *8.4.1.3–5*
When Cyrus had sacrificed and was celebrating his victory with a banquet, he invited in those of his friends (*philoi*) who showed that they were most desirous of magnifying his rule and of honouring him most loyally. . . . So when invited guests came to dinner, he (Gadatas) did not assign them their seats at random, but he seated on Cyrus's left the one for whom he had the highest regard, for the left side was more readily exposed to treacherous designs than the right; and the one who was second in esteem he seated on his right, the third again on the left, the fourth on the right, and so on, if there were more. . . . Accordingly, Cyrus thus made public recognition of those who stood first in his esteem, beginning even with the places they took when sitting or standing in his company. He did not, however, assign the appointed place permanently, but he made it a rule that by noble deeds anyone might advance to a more honoured seat, and that if anyone should conduct himself badly he should go back to one less honoured.

B3. The invention of inaccessibility

Herodotus, Histories *1.99–100*
Deioces had these fortifications [at Ecbatana] built to surround himself and his own palace. The people were required to build their houses outside the circuit of the walls. When the town was finished, Deioces proceeded to arrange the following ceremonial etiquette (and he was the first to do this): he allowed no one to have direct access to the person of the king, but made all communication pass through the

hands of messengers, and forbade the king to be seen directly by his subjects. He also made it a disgrace for anyone whatsoever to laugh or spit in the royal presence. His motive in creating all this formality was to create a distance between himself and his peers because they were brought up together with him, and were of as good family as he, and in no sense inferior to him in valour. He expected that if they did not see him personally, they would in time come to accept him as being different, more distinguished, from themselves, and thus they would not be moved to plot against him.

After completing these arrangements and firmly settling himself upon the throne Deioces continued to administer justice with the same strictness as before. Petitions were stated in writing and sent in to the king who passed his judgement upon the contents and transmitted his decisions to the parties concerned; besides which he had spies and eavesdroppers in all parts of his realm and if he heard of any act of disorder, he sent for the guilty party and made sure that the punishment met the crime.

B4. Invisible monarchs of the past

Ctesias F1n, F1pα = Athenaeus, Dinner of the Sophists
12.528f, 529a

In the third book of the *History of Persia*, Ctesias says that all those who ruled Asia were earnest in their pursuit of pleasure, especially Ninyas, the son of Ninus and Semiramis. And so because this man stayed inside living a life of luxury he was not seen by anyone apart from the eunuchs and his own wives. . . .

Such was Sarandapallus, too, whom some say was the son of Anacyndaraxes, others the son of Anabaraxares. And so Arbaces, one of the generals under his command and a Mede by birth, managed to get to see Sarandapallus through the help of Sparameizes, one of the eunuchs, and was permitted to do so with the King's consent, albeit with difficulty.

B5. The invisible king

Pseudo-Aristotle, De Mundo *348a*

The pomp of Cambyses and Xerxes and Darius was ordered on a grand scale and touched the heights of majesty and magnificence: the king himself, they say, lived in Susa or Ecbatana, invisible to all, in a marvellous palace with a surrounding wall flashing with gold, electrum and ivory; it had a succession of many gate-towers, and the gateways, separated by many stades from one another, were fortified with brazen doors and high walls; outside these the leaders and most eminent men were drawn up in order, some as personal bodyguards and attendants to the king himself, some as guardians of each outer wall, called 'guards' and the 'listening-watch', so that the king himself, who had the name of 'Master' and 'God' (*despotês kai theos*), might see everything and hear everything.

B6. Darius and Xerxes on the building of Persepolis

Elamite inscription of the southern terrace wall of Persepolis: DPf;
addition by Xerxes: XPf §36–43

On this terrace, where this fortified palace (*halmarraš*) was built, there no palace had been built before; by the favour of Ahuramazda I built this palace. And it was Ahuramazda's desire, and the desire of all the gods who are, that this palace should be built; and I built it, and at that time it was built firmly and excellently and exactly as I had ordered it to be.

When I became king, much that [is] superior I built. What had been built by my father, that I took into my care and other work I added. But what I have done and what my father has done, all that we have done by the favour of Ahuramazda.

B7. The creation of Darius' palace at Susa

Trilingual inscription of Darius I at Susa: DSf §7–14

This palace [*hadiš*] which I built at Susa, from afar its ornamentation was brought. Downward the earth was dug, until I reached rock in the earth. When the excavation had been made, then rubble was packed down, some 40 cubits in depth, another part 20 cubits in depth. On that rubble the palace was constructed. And that the earth was dug downward, and that the rubble was packed down, and that the sun-dried brick was moulded, the Babylonian people performed these tasks. The cedar timber, this was brought from a mountain named Lebanon. The Assyrian people brought it to Babylon; from Babylon the Carians and the Yaunâ [= Greeks] brought it to Susa. The *yakâ*-timber was brought from Gandhara and from Carmania. The gold was brought from Lydia and from Bactria, which here was wrought. The precious stone lapis lazuli and carnelian which was wrought here, this was brought from Sogdia. The precious stone turquoise, this was brought from Chorasmia, which was wrought here. The silver and the ebony were brought from

Egypt. The ornamentation with which the wall was adorned, that from Yaunâ was brought. The ivory which was wrought here, was brought from Nubia and from India and from Arachosia. The stone columns which were here wrought, a village named Abirâdu, in Elam – from there were brought. The stone-cutters who wrought the stone, those were Yaunâ and Lydians. The goldsmiths who wrought the gold, those were Medes and Egyptians. The men who wrought the wood, those were Lydians and Egyptians. The men who wrought the baked brick, those were Babylonians. The men who adorned the wall, those were Medes and Egyptians. Darius the King says: At Susa a very excellent work was ordered, a very excellent work was brought to completion. May Ahuramazda protect me, my father Hystaspes, and my country.

B8. The beauty of Darius III and his womenfolk

Plutarch, Alexander 21.6.11

The wife of Darius [III] was said to be the most beautiful princess of the age, just as Darius was the tallest and most handsome man in Asia; their daughters inherited their parents' looks. . . . When Alexander saw their beauty and stateliness, he took no more notice of them than to say, jokingly, 'These Persian women are a torment for our eyes!' He was determined to demonstrate his chastity and self-control by disregarding the beauty of their appearance – so he walked past them as if they were made of stone.

B9. Moulding the bodies of infant royalty

Plato, Alcibiades 121d

After [the birth] comes the nurture of the child, not at the hands of a low-born woman-nurse, but of the most high-ranking eunuchs in the king's service, who are charged with caring for the new-born child, and especially with the business of making him as handsome as possible by massaging his limbs into a correct shape; and while doing this they are held in high esteem.

B10. Cyrus the Great adopts Median dress, cosmetics, and deportment

Xenophon, Cyropaedia 8.1.40

Moreover, we can observe that Cyrus held the opinion that a monarch ought to excel his subjects, not only by being better than them, but by holding them under his spell. At any rate, he chose to wear the Median style of dress himself, and persuaded his followers to adopt it too because he thought that if anyone had a personal physical defect that this clothing would help conceal it and that it made the wearer look very tall and handsome. And they have shoes into which (without detection) they can insert lifts so that the wearer can appear taller than he actually is. And he also encouraged the fashion of painting beneath the eyes so that they might seem more lustrous than they are, and of using cosmetics to make the complexion look better than nature had made it. He also took care that his associates did not spit or blow their noses in public.

B11. The dress and good looks of Astyages of Media

Xenophon, Cyropaedia *1.3.2–3*

[Cyrus] noticed that his grandfather (Astyages) was adorned with eyeliner beneath his eyes, and had rouge rubbed onto his cheeks and was wearing a wig of false hair – in the Median mode. For all this is Median, as are their purple tunics, and their coats, the necklaces around their necks and the bracelets on their wrists. Yet the Persians, even of this day, have a much plainer style of dress and a more frugal way of life. However, observing his grandfather's adornment wide-eyed, [Cyrus] said, 'Oh my mother, see how handsome my grandfather is!' And when his mother asked him whom he thought the most handsome, his father or his grandfather, Cyrus straightaway answered, 'Mother, of all Persians, my father is by far the handsomest; but of the Medes – as far as I have seen any of them in the streets or at court – my grandfather here is the most handsome by far.'

Then his grandfather kissed him in return and gave him a beautiful robe to wear and, as a mark of special favour, adorned him with necklaces and bracelets. . . . As Cyrus was a boy fond of beautiful things and keen for distinction, he was pleased with his robe.

B12. Court beauticians and body servants

Xenophon, Cyropaedia *8.8.20*

Doormen, cooks, sauce-makers, wine-pourers, bath-attendants, waiters who bring dishes, waiters who take them away, bed-chamber assistants, assistants of the *royal Levée* (getting up – and getting dressed – ceremony), and the beauticians who paint and anoint and perform other services – now these are ones that the powers-that-be have made into nobility.

B13. Wigs or hair-pieces

Pseudo-Aristotle 2.14d

Noticing that the Lycians were fond of wearing their hair long, [Condalus, governor under Mausolus] said that a dispatch had come from the king of Persia ordering him to send hair to make false fringes and that he was therefore commanded by Mausolus to cut off their hair.

B14. Breaching the etiquette of sleeves

Xenophon, Hellenica *2.1.8*

In this year, Cyrus [the Younger] executed Autoboisakes and Mitraios, the sons of (Darius II's) sister [who was the daughter of Xerxes (or, more accurately, Artaxerxes I)] because, when they met with him, they did not put their hands into their long sleeves (*korē*). Now, the Persians do this only as a mark of respect for the king; this type of sleeve is longer than a normal sleeve so when one puts a hand into it, the hand is rendered harmless.

B15. Semiramis wears the king's robe and rules

Deinon F7 = Aelian, Historical Miscellany *7.1*

Semiramis the Assyrian is the subject of diverse accounts, for she was the most charming of women, even if her beauty was not the most notable. She met the Assyrian monarch because of her reputation for being a fascinating woman and the king fell in love with her at first sight. She asked the king to give her the royal robes as a gift, so that she could reign over Asia for five days and see her orders executed. And what she requested was made so. As soon as the king sat upon the royal throne, and she knew that the power was completely in her hands, she commanded the guards to kill him. And from thereon she took control of the Assyrians. As said by Deinon.

B16. Courtiers' muddy robes

Xenophon, Anabasis *1.5.8*

At one time they came across a very narrow muddy place where the going was tough for the carts. Cyrus [the Younger] halted with his entourage of courtiers and commanded Glous and Pigres to take some men from the barbarian troops and get the carts free from the mud. But he thought they were taking too long over the job and so, pretending to be angry, he told the Persian nobles in his entourage to help the carts get a move on. It then became possible to see a wondrous thing: they allowed their long purple coats to drop to the ground without caring where they stood and sprinted, as if they were running a race down a very steep hillside, while wearing their expensive tunics and trousers, with some of them even wearing necklaces and bracelets on their arms. As soon as they got there, they jumped into the muck in all their finery and heaved the carts free from the mud more quickly than would ever be thought possible.

B17. Royal punishment and clothing

Plutarch, Moralia *173D, 565A*

[Artaxerxes I] was the first to decree a type of punishment for those nobles who insulted him: instead of whipping their bodies and shaving the hair from their heads, they took off their outer garments and these were beaten; and they took off their headdresses and these were shaved. . . .

[In] Persia the robes and *tiaras* of the sufferers are shaved and whipped, as the tearful owners plead for mercy. . . .

B18. Intaphrenes and his wife

Herodotus, Histories *3.118–19*

Of the seven men who had revolted against the Magus, one of them, Intaphrenes met his death soon after the revolt, when he committed the following treasonous act: he had entered the palace wishing an audience with the king; indeed it was the rule that those who had rebelled against the Magus had free access to the king without being formally presented – unless the king happened to be having sex with a woman at that time. And so Intaphrenes, being one of the seven, thought it was acceptable for him to go to the king without being announced. But the Gatekeeper and the Messenger did not allow him to pass, telling him that the king was, at the time, preoccupied with a woman. Intaphrenes suspected them of lying, and so drawing his dagger he sliced off their noses and cut off their ears and attached them to his horse's bridle, which he then tied around their necks before releasing them.

In this state they presented themselves to the king and told him the cause of their mutilation. Fearing that the other six had conspired in this act, Darius sent for each one and questioned them individually about their thoughts on Intaphrenes' actions and asked them if they condoned what he had done. When he had ascertained that Intaphrenes had acted without their knowledge, he had Intaphrenes arrested together with his children and all his male relatives (he believed that Intaphrenes had conspired with his family in the plot). After Darius had had them imprisoned and condemned to death, and while they awaited execution, the wife of Intaphrenes began to wait at the gate of the king['s palace], weeping and lamenting. Her persistence persuaded Darius to take pity on her and he sent a messenger to her to say, 'Woman, Darius the king grants that you may save one of your relatives from imprisonment; whichever one you decide to select'. She thought for a moment and replied, 'If the king is truly granting me one life from all those who are imprisoned, I choose my brother'. Darius was surprised by this and sent his messenger back to her: 'Woman, the king wants to know: what was your reasoning in passing over your own husband and children to pick your brother to be the one who survives, since he is for sure more of a stranger to you than your children, and less beloved to you than your husband?' And she answered the king's question, 'Majesty, I may, god willing, have another husband and bear more children if I lose those I have now. But with my mother and father already dead, I will never have another brother. That is the reason for my answer'. Darius thought the woman had answered wisely, and was so delighted that he released not only the man she pleaded for, but her eldest son as well. He executed all the others; that is how one of the seven quickly met his end.

B19. The Gate of All Nations

Trilingual inscription (four surviving copies) of Xerxes on the main gateway at Persepolis: XPa §3

King Xerxes proclaims: By the favour of Ahuramazda I have constructed this Gate of All Nations. Much else [that is] good [was] built throughout this Parsa [i.e. Persepolis], which I have constructed and which my father has constructed. But whatever work appears [to be] good, all that we have done by the favour of Ahuramazda.

B20. Imagining Themistocles' royal audience

Philostratus, Imaginings 2.31

A Greek among foreigners, a real man among the unmanly, louche, and luxury-loving; he [Themistocles] is an Athenian to judge from his short rough cloak (*tribōn*). I think he pronounces some wise saying to them, trying to correct them. [Here are] Medes and the centre of Babylon . . . and the king on a throne decorated with ornamented peacocks. The painter does not ask to be praised for his fine depiction of the [royal] headdress (*tiara*) and the tasselled robe (*kalasiris*) and the sleeved tunic (*kandis*), nor the monstrous shapes of colourfully woven animals which are [typically] foreign . . . but he should be praised for . . . the faces of the eunuchs. The court is also gold . . . we breathe in incense and myrrh, with which the foreigners pollute the freedom of the air; one spear-bearer is conferring with another about the Greek, in awe of him as his great achievements begin to be realised. . . . For I believe that Themistocles the son of Neocles has come from Athens to Babylon after the immortal victory at Salamis because he has no idea where in Greece he might be safe, and that he is discussing with the king how indebted Xerxes was to him while he was commander of the Greek forces. His Median surroundings do not intimidate him, he is as confident as if standing on the rostrum; and his language is not his native one, but Themistocles speaks like a Mede, which he took the trouble to learn there. If you doubt this, look at his audience, how their eyes indicate that they understand him, and look at Themistocles, whose head tilts like one speaking, but his eyes show his hesitance, because what he is speaking is newly learned.

B21. Esther before the king

Hebrew Bible, Esther 5:1–3

On the third day Esther donned her royal robes and stood in the inner courtyard of the king's palace, facing the royal chambers. The king was sitting on his royal throne in the throne room, facing the entrance of the chambers. As soon as the king saw queen Esther standing in the courtyard she won his favour, and the king extended to Esther the golden sceptre which was in his hand. So Esther approached and touched the tip of the sceptre. 'What is it, queen Esther?' the king asked her. 'What is your request? [Ask for] up to half the kingdom, it shall be granted to you'.

B22. Overwhelming emotions of a royal audience

Greek Bible, Esther 15:5–7

And going through all the doors, [Esther] stood there before the king. And he was sitting upon his royal throne and he was clothed in a robe which manifested his status, gold all throughout and with expensive stones. And he was extremely awe-inspiring. And lifting his face which had been set afire in glory, he gazed directly at her – like a bull in the height of anger. And the queen was afraid, and her face changed over in faintness, and she leaned on the servant who was going in front of her. . . . [But] the king leaped down from his throne and he took her up in his arms.

B23. The royal footsool

Deinon F25a = Athenaeus, Dinner of the Sophists *12.514a*
Whenever the king alighted from his chariot, says Deinon, he neither jumped down (even though the distance to the ground was minimal), nor supported himself upon someone's arm; instead a gold footstool was placed out for him, and he put his feet upon this when he descended. The royal stool-bearer followed him about for this purpose.

B24. Alexander's makeshift footstool

Quintus Curtius Rufus, History of Alexander *5.2.13–15*
Alexander now sat on the royal throne, but it was too high for him and so, because his feet could not touch the floor, one of the royal pages placed a small table under them. Noticing the distress on the face of one of Darius' eunuchs, the king asked him why he was upset. The eunuch declared that the table was used by Darius to eat from, and he could not help his tears, seeing it consigned to such a disrespectful use. The king was struck with shame . . . and was ordering the table's removal when Philotas said, 'No, Your Majesty, don't do that! Take this as an omen: the table your enemy used for his feasts has become your footstool'.

B25. Carpets and thrones

Deinon F1 = Athenaeus, Dinner of the Sophists 12.514c
Through their court the king would proceed on foot, walking upon Sardis carpets spread on the floor, which no one else would walk upon. And when he reached the final court he would mount his chariot or, sometimes, his horse; but outside the palace he was never seen on foot. . . . The throne he sat upon was gold, and round it stood four short golden posts studded with jewels; these supported a woven canopy of purple.

B26. Obeisance to the king

Plutarch, Themistocles *27.4–5, 28.1*

'Amongst our many excellent customs, this we account the best, to honour the king and to worship him (*proskynein*), as the image of the god of all things (*eikōn theou*). If then you approve of our practices, fall down before the king and revere him, you may both see him and speak to him; but if you think otherwise, you will need to use messengers to intercede for you, for it is not our national custom for the king to grant audience to any man who does not pay him obeisance'. . . . When Themistocles was led into the king's presence, he kissed the ground in front of him and waited silently.

B27. Obsequious salutations to the pharaoh of Egypt

Akkadian document, Amarna Letter (EA) 320; Moran (1992: 350); Pritchard (1969: 490)

To the king, my lord, my god, my sun, the sun from the sky: message of Yidya, the ruler of Ashkelon, your servant, the dirt at your feet, the groom of your horses. I indeed prostrate myself, on the stomach and on the back, at the feet of my king, my lord, seven times and seven times. I am indeed guarding the place of the king where I am. Whatever the king, my lord, has written me, I have listened to very carefully. Who is the dog that would not obey the orders of the king, his lord, the sun of the sun?

C1. The king's lands

Old Persian inscription of Darius I at Bisitun: DB I §6

These are the lands which obey me, by the favour of Ahuramazda. I was their king: Persia, Elam, Babylonia, Assyria, Arabia, Egypt, those of the sea, Lydia, Ionia, Media, Armenia, Cappadocia, Parthia, Drangiana, Areia, Chorasmia, Bactria, Sogdiana, Gandhara, Scythia, Sattagydia, Arachosia, Maka: in all twenty-three lands.

C2. The Empire at large

Four trilingual texts on gold and silver tablets, Persepolis, DPh; two trilingual texts on a silver and gold tablet, Hamadan, DH

Darius the Great King, king of kings, king of countries. Son of Hystaspes, an Achaemenid. King Darius says: This [is] the kingdom which I hold: from the Saca who are beyond Sogdiana, from there to Kush, from the Indus as far as Sardis, which Ahuramazda the greatest of the gods bestowed on me. May Ahuramazda protect me and my house.

C3. The diverse Empire

Babylonian inscription, Persepolis, DPg §1
A great god [is] Ahuramazda, who is the greatest among the gods, who created heaven and earth, created mankind, who gave well-being to mankind to dwell therein and who made Darius king, and bestowed on Darius the kingship over this wide earth, in which there are many lands: Persia, Media, and the other lands of other tongues, of mountains and plains, from this side of the sea to that side of the sea, from this side of the desert to that side of the desert.

C4. Criss-crossing the Empire

Elamite tablets, Persepolis, PF 1318, PF 1404, PF 1550
11 BAR of flour Abbatema received. For his own rations daily he receives 7 BAR.

20 men received each 2 QA. He carried a sealed document of the king. They went forth from India. They went to Susa. 2nd month, 23rd year. Išbaramištima [is] his elite guide. The seal of Išbaramištima was applied [to this tablet].

4.65 BAR of flour Dauma received. 23 men [received] each 1½ QA. They went forth from Sardis. They went to Persepolis. 9th month. 27th year. [At] Hidali.

1 QA of wine [was] supplied by Karkašša. 1 woman went from Susa [to] Kandahar. She carried a sealed document of the king, and she received it. Zišanduš [is] her elite guide. 22nd year. 2nd month.

C5. Aršama the satrap of Egypt orders rations for a travelling party

Aramaic document from Susa or Babylon (Lindenberger 2003: 90–1)
This is to introduce my official, Nakhtor by name. He is on his way to Egypt. You are to issue him daily provisions from my estates in your respective provinces as follows: White flour – 2 cups

Fine flour – 3 cups

Wine or beer – 2 cups [. . .]

For his retinue (10 men in total), for each one daily:

Flour – 1 cup, plus sufficient fodder for his horses.

You are to issue too provisions for two Cilicians and one artisan (three in all), my servants who are accompanying him to Egypt:

Flour – 1 cup daily per man.

Issue these provisions, each official in turn, along the route from province to province, until he arrives in Egypt. If he stops at any place for more than one day, do not give him extra provisions for the additional days. Bagasrava has been informed of this order. Rašta was the scribe.

C6. Cyrus' search for an uninterrupted springtime

Xenophon, Cyropaedia *8.6.22*

Cyrus [II] made his home in the centre of his kingdom, and in winter he spent seven months in Babylon, for there the climate is warm; in the spring he spent three months in Susa, and in the height of summer two months in Ecbatana. By doing so . . . he enjoyed the warmth and coolness of perpetual springtime.

C7. The pleasure of relocation

Plutarch, Moralia *604C*

The kings of Persia were called happy because they spent the winter in Babylon, the summer in Media, and the most pleasant part of spring in Susa.

C8. Bigger is not better: criticising the king's migrations

Plutarch, Moralia *78D*

Also, Diogenes used to compare his moving between Corinth and Athens, and from Athens to Corinth again, with the journeys that the Persian king made to Susa in the spring, to Babylon in the winter, and Media in the summer. As Agesilaus used to say about the Great King, 'In what way is he greater than me, unless he is more just?'

C9. Relocating across Greece is better than traversing an Empire

Dio Chrysostom, Discourses (Orations) *6.1–7*

When Diogenes of Sinope was exiled from [his home city], he came to Greece and used to divide his time between Corinth and Athens, saying that he was following the practice of the Persian king. After all, that monarch spent the winters in Babylon and Susa, or occasionally in Bactra [capital of Bactria], which are the warmest parts of Asia, and the summers in Ecbatana in Media, where the air is always very cool and the summer is like the winter in the region of Babylon. . . . Diogenes thought that [Corinth and Athens] were far more beautiful than Ecbatana and Babylon, and that the Craneion [harbour of Corinth], and the Athenian acropolis with the Propylaea were far more beautiful structures than those royal cities, yielding to them only in size. . . . Besides, the king had a very long distance to travel when changing residences; he had to spend pretty much the larger part of the winter and summer on the road. [Diogenes] himself, on the other hand, by spending the night near Megara, could very easily be in Athens on the following day – or else, if he preferred, at Eleusis; otherwise, he could take a shorter way through Salamis, without passing through any deserts. So he had an advantage over the king and enjoyed greater luxury, since his housing arrangements were better. This is what he liked to say, jokingly; nonetheless, he intended to bring to the attention of those who venerated the wealth of the Persian and his so-called happiness that in reality his real life was nothing like they imagined.

C10. The luxury of traversing the Empire

Athenaeus, Dinner of the Sophists *12.513f*
The first people in history to become notorious for luxurious living were the Persians, whose kings spent the winter in Susa and the summer in Ecbatana (Susa got its name, according to Aristobulus and Chares, because of the beauty of its location, for *souson* is the [Persian] equivalent for the Greek word *krinon*, 'lily'). They spent the autumn in Persepolis, and were in Babylon for the remaining part of the year.

C11. The spawning of the mackerel – and the Great King

Aelian, On Animals *10. 6, 3.13*
It would appear that the mackerel of the Euxine River imitate the Persian king, who spends the winter in Susa and the summer in Ecbatana. . . .

[We admire] how cranes spend their summer and winter, but we continue to be obsessed with stories of the Persian king's comprehension of fluctuations in temperature and we go on endlessly about Susa and Ecbatana and this Persian's journeying back and forth.

C12. The Great King on the toilet

Aristophanes, Acharnians *81–3*

At the end of the fourth year we reached the king's court but he had left with his whole army to take a crap and for the space of eight months he was off, taking a shit, in the middle of the golden mountains. . . . After this he returned to his palace.

C13. An Empire on the move: Darius III and his court journey through Babylonia

Quintus Curtius Rufus, History of Alexander *3.3.8–16, 20–7*

It is an ancestral tradition amongst the Persians not to begin a march until after sunrise, and the day was already well advanced when the signal – from a horn– was given from the king's tent. Above the tent, so that it would be visible to all, a representation of the sun gleamed in a crystal case. The order of the line of march was as follows: in front, on silver altars, was carried the fire which the Persians called sacred and eternal. Next came the Magi, chanting a traditional hymn, and they were followed by 365 young men in scarlet cloaks, their number equalling the days of the year. . . . Then came the chariot consecrated to [Ahuramazda]; these were followed by a horse of extraordinary size, which they called the Horse of the Sun. Golden sceptres and white robes adorned the horse-riders. Not far behind were ten carts amply decorated with relief carvings in gold and silver, and these were followed by a cavalry of twelve nations of different cultures, variously armed.

Next in line were the soldiers whom the Persians call *Immortals*, some 10,000 in number. No other group were so well bedecked with barbaric splendour: golden necklaces, clothes interwoven with gold, long-sleeved tunics actually studded with precious stones. After a short interval came the 15,000 men known as the king's kinsmen, 15,000 men; this throng, with its almost ladylike elegance was conspicuous more for its luxury than its arms. The column next to these comprised the *Doryphoroi*, the Gentlemen of the Royal Wardrobe [probably meant to read *Dorophoroi* – literally, 'Gift Bearers'] . . . and these preceded the royal chariot on which rode the king himself, towering above all others. Both sides of the chariot were decorated with divine emblems in gold and silver; even the yoke was studded with gemstones and on it rose two gold statuettes, each a cubit high, of the king's ancestors: Ninus and Belus. Between these was a sacred golden eagle, its wings depicted outspread. . . . The chariot was followed by 10,000 spearmen carrying lances chased with silver and tipped with gold, and to right and left he was attended by 200 of his royal relatives. At the end of the column came 30,000 foot-soldiers, followed by 400 of the king's horses.

Next, at a distance of one *stade*, came Sisygambis, the mother of Darius, drawn in one carriage, and in another came his wife. A throng of women of the queen's household rode on horseback. There followed the fifteen so-called *harmamaxae* in which rode the king's children, their nurses and a herd of eunuchs who are not at all despised by these people. Next came the carriages of 365 royal concubines, all regally dressed and adorned and behind them 600 mules and 300 camels carrying the king's treasury, with a guard of archers in attendance. After this column rode the women of the king's relatives and friends, and hordes of camp-followers and servants. At the end, to close up the rear, were the light-armed troops with their respective leaders.
On the other hand, to look at the Macedonian army one would see something very different: its men and horses were not gleaming with gold and multi-coloured garments, but with steel and bronze; an army prepared to stand, or to chase, not over-burdened with baggage or excessive numbers.

C14. All the king's horses

Elamite tablets, Persepolis, PF 1793, PF 1943

Tell Harrena the cattle chief, Parnaka spoke as follows: '13 sheep and 5 portions issue to Bakatanna the horseman and his companions who feed [?] the horses and mules of the king and of the princes [at] Karakušan. [It?] has been changed [?]. 135 men, 1 sheep received by each 10 men.'

Month 7, year 19, this sealed document was delivered. Karkiš wrote [it]. Maraza communicated the message.

6 [BAR of grain], delivered [in accordance with] a sealed document of Iršena, Masana the hamarnabattiš received, and 1 young horse, maintained at Hadaran consumed [it as] rations. [For] 1 month, the 5th, [in] the 19th year; it consumed 2 QA daily. . . .

63 [BAR of grain], delivered [in accordance with] a sealed document of Iršena, Kunsuš the horseman, [for whom] Yaumanizza [does] the apportioning, received, and 1 ber [mature?] horse, maintained at Hadaran, consumed [it as] rations. For 7 months, from the 3rd through the 9th, in the 19th year, it consumed 3 QA daily.

C15. The Egyptian satrap commissions an equestrian statue

Aramaic papyrus from Egypt (AD 9 B; Lindenberger 2003: 97–8)
From Arshama to Nakhthor, Kenzasirma, and his associates.

Concerning: Hinzanay, a sculptor and a servant of mine, whom Bagasrava brought to Susa. Issue rations to him and his household, the same as those given to the other artisans on my staff.

He is to make a statue of a horseman [. . .]. They should be [. . .]. And he is to make a statue of a horse with its rider, just as he did previously for me, and other statues. Have them sent to me just as soon as you can!

Artavahya has been informed of this order.

Rašda was the scribe.

C16. King as horseman warrior

Trilingual inscription, tomb of Darius I, DNb §2h; Old Persian inscription, Persepolis, XPl §2h
As a horseman I am a good horseman. As a bowman I am a good bowman, both on foot and on horseback. As a spearman I am a good spearman, both on foot and on horseback.

C17. Horses sacrificed to Cyrus' memory

Arrian, Anabasis 6.29.7
The king used to provide [priests at Parsagade] a sheep a day, a fixed amount of flour and wine, and a horse each month to sacrifice to Cyrus.

C18. Royal camels

Elamite tablets from Persepolis, PF 1787, 1786
9.9 BAR of flour, supplied by Karma, Bawukšamira received, [for] rations of 33 camels belonging to the king. He carried a sealed document of Parnaka. He went forth to the king at Susa. First month, 22nd year.

9.9 BAR of flour Bawukšamira received [for] rations for camels [belonging to the king?]. Coming from Susa, he carried an authorisation of Bakabana. He went to Persepolis. 33 [royal?] camels consumed 3 QA. Second month, 22nd year.

C19. Clearing the king's path of scorpions

Aelian, On Animals *15.26*

On the second stage of the journey from Susa in Persia to Media there are said to be innumerable scorpions, so that when the king of Persia is going to pass that way he issues orders, three days in advance, that everybody is to hunt them; he gives gifts to the man who has caught the highest number. If this were not done, the region would be impassable because beneath every stone and under every clod of earth there waits a scorpion.

C20. Modest gifts of food and drink

Aelian, Historical Miscellany *1.31–3*

A custom very carefully upheld by the Persians when the king drives to Persepolis, is that every single one of them brings a gift, according to his means. Since they work as farmers and toil on the land and live on what they grow they bring no ostentatious offering or showy gift, but rather oxen, sheep, or grain, or in some cases wine. As the king rides past on his way, these things are laid out by every man and are designated as gifts, and the king regards them so. Men who are even poorer than the farmers bring him milk, dates and cheese, also locally grown fresh fruit and first fruits.

Here is another Persian story: they say that a Persian named Sinaetes met Artaxerxes [II] . . . some distance from his country estate. Taken by surprise, he was distressed – anxious about the local custom as well as his veneration of the king. Not knowing what to do under the circumstance, fearing for his good reputation, and not wanting to be thought of dishonouring the king by not offering a gift, he went as fast as he could go to the river that flowed nearby (it was called the Cyrus [i.e. the Kura, which flows into the Caspian Sea]), bent down and scooped up some water with both his hands, and said, 'King Artaxerxes, may you reign for ever! At this time I honour you as best I can, within my power and given the circumstances, so that you will not pass by unhonoured by me: I show my respect to you with the water of Cyrus. When you arrive at your destination, I will bring to you from my home the best and finest things I have, and in that way too I shall honour you, and so that I shall not lose face with those others who have bestowed gifts on you'. Artaxerxes was pleased with this and answered, 'My lord, I am pleased to accept your gift and I regard it as one of the most valuable I have had; I declare it to be equal in value to all the others, because, first, water is the best thing of all, and second, because it bears the name Cyrus. You must present yourself to me when you come to my residence'. With this, he commanded the eunuchs to accept the man's gift, and they rushed over to catch the water from his hands into a gold cup. When the king reached his pavilion, he sent his [Persian] subject a Persian robe, a golden cup, and a thousand darics. The man who delivered the gifts was instructed to say, 'The king requests that your heart rejoices with this golden object since you gladdened his heart by not letting him pass by without honour or reverence; instead you showed as much loyalty as possible and now he wants you to draw water from the river with this cup'.

As Artaxerxes was travelling through Persia, Omises offered him a huge pomegranate on a winnowing fan. Its size so amazed the king that he asked, 'From what estate have you brought me this gift?' He replied, 'From my own farmstead'. [The king] was delighted and sent the man royal presents, adding, 'By Mithras, in my opinion this man, by taking such good care of things, could turn a small town into a great city'.

C21. The origin of the king's largess towards women

Ctesias F8d §43*

When the Persians were in difficulties because of the enemy's greater numbers they began to flee to the mountain's summit, where their women were. And the women pulled up their dresses and shouted, 'Where are you off to, you cowards! Do you want to crawl back in where you came from?' (It is because of this episode that the king of the Persians, when he reaches Pasargade, presents gold to the Persian women and distributes to each of them the equivalent of 20 Attic drachmas.)

C22. *Baziš*: small livestock

Elamite tablet, Persepolis, PF 2010 (extract)

30 billy-goats
10 kids
45 nanny-goats
Total: 86 goats [sic]
221 rams
8 lambs – total 229 males
339 ewes

2 lambs – total 341 females
Total: 570 sheep

C23. Gifts of abundance

Theopompus F263a/b

What city or people did not send embassies to the king? Is there anything of beauty or value, any product of the workshops that they did not bring as gifts to set before the king? There were many splendid textiles and cloths, purple and multi-coloured weavings, others white; many tents fitted out in gold and equipped with everything necessary. There were garments and expensive couches, and then drinking cups and bowls of chased silver and gold, some covered with precious gemstones, others beautifully and elegantly wrought. Above and beyond all this, there were myriads of arms – both Greek and barbarian, and team after team of horses, and animals fattened for sacrifice, and *medimnoi* of spices, numerous leather bags and sacks and huge quantities of [papyri?] and every other thing thought necessary for living – and so much salted meat that travellers approaching from some distance away mistook the huge piles for hills and mountains rising up before them.

C24. Figs from Athens

Deinon F12a = Athenaeus, Dinner of the Sophists *14.652b–c*

Now with respect to dried figs: those which came from Attica were always considered a great deal the best. Accordingly Deinon, in his *Persica*, says:

And they used to serve up at the royal table all the fruits which the earth produces as far as the king's dominions extend, being brought to him from every district as a sort of first-fruits. And Xerxes did not think it right for the kings either to eat or drink anything which came from any foreign country [that is, beyond the borders of the Empire]; and this idea gradually acquired the force of a law. For once, when one of the eunuchs brought the king, among the rest of the dishes at dessert, some Athenian dried figs, the king asked where they came from. And when he heard that they came from Athens, he forbade those who had bought them to buy them for him anymore, until it should be in his power to take them whenever he chose, and not to buy them. And it is said that the eunuch did this on purpose, with a view to remind him of the expedition against Attica.

C25. Cyrus' camp and tent

Xenophon, Cyropaedia 8.5.2–14

I will comment on how orderly the operation to pack up the baggage train was carried out, vast though it was, and I will note how quickly they reached the place they were heading for. For wherever the king encamps, all his entourage follow him onto the land with their tents, whether it be summer or winter. Cyrus . . . made the rule . . . that his tent should be pitched facing the east; and then he determined, first how far from the royal pavilion the spearmen of the guard should have their tent. Then he assigned a place on the right for the bakers, and on the left for the cooks, on the right for the horses, and the left for the remainder of the pack animals. Everyone knew his place – things were so well organised. . . . And when they came to repacking, everyone knew he had to pack what he used and others packed the animals, so that the baggage men all came at the same time to collect the things they were supposed to carry, and at the same time load up the animals with the baggage. The time required for taking a down a single tent is the same for all people.

The unpacking proceeds in the same way, and in order to be completely ready at the right time, everyone has a specific job to do. Therefore the time required to do any job is equitable.

Just as the servants in charge of provisions had a set place in the camp, so too the soldiers of every troop knew exactly where to encamp – and all this meant that everything was undertaken with no hint of friction. . . .

[Cyrus] himself first took up position in the middle of the camp in the belief that this was the most secure position. Then came his most trustworthy followers, just as he was accustomed to have them about him in his palace, and next to them in a circle he had his horsemen and charioteers. . . . And all (his) officers had banners over their tents so . . . [everyone] in the camp knew the location of the various officials.

C26. Tented luxury

Athenaeus, Dinner of the Sophists 2.48e–f

Artaxerxes bestowed on [Themistocles] a tent of extraordinary beauty and size, and a silver-footed bedstead; he also sent rich coverings and a slave to spread them. . . . The king [also] sent Entimus a silver-footed bed with its coverings, a tent with a richly embroidered canopy, a silver throne, a gilded parasol, 20 gold saucers sets with jewels, 100 saucers of silver and silver mixing bowls, 100 concubines, 100 slaves, and 6000 pieces of silver.

C27. Alexander commandeers the royal tent

Plutarch, Alexander 20.11–13

[Alexander] found his Macedonians carrying off the wealth from the camp of the Barbarians, and the wealth was of extraordinary quantity, although its owners had come to the battle in light marching order and had left most of their baggage in Damascus; he also found that his men had picked out for him the tent of Darius, which was full to bursting with dazzling table-ware and furniture, and many treasures. Straightway, then, Alexander took off his armour and went to the bath, saying: 'I shall go and wash off the sweat of battle in Darius' bath'. 'But no', said one of his companions, 'rather in that of Alexander; for the property of the conquered must belong to the conqueror, and be called his'. And when he saw the basins and pitchers and tubs and caskets, all of gold, and finely crafted, while the apartment was heady with fragrant smells of spices and unguents, and when he passed from this into a tent which was worthy of wonder for its size and height, and for the adornment of the couch and tables and the banquet prepared for him, he turned his eyes to his companions and said, 'This, it seems, is what it means to be a king'.

C28. Alexander's marriage tent

Chares F4 = Athenaeus, Dinner of the Sophists 538b–9a

When he overcame Darius [III], he concluded marriages of himself and of his friends besides, constructing 92 bridal chambers in the same place. The structure was large enough for 100 couches and in it every couch was adorned with nuptial coverings.... Moreover, the structure was decorated sumptuously and magnificently with expensive draperies and fine linens and underfoot with purple and crimson rugs interwoven with gold. To keep the tent firmly in place there were columns thirty-foot high, gilded and silvered and studded with jewels. The entire enclosure was surrounded with rich curtains having animal patterns interwoven in gold, their rods being overlaid with gold and silver. The perimeter of the courtyard measured four *stadia*.

C29. Alexander's royal tent and court

Polyaenus, Stratagems *4.3.24*

When deciding legal cases among the Macedonians or the Greeks, Alexander opted to have a modest and common courtroom. But when among the barbarians, he preferred to hold a brilliant court, suitable for a military general, astonishing the barbarians even by the room's appearance. When deciding cases among the Bactrians, Hycarnians, and Indians, he had a tent made as follows: the tent was large enough to hold 100 couches; fifty gold pillars supported it; embroidered gold canopies, stretched out above, covered the whole space. Inside the tent 500 Persian Apple Bearers stood first, dressed in purple and yellow clothing. After the Apple Bearers stood an equal number of archers in different clothing, for some wore flame-coloured robes, some dark blue, and some scarlet. In front of these stood the Macedonian Silver Shields – 500 of the tallest men. In the middle of the room stood the gold throne, on which Alexander sat to hold audience. Bodyguards stood on each side when the king heard cases.

In a circle around the tent stood the corps of elephants Alexander had equipped, and 1,000 Macedonians wearing Macedonian dress. Next to these were 500 Elamites dressed in purple, and after them, in a circle around them, 10,000 Persians, the handsomest and tallest of them, adorned with Persian decorations, and all carrying short swords. Such was the room Alexander used for court among the barbarians.

C30. The cost of feeding a peripatetic court

Herodotus, Histories *7.187*

No one could calculate the precise number of others who followed along [besides Xerxes' army] – the women who prepared the food, the concubines, the eunuchs, or of the pack animals and other beasts of burden and the Indian dogs; the number was so huge, there is no possible way to express it. To me it is no wonder that some rivers ran dry, but it is a wonder to me that there were enough provisions for so many tens of thousands of people. If my calculations are correct, every person received a daily ration of one quart of wheat, but no more than that, meaning that 110,340 *medimnoi* would be consumed every day, although I have not included in this calculation anything for the women, eunuchs, pack animals or dogs.

C31. Expenditure on food

Ctesias F39/Deinon F24 = Athenaeus, Dinner of the Sophists *4.145a*
But the Persian king, as Ctesias and Deinon (in their *Persica*) say, used
to dine in the company of 15,000 men, and 400 talents were spent on
the dinner. This amounts, in the coinage of Italy, to 2,400,000 *dinarii*,
which divided among 15,000 men make 160 *dinarii* per head.

C32. Food as tribute

Theopompus, Philippica *F298 = Athenaeus 4.145a*
Whenever the Great King visits any of his subjects, twenty or even
thirty talents are spent on his dinner; others spend even more. For, as
with tribute, the dinner has, for many years past, been imposed upon
all cities in proportion to their size of population.

C33. The king's dinner

Polyaenus, Stratagems *4.3.32*
In the palace of the Persian monarch Alexander read a bill of fare for
the king's dinner and supper that was engraved on a column of brass:
on which were also other regulations, which Cyrus had directed. It ran
thus:

Of fine wheat flour four hundred *artabae* (a Median *artaba* is an Attic
bushel). Of second-rate flour three hundred *artabae*, and of third-rate
flour the same: in the whole one thousand *artabae* of wheat flour for
supper. Of the finest barley flour two hundred *artabae*, of the second-
rate four hundred, and four hundred of the third-rate: in all one thousand *artabae* of barley flour. Of oatmeal two hundred *artabae*. Of paste
mixed for pastry of different kinds ten *artabae*. Of cardamom (cress)
chopped small, and finely sifted, and formed into a kind of *ptisan*
(treated barley?), ten *artabae*. Of mustard-seed the third of an *artabae*.
Male sheep four hundred. Oxen a hundred. Horses thirty. Fat geese
four hundred. Three hundred turtle-doves. Small birds of different
kinds six hundred. Lambs three hundred. Goslings, a hundred. Thirty
gazelles. Of fresh milk, ten *marises*. Of sour milk sweetened with whey,
ten *marises*. Of garlic, a talent's worth. Of strong onions half a talent's
worth. Of knot grass an *artaba*. Of the juice of benzoin (silphium
juice?) two *minae*. Of cumin, an *artaba*. Of benzoin a *talent* worth. Of
rich cider the fourth of an *artaba*. Of millet seed three *talents'* worth.

Of anise flowers three *minae*. Of coriander seed the third of an *artaba*. Of melon seed two *capises*. Of parsnips ten *artabae*. Of sweet wine five *marises*. . . . Of pickled capers five *marises*. Of salt ten *artabae*. Of Ethiopian cumin six *capises*. . . . Of dried anise thirty *minae*. Of parsley feed four *capises*. Oil of sesame ten *marises*. Cream five *marises*. Oil of cinnamon five *marises*. Oil of acanthus five *marises*. Oil of sweet almonds three *marises*. Of dried sweet almonds three *artabae*. Of wine five hundred *marises*. And if he was at Babylon or Susa, he had one half palm-wine, and the other half grape-wine.

Two hundred load of dry wood, and one hundred load of kindling. Of fluid honey a hundred square cakes, containing the weight of about ten *minae*.

When he was in Media he doled out the following:

Of false-saffron (seed) three *artabae*: of saffron two *minae*. This was for drink and dinner.

He also distributed in largesse five hundred *artabae* of fine wheat flour. Of fine barely flour a thousand *artabae*: and of other kinds of flour a thousand *artabae*. Of rice five hundred *artabae*. Of corn five hundred *marises*. Of corn for the horses twenty thousand *artabae*. Of straw ten thousand load; five thousand wagon loads. Of oil of sesame two hundred *marises*. Of vinegar a hundred *marises*. Of cardamom cresses chopped small thirty *artabae*.

All that is here enumerated was distributed to the soldiers; this is what the king consumes in a day: his lunch, dinner and in largess.

C34. The royal table and food distribution

Heraclides F2 = Athenaeus, Dinner of the Sophists *4.145*
What is referred to as 'The King's Dinner', [Heraclides] says, will seem ostentatious if one hears it described, but if examined carefully, it becomes clear that it has been carefully arranged with economic rigour, like the meals given by other Persian elites too. One thousand sacrificial animals are butchered for the king each day, including horses, camels, oxen, donkeys, and deer; the majority though are sheep and goats. Lots of birds are eaten too: ostriches (a very large creature), geese, and chickens. Each of the king's guests is served with a modest food portion and takes home the leftovers for food the following day. But the majority of the cooked meat and breadstuffs are taken out into the courtyard for the bodyguards and the household troops which the king supports. They break up the half eaten meat and bread there into portions, divided equally. Just as Greek mercenary soldiers get wages in

silver, so these men get food from the monarch to pay for their services. So too in the estates of other eminent Persians, all the food is placed together on a table and when the guests are through with eating, the steward in charge of the table gives some of the leftover food (mainly meat and bread) to individuals in the household, which is how they get their daily provisions. The most esteemed guests therefore visit the king for lunch only, for they ask to be excused from returning again so that they themselves can entertain their own dinner guests.

C35. *Paradeisoi* as royal storage units

Elamite tablet, Persepolis, PF 158
60 BAR [of] royal dates is to be kept [at] the *paradeisos* called Mishdukba, at the palm garden called Duhutrasa. It has been deposited to [the account of] Mishparma, chief of workers, who is responsible. Year 28.

C36. *Paradeisoi* of the satrap Pharnabazus at Daskyleion

Xenophon, Hellenika 4.1.15–16, 33–6
The place where the palace of Pharnabazus was located was surrounded by many large villages, all with abundant stores, and there were many wild animals found around about – some in enclosed *paradeisoi*, others in open areas. There was also a river teaming with fish flowing near by the palace. And besides all this there was winged game in plenty for those who knew how to get it.

C37. A *paradeisos* near Uruk?

Babylonian cuneiform text (Cuneiform Texts from Babylonian Tablets in the British Museum 22, no. 198)
Šapik-zeri has received 1 shekel of silver from Marduk-rimanni for the shift-workers of the *pardēsu* in the presence of Apla, son of Tabnea and Nadin, his third man (on the chariot). Month of Tebetu, 22nd day, 5th year of Cyrus, King of Babylon, King of all Lands.

C38. Cyrus generates a storm

Ctesias F8d* §41–2
And in some way or other Cyrus arrived at his ancestral home where he used to sleep when he was a young goatherd and he made a sacrifice

there. He found some flour and after setting cypress wood and laurel underneath it, he lit a fire by rubbing sticks together, just like a poor man who had fallen on hard times. And straightaway there was thunder and lightning on his right-hand side and Cyrus prostrated himself and auspicious birds settled on his home presaging that he would reach Pasargade.

After this, they prepared dinner and slept on the mountain. And the following day, trusting in the birds, they went down to fight the enemy who were already creeping up the mountain. And they fought bravely for a long time.

C39. Artaxerxes II controls the weather

Ctesias F45 §9

There is iron at the bottom of the spring from which Ctesias says two swords were fashioned and given to him; one was from the king the other from the king's mother Parysatis. He maintains that the sword if stuck into the ground can ward off clouds, hail and hurricanes, an act he claims to have personally witnessed the king perform on two occasions.

D1. Greek speculations on Persian moral and cultural decline and the idea of harem upbringing

Plato, Laws *694b–96a*

ATHENIAN: So how are we to explain the disaster under Cambyses, and the almost total recovery under Darius? To help our reconstruction of events, shall we have a go at guessing?

CLEINIAS: Yes, certainly this topic we've embarked on will help our investigation.

ATHENIAN: My guess about Cyrus, then, is that although, doubtless, he was a great commander and a loyal patriot, he never, even superficially, considered the problem of decent education. As for running his household, I'd say he never paid any attention to that at all!

CLEINIAS: And how should we interpret that kind of statement?

ATHENIAN: I mean, he probably spent his life after adolescence on campaign and handed over his children to the women to bring up. These women reared them from their formative years as though they were already 'Heaven's Chosen-Ones', and fawned over them accordingly. They wouldn't allow anyone to scold their god-sent darlings in anything, and they forced everyone to rhapsodize about whatever the child said or did. You can imagine the type of person they produced.

CLEINIAS: A great education it must have been, to judge from what you say!

ATHENIAN: It was a womanish education, conducted by the royal harem. The teachers of the children had recently come into considerable wealth, but they were left all alone, without men, because the army was preoccupied in the field.

CLEINIAS: That makes sense.

ATHENIAN: The children's father . . . just didn't notice that women and eunuchs had given his sons the education of a Mede [i.e. of great luxury] and that it had been debased by their so-called 'heaven-sent' status. That is why Cyrus' children turned out as children naturally do when their teachers have never corrected them. So when, on the death of Cyrus, they succeeded to their inheritance they were living in a riot of unrestrained luxury. . . . [But] Darius was no royal prince, and his upbringing had not encouraged him to self-indulgence. . . . But Darius was succeeded by Xerxes, whose education reverted to the old royal practice of pampering. . . . So Xerxes, being a product of this kind of tutoring, naturally had a career that resembled that of the unfortunate Cambyses, and ever since hardly any king of the Persians has been truly 'great' except in title and magnificence. I hold that the reason for this is not just bad luck, but the shocking life that children of despots and fantastically wealthy parents almost always lead.

D2. The honour of the king's wife

Plato, Alcibiades *1.121c*

The Persian king is so superior to us that no one has a suspicion that he could have been born of anybody but the king before him; therefore the king's wife has nothing to guard her except fear.

D3. 'Oriental' seclusion

Plutarch, Themistoces *26.5*

As a rule, the barbarian peoples are excessively jealous of their wives, and the Persians outdo all others in this respect. Not only their wives, but also the female slaves and concubines are rigorously watched, and no outside eye is allowed to see them. At home they live shut up in their own quarters, and if they have to take a journey, they do so in carriages hung around on all four sides with tented curtains and set upon a *harmamaxa.*

D4. Breaching etiquette

Plutarch, Artaxerxes *5.6*

What gratified the Persians the most was the sight of . . . Stateira's carriage, which always appeared with its curtains up, and thus permitted the women of the people to approach and greet the queen. This made her the beloved of the common folk.

D5. Keeping a distance from the royal concubines

Plutarch, Artaxerxes *27.1*

The barbarians are very jealous, especially about anything that pertains to love-lives, so that it is death for anyone merely approaching and touching a royal concubine, but even when somebody, during a journey, overtakes or crosses the path of the *harmamaxae* in which they are transported, he is punished with death.

D6. Concubines show deference to royal wives

Athenaeus, Dinner of the Sophists *13.556b*

Among the Persians the queen (Greek, *basileia*) tolerates an enormous number of concubines because the king rules his legal wife like a master rules his slaves, but also for another reason, as Deinon tells in his *Persica*: the queen is treated with deference by the concubines; in fact, they do obeisance in front of her (*proskynousi goun autēn*).

D7. Prestige of royal ladies

Plutarch, Artaxerxes *5.3*

Again, no one shared the table of the Persian king except his mother or his wedded wife, the wife seated below him, the mother above him.

D8. Dynastic politics and the king's mother

Ctesias F14 §39–43

Amestris was deeply vexed about [the death of] her son, Achaemenides, because she had not had vengeance on Inarus and the Greeks [who had killed him]. She asked for this from the King but he did not grant it. Then she asked for it from Megabyzus, who sent her away. Then, because she kept on bothering her son about it, she got her way. After five years she was given Inarus and the Greeks by the King. And she impaled him on three stakes; and she beheaded as many Greeks as she was able to get hold of – fifty in all. . . . Artarius sent a messenger to Megabyzus and advised him to make a treaty with the King. Megabyzus made it clear that he wanted to make a treaty too but did not want to go to the King – rather he would only do it on condition that he could stay in his own land. The King was told this and both the Paphlagonian eunuch, Artoxares, and Amestris, too, advised him to make a peace treaty quickly. And so Artarius himself was sent, as were Amytis, Megabyzus' wife, Artoxares . . . and Petesas, the father of Urisis and Spitamas. They made full assurances to Megabyzus with numerous speeches and oaths, but nevertheless had great difficulty persuading him to come to the King. When Megabyzus did return, the King finally sent him news that he was forgiven for the wrongs he had done. . . . The King went out hunting and was attacked by a lion. Megabyzus struck the beast with a javelin as it was flying through the air and killed it. And Artaxerxes was annoyed because Megabyzus had struck it before he could hit it himself. And he ordered that Megabyzus should be beheaded. His life was spared because of the entreaties of Amestris, Amytis and others, but he was forced to emigrate to a city by the Red Sea called Cyrta. The eunuch Artoxares was also banished to Armenia because he had often spoken to the King on Megabyzus' behalf.

Megabyzus spent five years in exile, then ran away disguised as a [leper]. . . . So he ran away and went home to Amytis and was barely recognized. And the King was reconciled with him thanks to Amestris and Amytis and made him a messmate [*homotrapezus*], as he had been before.

D9. Sexual shenanigans and punishment

Ctesias F14 §44

When [Princess] Amytis was ill – albeit only mildly and not seriously – Apollonides, the doctor from Cos, who was in love with her, told her that she would recover her health if she consorted with men because she had a disease of the womb. When his plan succeeded and he started sleeping with her, the woman began to waste away and he put an end to their sexual relations. So since she was dying she told her mother [Amestris] to take revenge on Apollonides. And her mother told King Artaxerxes everything: how Apollonides had been sleeping with her, how he then stopped after he had abused her and how her daughter had asked her to take revenge on him. And he let her mother deal with the situation herself. And she took Apollonides, bound him and punished him for two months. She then buried him alive and at this time Amytis died too.

D10. A ration of sheep to Queen Irtašduna

Elamite tablet, Persepolis, PF 6764

Say to Harrena the overseer of cattle, Parnaka spoke thus: 'Darius the king ordered me, saying, "100 sheep from my estate are to be issued to the *dukšiš* Irtašduna."' And now Parnaka says: 'As the king ordered me, so I am ordering you. Now you are to issue 100 sheep to the *dukšiš* Irtašduna, as was commanded by the king'.

First month, year 19.

Ansukka wrote [the text]; Maraza communicated the contents.

D11. The king commands that virgins be brought to the royal harem at Susa

Hebrew Bible, Esther 2:2-3, 8-9

Let beautiful young virgins be selected for the king! And let the king appoint officers in all the provinces of the kingdom to bring all these beautiful young virgins into the citadel of the city of Susa. Let them be given into the care of Hegai, the king's eunuch in charge of women, and let cosmetics be provided for them. . . . So when the king's order and his edict were proclaimed, and when many maidens were gathered in Susa the capital in custody of Hegai, Esther was also taken into the king's palace and put in custody of Hegai who had charge of the women. And the maiden pleased him and won his favour; and he quickly provided her with ornaments and her portion of food, and with seven maids chosen from the king's palace and advanced her and her maids to the best place in the harem.

D12. The 'second harem': concubinage as a royal 'finishing school'

Hebrew Bible, Esther 2:12-14

Now when the turn came for each maiden to go in to king Xerxes (Hebrew, Ahasuerus), after being twelve months under the regulations, since this was the regular period of their beautifying, six months with oil of myrrh and six months with spices and ointments for women – when the maiden went into the king in this way she was given whatever she desired to take with her from the harem into the king's palace. In the evening she went back and in the morning she came back to the second harem in custody of Shashgaz, the king's eunuch who was in charge of the concubines; she did not go into the king again, unless the king delighted in her and she was summoned by name.

D13. Captive Sidonian women enter the Babylonian palace of Artaxerxes III

Babylonian chronicle (Glassner 2004: 240 no. 28)
[Year] 14, Umasu, who is called Artaxerxes: In the month of Tashritu [i.e. 11 October–9 November 345 BCE], [were brought] the prisoners of war which the king took from Sidon to Babylon and Susa. That month, day 13, some o[f them] entered Babylon. Day 16, the remaining women prisoners which the king sent to Babylon, that day they entered the palace of the king.

D14. The capture of concubines as part of the royal household

Athenaeus, Dinner of the Sophists *13.608a*
Even princes were often aroused by flute-girls and harp-girls, as is made clear by Parmenio in the *Letter to Alexander* dispatched to him after the capture of Damascus, when he came into possession of Darius' household. Having caused an inventory to be made of the captured things, he writes also the following: 'I found 329 concubines of the king who played musical instruments; 46 men employed to weave garlands; 277 who cook fancy titbits; 29 caterers; 13 milk-dish makers; 17 bartenders; 70 men who strain wine; 14 perfumiers'.

D15. The lower status of concubines

Ctesias F13a
For when Cambyses learnt that Egyptian women were superior to others when it came to sexual intercourse, he sent to Amasis, the Egyptian King, asking for one of his daughters in marriage. But the King did not give him one of his own, since he suspected that she would have the status not of a wife but that of a concubine.

D16. Concubines as mothers of kings

Ctesias F15 § 47
Artaxerxes [I] had seventeen 'illegitimate' sons [i.e. sons by concubines], one of whom was Secyndianus whose mother was Alogyne,

a Babylonian. And there were also Ochus and Aristes, too, whose mother was Cosmartidene: also a Babylonian. And Ochus [Darius II] was later king, too. He had more children in addition to those already mentioned: Bagapaeus and Parysatis, whose mother was Andia, also a Babylonian. It is this Parysatis who was the mother of Artaxerxes [II] and Cyrus [the Younger]. His father, when he was alive, made Ochus Satrap of the Hycanians and gave him a wife, too, called Parysatis, who was the daughter of Artaxerxes [I] and was Ochus' own [half-] sister.

D17. The 360 concubines of Artaxerxes II

Plutarch, Artaxerxes *27*

[Artaxerxes] had ... no fewer than three hundred and sixty concubines, selected for their beauty.

D18. The 360 concubines of Darius III

Athenaeus, Dinner of the Sophists *13.557b*

For Darius, although engaged in a war which put his entire empire at stake, took round with him three hundred and sixty concubines, according to the account given by Dicaearchus in the third book of his *History of Greece*.

D19. The Persian concubines of Alexander the Great

Diodorus, Library *17.7.77*

[Alexander] added concubines to his retinue in the manner of Darius [III], no less than the days of the year in number, and outstanding in beauty as selected from all the women of Asia. Each night these paraded about the couch of the king so that he might select the one with whom he would lie that night.

E1. A concubine's song

*Ctesias F8d**

Towards evening, while drinking, [Astyages] summoned those of his concubines that were dancers and cithara players. And one of them sang the following words in her song: 'Although the lion had the wild boar in his power, he let him go into his lair; he has become mightier there and will give the lion much grief and despite being weaker will end up subduing one stronger'. As she sang, Astyages took her words as referring to him.

E2. Songs about Cyrus

Xenophon, Cyropaedia *1.2.1*
Cyrus is still celebrated to this day by the barbarians in story and in song as the most handsome and generous of men, devoted to wisdom yet ambitious; he endured all kinds of danger and faced hardship in order to gain renown.

E3. Angares, a Persian bard

Deinon F9 = Athenaeus, Dinner of the Sophists *14.633c–e*
After all, it was singers who foretold the courage of the first Cyrus and the war he would wage against Astyages. It was a time, says Deinon, when Cyrus had asked to visit Persia – earlier he had been in charge of the sceptre-bearers and the weapon-bearers – and then he left. Astyages held a banquet for his friends and a man named Angares, the most famous of all singers, was invited. He began to sing the usual songs and at the end he sang of how a mighty wild animal, more ferocious than a wild boar, had been set free in the marshes. If it came to dominate the area round about it would soon fight a multitude without any effort. When Astyages asked, 'What is this wild animal?' Angares replied, 'Cyrus the Persian'.

E4. A Persian love story

Athenaeus, Dinner of the Sophists *13.575*
We should not wonder that people have fallen in love at first sight, seeing that Chares of Mytilene in the tenth book of his *Histories of Alexander* asserts that many people having seen in a dream certain persons whom they had never seen before, fall in love with them; he tells it thus:

Hystaspes had a younger brother named Zariadres; the locals say that they were both the sons of Aphrodite and Adonis. Now Hystaspes was overlord of Media and the territory below it, whereas Zariadres ruled over the region above the Caspian gates, as far as the Tanais river. Now, Homartes, who was king of the Marathi, beyond the Tanais, had a daughter named Odatis; it is recorded in the histories that she saw Zariadres in a dream and became besotted with him, while the same passion for her overcame him in the same way. At any rate they continued to long for each other in the dreams of sleep. Now Odatis was the most beautiful woman in Asia, and Zariadres also was handsome of men. So Zariadres sent to Homartes in his eager desire to marry the girl, but Homartes would not agree to the match, because he lacked male heirs and wanted to give her to a man of his own court.

After a brief interval Homartes gathered together the princes of the kingdom and also his friends and relatives, and proceeded to celebrate a wedding without announcing to whom he intended to give his daughter. Well, when the drinking was at its height the father summoned Odatis to the symposium, and in the earshot of all the guests he said: 'My daughter Odatis, today we are celebrating your wedding. Look around, therefore, and after inspecting all the men take a gold cup, fill it with wine, and give it to the man to whom you wish to be married; for you shall be called his wife'. And the poor girl, after looking all around, turned away in tears, longing as she did to see Zariadres; for she had warned him that the nuptials were to be celebrated. He, meanwhile, was encamped at the Tanais river, which he crossed without the knowledge of his army, and accompanied solely by his charioteer he started off at night in his chariot, traversing a large territory for a distance of about 800 *stades*. And approaching the village in which they were celebrating the wedding he left the chariot-driver with the chariot in a certain place and proceeded on his way disguised in Scythian clothes. Passing into the court he spied Odatis standing in front of a table weeping while she slowly mixed the wine; and taking his place beside her he said, 'Odatis, I am here according to your desire, I, Zariadres'. And, noticing that the stranger was handsome and like the one she had seen in her dreams, she was overjoyed, and gave the cup to him; he, lifting her up, carried her off to his chariot and escaped with Odatis as his bride. Meanwhile the slaves and the serving-maids, conscious that this was a love affair, fell silent, and although the father commanded them to speak, they professed not to know where the young man had gone.

Now this love affair is very well-known among the barbarians who live in Asia and it is exceedingly popular; in fact they picture this story in their temples and palaces and even in private dwellings; and most princes bestow the name Odatis on their own daughters.

E5. Professional wrestlers at the court of Darius II

Pausanias, Description of Greece *6.5.7*
The bastard son of Artaxerxes [I], who ruled the Persians and seized the throne from his legitimate son, Sogdius, having become king sent messengers to Poulydamas, because he knew of his amazing feats, and persuaded him, with pledges of gifts, to come to Susa for Darius [II] to see him. At Susa Poulydamas challenged three of those Persians called the Immortals and fought alone against three of them together and slew them.

E6. Etiquette of the king's dinner

Heraclides F2 = Athenaeus, Dinner of the Sophists *4.146a*
Whenever the monarch throws a drinking party (as he often does), he is joined by a dozen people. After they have finished dinner, the king being alone by himself, and his guests separately, one of the eunuchs summons the men who are going to drink with him. Once they come in they drink in his presence, although not the same wine; they do so sitting on the floor, whereas he lies on a gold-footed couch. After they have become very drunk, they leave. The king usually lunches and dines alone, but every now and then his wife and some of his sons eat with him.

E7. The pleasure of a royal banquet

Hebrew Bible, Esther 1:3–9
In the third year of his reign [Xerxes] gave a banquet for all the officials and courtiers – the administrators of Persia and Media, the nobles and the governors of the provinces in his service. For no fewer than 180 days he displayed the vast riches of his kingdom and the splendid glory of his majesty. At the end of this period, the king gave a banquet for seven days in the court of the king's palace garden for all the people who lived in the city of Susa, high and low alike. [There were hangings of] white cotton and blue wool, caught up with cords of fine linen and purple wool to silver rods and alabaster columns; and there were couches of gold and silver on a pavement of marble, alabaster and mother-of-pearl, and mosaics. The drinking-ware was golden beakers, beakers of varied design. And there was royal wine in abundance as befits a king. And the rule for the drinking was, 'No restrictions!' For the king had given orders to every palace servant to comply with each

man's wishes. In addition, Queen Vashti gave a banquet for women in
the royal palace of king Xerxes.

E8. Frustrations of hunting in a *paradeisos*

Xenophon, Cyropaedia *1.4.5, 11, 14–15*

[Cyrus] before too long had exhausted the supply of animals in the
park by hunting, shooting, and killing them, so that Astyages could
no longer supply animals quickly enough for him. . . . [Cyrus said to
Astyages], 'How foolish it is to hunt game in a park. It seems to me that
it was like hunting trussed-up game: for in the first place they were in
a confined space, and moreover, they were lean and mangy; one was
lame, another maimed. But the animals out on the mountains and
plains – how fine they look: big and sleek!'...

Wishing to bring [Cyrus] joy Astyages took him out hunting; he
had gathered together a group of boys and a large party of men on foot
and horseback, and after he had driven the wild animals out into the
country best suited for riding, he instituted a great hunt. And as he was
to be present himself, he issued a royal command that no one should
throw a spear before Cyrus had had his fill of the chase. But Cyrus did
not permit this interference, saying, 'Grandfather, if you want me to
enjoy the hunt then let all my comrades give chase and try to outdo
one another, each doing his very best!' And so Astyages acquiesced
and from his position he watched them rushing upon their animal
foes, vying eagerly with each other in giving chase and throwing their
spears. He was delighted to see that Cyrus was unable to keep silent
from delight, but like a well-bred hound, he hollered when an animal
came close and urged on each of his companions by name. And the
king was delighted to see him laugh at one and laud another without
the least bit of jealousy. At long last, Astyages returned home with a
quantity of game and he was so happy with the hunt that, from thereon
in, whenever possible he went out with Cyrus and took along with him
many others, including the boys, for Cyrus' sake.

E9. The splendour of the royal chase

Chariton, Callirhoe *6.4*

A magnificent hunt was announced. Horsemen rode out, splendidly
attired – Persian courtiers and the elite of the army. Every one of
them was a sight to behold, but the most impressive was the king
himself; he was riding a powerful and striking Nisaean horse whose

trappings – bit, cheekpieces, frontlet, breastplate – were all of gold; he was wearing a mantle of Tyrian purple made from Babylonian cloth and his *tiara* was the colour of hyacinths; he had a sword at his waist and carried two spears, and slung over his shoulder was a bow and quiver of the finest Chinese craftsmanship. He was an impressive sight in the saddle. . . . Soon the mountains were full of people shouting and running, dogs barking, horses neighing, game fleeing. The excitement and the noise they were making would have driven Love himself out of his senses; delight was mixed with anguish; joy with fear, danger with enjoyment.

E10. Royal Egyptian lion hunts

Egyptian hieroglyphic text, lion scarab of Amenhotep III (Breasted 1906: vol. II, p. 347)

Amenhotep, ruler of Thebes, given life, (and) the Great Royal Wife, Tiy, who lives. Statement of lions which his majesty brought down with his own arrows from year 1 to year 10: fierce lions: 102.

E11. Royal Assyrian lion hunts

Akkadian inscriptions carved onto hunting reliefs from Nineveh (Luckenbill 1989: 391–2)

I am Ashurbanipal, king of the universe, king of Assyria. . . . The lions which I slew – the terrible bow of Ishtar, lady of battle, I aimed upon them. I brought an offering, I poured out wine over them.

I am Ashurbanipal, king of the universe, king of Assyria. For my pleasure, on foot I seized a fierce lion by the tips of his ears. . . . I pierced his body with the lance of my hands.

I, Ashurbanipal, king of the universe, king of Assyria, in my kingly sport I seized a lion by the end of his tail . . . I smashed his skull with the club of my hand.

I, Ashurbanipal, king of the universe, king of Assyria, in my kingly sport, they let a lion of the plain out of his cage and on foot with my spear shaft I . . . [] . . . but did not end his life. . . . I stabbed him later with my iron girdle dagger and he laid down his life. . . .

I, Ashurbanipal, king of the universe, king of Assyria . . . I went forth. In an open space in the plain, fierce lions, dreadful children of the mountains, came out. They surrounded the chariot, my royal vehicle . . . I shattered the might of those lions. . . .

E12. Alexander kills a lion

Quintus Curtius Rufus, History of Alexander *8.1.14–16*

A lion of remarkable size rushed forward to pounce on [Alexander] himself. Lysimachus . . . happened to be standing by Alexander's side and had lifted his hunting spear to take aim at the animal when the king pushed him to one side and told him to get out of the way, adding that he was as capable as Lysimachus of killing a lion single-handed. . . . He not only took on the animal but he dispatched it with a single stab. . . . After 4,000 animals had been slain, then Alexander feasted with the entire army in the wood.

E13. Artaxerxes I's new hunting etiquette

Plutarch, Moralia *173d*

[Artaxerxes I] was the first to pass a command saying that his hunting companions might, if they were able, cast their spears without waiting for him to throw first.

E14. Rivalry and revenge: Xerxes' women

Herodotus, Histories *9.109–11*

Amestris, Xerxes' wife, gave him a long robe of well-woven colours; it was very beautiful and she had created it with her own hands. Very pleased with it, he put it on and, still wearing it, went to visit Artaÿnte – who pleased him no less, with the result that he told her to ask for anything she desire as a reward for her favours, and he promised to grant it. Doomed to come to a bad end (with the rest of her family), Artaÿnte asked if His Majesty really meant what he said and that she could ask for whatever she wished and Xerxes, never suspecting what her request would be, pledged his word to do so. Thereupon she boldly demanded the robe. Xerxes did all he could to get out of his promise because he was afraid of Amestris, who had already guessed what was going on, and would, he feared, have all her suspicions confirmed. He offered her cities, unlimited gold, an army of her own (a very Persian gift) – but all to no effect. Nothing would do for her but the robe. So he gave it to her and she, delighted, wore it, and gloried in wearing it. Soon afterwards Amestris discovered that Artaÿnte had the robe, but her anger was not directed against her. On the contrary, Amestris thought that the girl's mother, Masistes' wife, was the person responsible for all the trouble and therefore she plotted her destruction. Amestris waited for the day when her husband gave his Royal Supper – a once-a-year occasion, held on the king's birthday. . . . It is the one time of the year when the king anoints his head and bestows gifts on the Persians. When, then, the day of the supper arrived, she asked Xerxes for a present: Masistes' wife. Fully understanding the reason for her request, Xerxes was horrified, not just at the prospect of handing over his brother's wife, but also because he knew that she was completely innocent. But Amestris persisted – moreover, the law of the Royal Supper stated that on that day no one should be refused a request. So, at last, and much against his will, Xerxes was forced to consent. Then, having told his wife to do with the woman as she pleased, he sent for his brother. 'Masistes', he said, 'you are my brother and the son of Darius; moreover, you are a good man. Do not live with your wife any longer – I will give to you instead the hand of my own daughter. Marry her and repudiate your present wife – I do not approve of you keeping her'.

Masistes replied in astonishment, 'My lord, this is a strange suggestion! Why would you tell me to repudiate my wife who is the mother of grown up sons and daughters – one of whom [Artaÿnte] married your own son. Besides, my wife is everything I could wish for, so why should I marry your daughter? Sire, no, I will do neither of these things, despite the pride I feel at being thought worthy of your daughter. I beg you, do not force this request upon me, but allow me to live peacefully with my wife. You will find another man as worthy as I for your daughter's hand'. This reply angered Xerxes and he shouted, 'Very well! I tell you now Masistes the damage you have done for yourself. I will no longer offer you my daughter. Thus may you learn to accept a proffered gift'. 'Master', replied Masistes, 'you have not killed me yet!' And without saying another word he left the room.

In the meantime, while Xerxes and Masistes were talking, Amestris sent for soldiers from the royal bodyguard and had Masistes' wife dreadfully mutilated: her breasts, nose, ears, and lips were cut off and thrown to the dogs; then her tongue was torn out and, in this dire state, she was sent home. Masistes, who as yet knew nothing of this, suspected mischief of some sort and quickly returned home; when he saw his wife's gruesome mutilations, he took immediate council with his sons and they all, with certain other friends, set off for Bactria, with the aim of stirring up rebellion and of bringing great harm to the king.

E15. Bad feelings among the royal ladies

Deinon F15a = Plutarch, Artaxerxes 6.6

Therefore Parysatis hated Stateira, and being naturally of a harsh temper and savage in her wrath and resentment, she plotted to kill her.

E16. Poisoning the king's wife

Ctesias F29b/Deinon F15b = Plutarch, Artaxerxes 19

And so Parysatis, who had felt hatred and jealousy towards Stateira from the very beginning, seeing that her own influence with the king stemmed from the respect and esteem he felt for her, but that Stateira's influence – based on love and trust – was steadfast and secure, plotted against her, playing for what in her opinion were the highest possible stakes. She had a trusted servant called Gigis who held great influence with her: Deinon says that she helped in the poisoning, Ctesias only that she was unwillingly in on the secret. Ctesias says the man who procured the poison was called Belitaras, whereas Deinon says it was Melantas. After their former suspicion of each other and their differences, although they had begun to frequent the same places again and to dine together, their mutual fear and caution nevertheless led them to eat the same food as each other served on the same dishes.

The Persians have a small bird, every part of which can be eaten since it is entirely full of fat inside – and for this reason they think that this animal feeds on air and dew. It is called a *rhyntaces*. Ctesias says that Parysatis cut a bird of this kind in two with a small knife smeared with poison on one side, thus wiping the poison off on just one part of the bird. And she put the undefiled, clean part in her mouth and ate it, but gave the poisoned half to Stateira. Deinon says that it was not Parysatis but Melantas who did the cutting with the knife and gave the poisoned meat to Stateira.

And so this woman died in convulsions and in considerable agony. And she was herself conscious of the evil that had befallen her and made her suspicions about his mother known to the King, who was aware of his mother's brutal nature and implacability.

For this reason he set out in search of his mother's servants and attendants at table, arrested them and tortured them. Parysatis kept Gigis at home with her for a long time and she would not surrender her when the King asked, but when Gigis later asked for leave to go home at night, the King got wind of this, set an ambush, seized her and condemned her to death. In Persia the law prescribes that poisoners be killed in the following way: there is a broad stone on which they place the poisoners' heads and with another stone they pound and crush until their face and head are mashed to a pulp. So it was like this that Gigis died and Artaxerxes neither reproached nor harmed Parysatis in any other way, but sent her to Babylon in accordance with her wishes, saying that so long as she lived, she would not see Babylon again. And so this was the state of affairs in the King's household.

E17. Poison at the Persian court

Xenophon, Cyropaedia *8.8.14*

Whereas in the past the children [at court] would learn about the powers of plants which grew naturally in the earth in order to make use of the helpful ones and avoid the ones which might do harm, today it appears that they are only taught about the ones that do the most harm. In any event, nowhere are so many men killed or ruined because of poisonous drugs [than at the Persian court].

E18. Cup-bearer and taster

Xenophon, Cyropaedia *1.3.8, 10*

Now, it is a well-known fact that the king's cupbearer, when they proffer the cup, draw off some of it with a ladle, pour it into their left hand and swallow it down – so that if they should put poison in it, they will not benefit from it. . . .

Astyages said jokingly, 'Cyrus, since you mimicked Sakas [the cup-bearer] in all other ways, why didn't you swallow some of the wine?'

'By God!', he responded, 'Because I was afraid that there might have been poison in the cup – after all, when you entertained your friends on your birthday, I quickly realized that he had added poison for you all'.

E19. Exclusive Indian poison at the Persian court

Ctesias F45m = Aelian, History of Animals *4: 41*

There is a species of very small Indian birds which build their nests both within the high rocks and also the so-called 'soft cliffs'. The little bird is the size of a partridge egg and I believe its colour is orange. In their language the Indians call it *Dikairon*, but the Greeks, as I understand it, call it *Dikaion*. If someone should swallow a speck of its dung placed in a drink, he would die by the evening. The death is like sleep – very agreeable and free of pain – the sort the poets like to call 'limb-relaxing' and 'easy'. This death would bring freedom from pain and therefore is most pleasing for those in need of it. The Indians go to enormous lengths to get it, for they think of it as the source of forgetfulness of all our troubles. The Indians also include this substance among their most precious tribute for the Persian king who receives it as a gift revered above all others; he hoards it as a remedy and antidote for incurable illness – should he contract one. No one else in Persia owns this substance except the king himself and his mother.

E20. Poison and the death of Alexander

Arrian, Anabasis of Alexander *7.27.1–2*
I am aware of many other versions of Alexander's death . . . for example, that Antipatros sent Alexander a drug that caused his death . . . and given to Alexander by Iollas . . ., since Iollas was a royal wine-pourer.

E21. A eunuch king-maker

Diodorus, Library *17.5.3–5*
Ochus [Artaxerxes III] ruled the Persians and oppressed his subjects cruelly and harshly. Since his savage nature made him hated, the chiliarch Bagoas, a eunuch in physical fact and an insubordinate reprobate in temperament, killed him by poison which was administered by a certain physician; he placed upon the throne the youngest of [Ochus'] sons, Arses [Artaxerxes IV]. He likewise murdered the brothers of the new king, who were barely of age, in order that the young man might be isolated and therefore obedient to his control. But the young king let it be known that he was offended at Bagoas' previous contemptible behaviour and that he was prepared to punish him for his crimes, so Bagoas anticipated his intentions and killed Arses and his children also while he was still in the third year of his reign. The royal house was thus extinguished, and there was no one in the direct line of descent to claim the throne. Instead Bagoas selected a certain Darius, a member of the court circle, and secured the throne for him [as Darius III]. He was the son of Arsanes, and grandson of that Ostanes who was a brother of Artaxerxes [II], who had been king.

E22. Succession struggles: the 'Dynastic Prophecy'

Akkadian text, probably from Babylon (Grayson 1975)
For two years [he will exercise kingship].
That king a eunuch [will murder].

A certain prince [. . .]
will set out and [seize] the thr[one]
Five years [he will exercise] king[ship]
Troops of the land of Hani [. . .]
will set out a[nd?]./-ship?\ th[ey will? . . .]

E23. A Babylonian account of Xerxes' assassination

The Babylonian Eclipse Lists *(BM 32234; Stolper 1988: 196–7)*
. . . in 18 [. . .]; 40 (duration) of onset, to[tality and clearing up], the
'garment of the sky' was present; (the moon) was eclipsed in the area
of the rear group of four stars of Sagittarius. (There was an) intercalary
month Ulul. On the fourteenth (?) day of the month Ab [i.e. 5th June
465 BC], Xerxes – his son murdered him.

E24. Accounts of the death of Xerxes

Ctesias F13 §33–4; Ctesias F13b* = Aelian, Historical Miscellany
13.3
[The eunuch] Artapanus, who held a lot of influence with Xerxes,
plotted with the eunuch Spamitres, who also held a lot of influence,
to kill Xerxes. And they did kill him. And they persuaded his son,
Artaxerxes, that his other son, [Crown Prince] Darius had killed him.
Artaxerxes arrived at Darius' house, brought there by Artapanus.
Darius shouted a good deal and refuted all claims that he was his
father's murderer: he was killed. Artaxerxes [I] became king, thanks to
Artapanus' exertions.
. . . For after gathering 700,000 men to fight the Greeks [Xerxes]
came off badly, and then after returning he died in the most shameful way a man can die, by having his throat cut by his son in bed at
night.

E25. Patricide and regicide: the death of Artaxerxes II

Justin, Epitome of the Philippic History of Pompeius Trogus
10.1.4–3.1
But Darius, after such an extraordinary proof of his father's affection,
conceived the design of killing him. He would have been bad enough, if
he had meditated the murder alone, but he became so much the worse,
by enticing fifty of his brothers to participate in his crime – making
them parricides too. It was miraculous that, among so many involved,

the assassination should not only have been plotted, but concealed, and that of fifty children there was not one who respected their father's dignity, or had reverence for an old man, or gratitude for paternal kindness; nothing could deter them from so horrible a purpose. Was the name of 'father' so cheap among so many sons? With such a retinue Artaxerxes should have been protected from all his foes; instead, surrounded by his treacherous sons, he was in less danger from his enemies than from his sons.

The motive of the anticipated parricide was even more atrocious than the crime itself; for after Cyrus [the Younger] was killed in the war against his brother ..., Artaxerxes [II] had married Aspasia, the concubine of Cyrus; and Darius had required that his father should hand her over to him just as he had handed him the crown. Artaxerxes, typically indulging his children, said at first that he would do so, but afterwards he changed his mind, and in order to plausibly refuse what he had thoughtlessly promised, he made her a priestess of the sun, an office which obliged her to life-long chastity. The young Darius, being incensed at this, broke into an outburst of quarrels with his father, and subsequently entered into this conspiracy with his brothers. But while he was plotting his father's destruction, he was discovered and apprehended with his accomplices, and paid the penalty of his crime to the gods who avenge paternal authority. The wives and children of all the conspirators were also put to death, to eliminate every last trace of this wickedness. Soon after this Artaxerxes died of a malady brought on by grief, having been more successful as a king than as a father.

The kingdom now passed to Ochus [Artaxerxes III] who, fearing a similar conspiracy, filled the palace with his family's blood and with the slaughter of his most prominent courtiers. Nothing moved him to compassion – not family-bonds, not sex, not age. He simply did not want to be thought weaker than his murderous brothers.

E26. Court conspiracy: the plot and execution of Prince Darius

Plutarch, Artaxerxes 28–9

But Artaxerxes [II], being now advanced in years, saw that his sons were forming rival parties among his friends and chief courtiers with reference to the royal succession. For the conservatives thought it right that, as he himself had received the royal power by virtue of seniority, so he should leave the throne to Darius. But his youngest son, Ochus, who was of an impetuous and aggressive nature, not only had many adherents at court, but hoped for most success in winning over his father through the aid of [his sister] Atossa. For he sought to gain Atossa's favour by promising that she should be his wife and share the throne with him after the death of their father. And there was a report that even while his father was alive Ochus had secret sexual relations with Atossa. But Artaxerxes was ignorant of this; and needing to shatter for once and for all Ochus' ambitions (so that he might not venture upon the same course as Cyrus [the Younger] and so involve the kingdom again in wars and contests), he proclaimed Darius, then fifty years of age, his successor to the throne, and gave him permission to wear the upright *kitanis*, as the *tiara* was called.

Now, there was a custom among the Persians that the one appointed to the royal succession should ask a favour, and that the one who appointed him should give whatever was asked, if it was within his power. Accordingly, Darius asked for Aspasia, who had been the special favourite of Cyrus [the Younger], and was then a concubine of the king. . . . He thereby offended his father; for the barbarians are very jealous, especially about anything that pertains to love-lives, so that it is death for anyone merely approaching and touching a royal concubine. . . . And yet there was Atossa, whom the king passionately loved and had made his wife. . . . However . . . the king gave her to Darius under constraint of the custom, but a little while after he had given her, he took her back again and appointed her a priestess of Artemis of Ecbatana, who bears the name of Anaitis [Anahita] in order that she might remain chaste for the rest of her life, thinking that in this way he would inflict a punishment upon his son. . . . Darius' resentment knew no bounds, partly because he was deeply stirred by his passion for Aspasia, and because he thought that he had been insulted and mocked by his father.

And now Teribazus, who became aware of the prince's feelings, sought to embitter him still more . . . and was forever telling him that the upright *tiara* was of no use to those who did not seek by their own efforts to stand upright in affairs of state, and that he was very foolish if, when his brother was insinuating himself into affairs of state by way of the harem, and his father was of a nature so fickle and insecure, he could suppose that the succession to the throne was securely his. . . . Accordingly, Darius put himself in the hands of Teribazus and soon, when many people were involved in the conspiracy, a eunuch told the king about the plot, having accurate knowledge that the conspirators had resolved to enter the king's chamber by night and kill him in his bed. When Artaxerxes heard the eunuch's story, he ... instructed the eunuch to watch the conspirators closely; meanwhile he himself cut away the wall of his chamber behind the bed, put a doorway there, and covered the door with a tapestry. Then, when the appointed hour was at hand and the eunuch told him the exact time, he went to bed and did not rise from it until he saw the faces of his assailants and recognised each man clearly. But when he saw them advancing upon him with drawn swords, he quickly drew aside the tapestry, retired into the inner chamber, closed the door with a slam, and raised a cry.

The murderers, accordingly, having been seen by the king, and having accomplished nothing, fled back through the door by which they had come, and told Teribazus and his friends to be off since their plot was known. The rest, then, were dispersed and fled; but Teribazus slew many of the king's guards as they sought to arrest him, and at last was smitten by a spear at long range, and fell. Darius, together with his children, was brought to the king, who handed him over to the royal judges for trial.

The king was not present in person at the trial, but others brought in the indictment. However, the king ordered clerks to take down in writing the opinion of each judge and bring them all to him. All the judges were of one opinion and condemned Darius to death, whereupon the servants of the king seized him and led him away into a chamber nearby, whither the executioner was summoned. The executioner came with a sharp knife in his hand (the type used for cutting off the heads of condemned persons) but when he saw Darius, he was confused and retired towards the door with averted gaze, declaring that he could not and would not take the life of a king. But since the judges outside the door threatened and commanded him, he turned back, and with one hand clutching Darius by the hair, dragged him to the ground, and cut off his head with the knife.

Some say, however, that the trial was held in the presence of the king, and that Darius, when he was overwhelmed by proof, fell upon his face and begged and sued for mercy; but Artaxerxes rose up in anger, drew his scimitar, and smote him till he had killed him; then, going forth into court, he made obeisance to the sun and said. 'Depart in joy and peace, Persians, and say to all you meet that those who have contrived impious and unlawful things have been punished by great Orosmasdes [Ahuramazda]'.

E27. Fratricide at court

Plutarch, Artaxerxes *30*

And now Ochus was drunk with the hopes which [his sister] Atossa inspired in him, but he was still afraid of Ariaspes, the only legitimate son of the king still alive, and also of Arsames of his father's illegitimate sons [i.e. born to concubines]. For Ariaspes . . . was deemed by the Persians to be worthy of the crown; Arsames, however, was thought to have wisdom, and the fact that he was especially loved by his father was not unknown to Ochus. Accordingly, he plotted against the lives of both, and being at once devious and bloody-minded, he brought the cruelty of his nature into play against Arsames, but his villainy and craft against Ariaspes. For he secretly sent to Ariaspes the eunuchs and friends of the king, who constantly brought him word . . . that his father had decided to put him to a cruel and shameful death. Since they pretended that these . . . reports of theirs were secrets of state…, they so terrified the prince . . . that he drank a deadly poison which he had prepared, and thus took his own life. When the king was informed of the manner of his death, he lamented the loss of his son but suspected what had caused his death, but being unable by reason of his age to search out and convict the guilty one, he began to hold Arsames in greater esteem than ever before, and clearly made him his chief support and confidant. This did not stop Ochus's ambitions and he commanded Arpates, a son of Teribazus, to kill the prince. Now Artaxerxes, by reason of his age, was already hovering between life and death; and when the sad fate of Arsames came to his ears, he could not hold out even a little while, but straightway died of grief and despair.

F1

Doorjamb from the Tripylon (Council Hall) at Persepolis depicting the Great King and two courtiers (represented on a smaller scale than the king) in procession. All wear the impressive 'court robe' and have well set coiffures; the Great King's beard reaches down to his chest. The courtier at the rear holds a fly whisk and folded cloth while the other courtier holds a long-handled parasol above the monarch's head. Ahuramazda, sitting in a winged disk, is located above the scene. (Author's photograph.)

F2

Mohammad Reza Shah Pahlavi, Iran's last monarch, crowns himself
with a Sasanian-style crown during his coronation ceremony held
at the Golestan Palace in Tehran in October 1967. (Original Iranian
newspaper clipping in the author's collection.)

F3

Re-creation of the Treasury relief, Persepolis. On a raised platform, Darius I (or possibly Xerxes) is seated on his high-backed lion-legged throne, his feet resting upon a footstool. He is accompanied by the crown prince, courtiers, and guards. Incense burners in front of the king purify and sweeten the air and a canopy decorated with a winged disc, striding lions, and a tassel boarder demarcates the royal ceremonial space. (Courtesy of Persepolis 3d.com.)

F4

A tiny lapis lazuli head of an Achaemenid courtier from Persepolis, now in the National Museum in Tehran. The head may represent a young beardless man (a prince, perhaps), a eunuch, or even a woman. The face is full and fleshy and the nose and lips are delicately sculpted. The eyes and eyebrows are stylistically but elegantly rendered and show kohl make-up lines. The short, full, curly hairstyle (shared by men and women) is set off by a tall crenulated crown. (Author's photograph.)

F5

Darius I's relief and inscription at Bisitun. The king, bow in one hand, raises his other in adoration of Ahuramazda, who hovers above him. Rebel leaders, chained and fettered, are led before the king (he steps upon the belly of Gaumata). Darius is accompanied by courtiers holding weapons as emblems of their courtly offices. (Author's photograph.)

F6

The Elamite king Anubanini, from a rock relief at Sar-i Pol, Luristan. The monarch, bow in one hand, axe in the other, stands in front of the warrior-goddess Ishtar and receives the bound and naked bodies of prisoners. He places his sandaled foot on the belly of a fallen captive.

F7

An Achaemenid king (possibly Xerxes or Artaxerxes I) in his role as 'Persian hero' kills an Asiatic lion, a symbol of chaos and disorder, by stabbing it in the belly. The Great King wears the court robe but turns it into a practical garment for slaughter by girding the skirt and hitching it into his belt, and freeing his arms from the sleeve-like overhang. From Persepolis. (Author's photograph.)

F8

Detail of a glazed brick wall depicting an Immortal guard with a quiver and bow slung over his shoulder; from Susa, now in the Louvre, Paris. The spear-bearing soldier wears a court robe decorated with appliqué rosettes as a kind of 'dress uniform' or livery. Fine jewellery decorates his wrists and a twisted headband adorns his well curled hair. (Author's photograph.)

F9

A eunuch or beardless courtier from the palace of Darius, Persepolis. The elegant courtier, his hair dressed into a low chignon, and his ears pierced with hoop earrings, holds a folded cloth or towel and a small bottle probably containing perfume or sweet-smelling oil. It is possible that we have here a representation of one of the Great King's personal body servants. (Author's photograph.)

F10

Egyptianising monumental statue of Darius I from Susa (originally one of a pair) now in the National Museum in Tehran. The headless statue depicts Darius wearing the court robe, the belt of which is inscribed in Egyptian hieroglyphics and Old Persian cuneiform and pronounces the king's titles. (Author's photograph.)

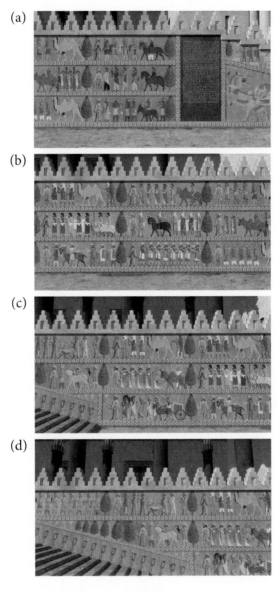

F11

(a–d) Reconstructed details of the Apadana north staircase, Persepolis, depicting tribute-bearers from across the Empire bringing gifts of textiles, precious metals, jewellery, and livestock to the Great King. Note the presence of the military and courtiers, and the image of a bull being attacked by a lion, which is found repeatedly in Achaemenid art. (Courtesy of Persepolis 3d.com.)

F12

The peoples of the Empire support the king's throne. East doorjamb of the eastern doorway of the southern wall of the Hall of a Hundred Columns, Persepolis. The king is seated on a throne beneath a baldaquin (above which hovers Ahuramazda) and is attended by a courtier with a fly whisk. The throne is set on a giant *takht* or platform. (Line drawing after Curtis and Tallis 2005: 76.)

F13

Achaemenid courtier in the 'riding habit' composed of sleeved tunic, trousers, long-sleeved coat draped over the shoulders, soft shoes or boots, and a felt cap. (Adapted from the Apadana east frieze by the author.)

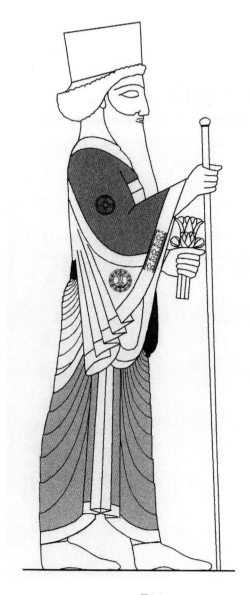

F14

Line drawing of an Achaemenid king wearing the court robe. The artist created a schematic two-dimensional rendering of the garment which suggests constructed sleeves but this is a fallacy. Bands of colour are represented by the shading, as are details of the embroidery, woven patterns, or appliqué decoration. The king wears a plain cylindrical crown and carries a long sceptre and lotus blossom. (After Rehm 2006.)

F15

Reconstruction of Xerxes' Gate of All Nations. This monumental gateway into the Persepolis palace complex was flanked by two vast bull figures. This particular animal appears many times at Persepolis, in the form of wall reliefs and column capitals. Representing strength and vitality, at Xerxes' Gate they had an apotropaic function. (Courtesy of Persepolis 3d.com.)

F16

(a) Reconstructed view of the north elevation of the Apadana at Persepolis as seen from the courtyard. Note the bull capitals supporting the portico and the scenes of tribute bearers and royal audience decorating the multiple staircases. (Courtesy of Persepolis 3d.com.)

(b) The north staircase and portico of the Apadana. The staircase reliefs depict tribute-bearers, royal chariots, lions, and bulls and, in the centre panel, an audience scene. (Courtesy of Persepolis 3d.com.)

F17

Throne-bearers from across the Empire support Darius I as he worships Ahuramazda. The Great King, bow in hand, stands on a raised platform in front of a fire altar. The god emerges from a winged disc and proffers Darius a ring – possibly symbolising the kingship itself. Detail from the façade of the tomb of Darius I at Naqš-i Rustam. (Author's photograph.)

F18

Darius I's name seal. The king hunts lions from a chariot in a date-palm grove while Ahuramazda hovers above. (Line drawing based on BM ANE 891232; Curtis and Tallis 2005: no. 398).

F19

A small part of the extensive L-shaped harem block at the southern end of the Persepolis platform as seen from Xerxes' palace, above. The staircase (one of two) leads directly from the palace to the harem. The regularly proportioned pillared rooms (with some surviving stone column bases) and antechambers are clear to see, as are two long corridors which run the entire length of the building. (Author's photograph.)

F20

A female audience scene. An enthroned veiled female is attended by a young girl carrying a bird and a more mature crowned and veiled woman standing behind an incense burner. While this possibly represents a scene of veneration towards the goddess Anahita, the many details which correspond to the standard (male) royal audience scene (F3) make a court setting for this scene more likely. (Line drawing of a cylinder seal, Louvre AO 22359, after Brosius 2010a: fig. 13.9; and Lerner 2010: fig. 14.2.)

F21

The cruciform-shaped tombs of several successive Achaemenid Great Kings are carved high into a rock face at Naqš-i Rustam (ancient Nupistaš), near Persepolis. Located here are the tombs of Darius I, Xerxes I, Artaxerxes I, and Darius II. It is possible that in front of the Achaemenid tombs there was a *paradeisos*, since one of the Persepolis texts refers to a park at Nupistaš. Other kings (Artaxerxes II, Artaxerxes III, and Darius III) had tombs cut into the mountainside that overlooks Persepolis. (Author's photograph.)

Further Reading

Part I Debates

There are a number of edited volumes covering the rudiments of ancient court societies. See Spawforth (2007b) for a solid collection of essays which focus variously on the ancient courts of the Near East, Egypt, the Hellenistic world, Rome, Byzantium, and China, while the edited volume by Lanfranchi and Rollinger (2010) explores aspects of ancient kingship but offers much good comment on court systems. Duindam et al. (2011) incorporate a wide-ranging series of essays on court life from antiquity to the nineteenth century, but of particular interest are the articles by Strootman on the Hellenistic court and Barjamovic on the Neo-Assyrian court. Erskine et al. (2013) provide a study of the Hellenistic court with many references to earlier Achaemenid traditions. The only full-scale study of the Achaemenid court is the edited volume by Jacobs and Rollinger (2010), which contains many important articles on Persian court life, structure, and rationale. In addition Brosius (2007) gives a synthesised but informative account of key aspects of the ancient Persian court.

Elton (1983), Elias (1983), and Duindam (2003) provide important models for thinking about court societies in general, although their focus is on early modern European courts. Of greater relevance as models for the Achaemenid court are the studies of early modern eastern courts by Babaie (2008), Huff (2010), and Lal (2005).

Generally – but importantly – on kingship and the gods see Briant (2002: 204–54) and Kuhrt (2007: 469–507). Gressmann (1929) offers an influential reading on the god-like qualities of Near Eastern rulers and Battesti (2011) on the theme of *xvarnah*. Most importantly Henkelman (2008) investigates evidence from the Iranian and Elamite pantheon as located in the Persepolis texts, while Briant (2002: 93–4, 250–4) has much else of value on the background to Achaemenid religion. The

Elamite connection to the Achaemenids has been recently explored by Álvarez-Mon and Garrison (2011) and by Potts (2011). Henkelman (2011b) looks in more detail at Achaemenid religious traditions deriving from Elamite archetypes. Widengren (1959, 1965, 1968) influentially but mistakenly deals with the Indo-European construction of Persian monarchy and its relationship to the gods, although much of his work has been overturned by Gnoli (1974a, 1974b). On crown princes and possible co-regencies see especially Henkelman (2010b), Calmeyer (1976), and Borchhardt (1976). Keaveney (2010) looks at the role of the chiliarch, primarily from a Greek perspective.

Briant (2002: 302–54) provides an in-depth analysis of the relationship between the king and his hereditary nobility (see also Tuplin 2010a). Henkelman (2003a) has tackled the thorny issue of court titles. Doctors at court are explored by Llewellyn-Jones and Robson (2010), Stronk (2004–5), and Griffiths (1987), while Greeks at the Persian court have been studied by Hofstetter (1978) and Brosius (2011). For the Achaemenid military see Head (1992); much is still to be done on this neglected topic but we can expect much of Tuplin's forthcoming work on the army. For Persian eunuchs see Llewellyn-Jones (2002) and comments by Tougher (2008); for the 'mechanics' of eunuchism see Bullough (2002). Eunuchs at the Neo-Assyrian, Israelite, and Babylonian courts are explored by Guyot (1980), Grayson (1995), Deller (1999), and Pirngruber (2011).

On the concept of the invisible ruler and its use in Classical texts see especially Lanfranchi (2010) and Allen (2005b), who treats the subject of the audience as represented in art and literature in a lively and thought-provoking manner; Brosius (2007, 2010b) also explores audience (and other) ceremonies. The motif of the audience ceremony is also noted by Tilia (1972, 1978), who studies the creation and positioning of the audience reliefs at Persepolis. For *proskynesis* see especially Frye (1972) and Fredricksmeyer (2000).

On the royal residences see especially Nielsen (1999) (generally on Persian palaces as a forerunner for later Hellenistic buildings), Matheson (1972), and Stronach (1978, 1997a, 1997b) (on Parsagade), Perrot (2010) (on Susa), and Wilber (1969), Shahbazi (2004), and Mousavi (2012) (on Persepolis). A controversial reading of Persepolis as a religious structure is provided by Razmjou (2010). On the royal monumental iconography of Persepolis and other Achaemenid monuments and the visualisation of the king see particularly Root (1979).

On the body in Achaemenid art see Azarpay (1994) together with

Bertelli (2001), Hamilton (2005), Sommer (2009), and Llewellyn-Jones (forthcoming b). Persian dress and hairstyles have been examined by Llewellyn-Jones (2010b, 2011), Root (2011), Beck (1972), Goldman (1964, 1991), and Volgelsang (2010). Crowns and headgear are well treated by Henkelman (1995–6) and Tuplin (2007c).

On the lands of the Empire and its demographic see Wiesehöfer (2009) as well as Sancisi-Weerdenburg (1998) for the concept of Empire-wide tribute. Gift-giving and nomadism are discussed by Briant (1988) while the roads and settlements of the Empire (as revealed by the Persepolis texts) are thoroughly explored by Arfaee (2008). Briant (2009) has some lively observations to make on the royal entry into cities, and royal tents are well explored by Miller (1997) and Spawforth (2007a). The most comprehensive and worthy discussion of the royal migration (and the reasoning behind the regular relocations of the court) is by Tuplin (1998b), who also (2010b) discusses the horse in Persian elite society. For camels in ancient Persia see especially Bulliet (1975).

The conspicuous use of food by the court has been dealt with extensively by Sancisi-Weerdenburg (1995, 1997), Lenfant (2007b) (on Greek concepts of Persian luxury), and Henkelman (2010a), who examines food in the Persepolis texts and the idea of 'the king's dinner'. Janković (2008) and Potts (2008) deal with food rationing and the practicalities of distribution. Tuplin (1996) gives a full and fluent account of the Persian conception of *paradeisoi*, while an interesting take on the psychology of hunting game is provided by Allsen (2006).

On women in ancient Persia see most importantly Brosius (1996), who explores both Greek and Near Eastern sources; see also her assessment of the female audience scene (2010a). For individual women see, for example, Henkelman (2010a, 2010b, 2011a, 2011b) on Darius' wives and (possible) mother. For the Persian harem see Balcer (1993), Llewellyn-Jones (2002, 2009b), and Llewellyn-Jones and Robson (2010) and for the Near Eastern harem see Marsman (2003) and Solvang (2003). On the physical structure at Persepolis being identified as a 'harem' see Schmidt (1953) and Shahbazi (2004). For the political aspects of the Ottoman harem against which the Achaemenid harem can be read, see Peirce (1993). Court intrigues and the themes of revenge and cruelty are very well treated by Keaveney (2003), Wiesehöfer (2010), and Rollinger (2004, 2010). The death of Xerxes is explored by Stolper (1988) and cultic offerings for dead kings are well examined and clearly explained by Henkelman (2003a).

Part II Documents

For those wishing to read beyond the extracts found in Part II, translations of most of the Greek and Latin sources are easily accessed through translations in the Loeb Classical Library, which produces the text of the original language alongside an English translation. The Oxford World Classics and the Penguin Classics series also give lively translations. Exceptions, however, are the following:

- Ctesias, *History of Persia*, L.Llewellyn-Jones and J.Robson, *Ctesias' History of Persia. Tales of the Orient*. London, 2010.
- Ctesias, *On India*, A. Nichols, *Ctesias. On India. Introduction, Translation and Commentary*. London, 2011.

There is not, as yet, a full English translation of Deinon or Heraclides; translations of the necessary fragments can be accessed via Kuhrt (2007), but the translations encountered here are the author's own.

Those wishing to read fuller versions of the Near Eastern texts will find full translations of the Persepolis Fortification texts in Hallock (1969). Royal inscriptions and other translations from Old Persian, Elamite, and Babylonian texts are primarily adapted and amended from Brosius (2000) and Kuhrt (2007) alongside the original translations both author's cite. Both these books are admirable for the range of sources they collate, although Kuhrt's in particular is exceptionally comprehensive and exhaustive. Here, Egyptian texts are predominantly drawn from Lichtheim (1980); Akkadian texts come from Pritchard (1969), and Aramaic sources come from Lindenberger (2003). Hebrew Biblical texts are adapted from the *New International Version* of the Bible and from the *Jerusalem Bible*. Other translations from Near Eastern sources are cited in the text and can be followed up by the enthusiastic reader.

Internet Resources

The following sites provide links to a wide range of Achaemenid-related resources and are well worth exploring:

Gateways

http://www.achemenet.com/
http://www.iranicaonline.org
http://www.cais-soas.com/index.htm
http://www.livius.org/persia.html

More generally on the Near East, visit:
http://www.aakkl.helsinki.fi/melammu/home/home.php

An amazing selection of Persian-related books and materials for downloading is available at:
http://oi.uchicago.edu/research/pubs/catalog/persia.html

Royal inscriptions and Old Persian

http://www.livius.org/aa-ac/achaemenians/inscriptions.html
http://www.fas.harvard.edu/~iranian/OldPersian/index.html

Achaemenid Aramaic and the Aršama Dossier

http://arshama.classics.ox.ac.uk

Persepolis

http://www.persepolis3d.com

Bibliography

Abdi, K. 2010. 'The Passing of the Throne from Xerxes to Artaxerxes', in J. Curtis and S. Simpson (eds), *The World of Achaemenid Persia*. London. 275–84.

Albright, W. F. 1982. 'The Lachish Cosmetic Burner and *Esther* 2.12', in C. A. Moore (ed.), *Studies in the Book of Esther*. New York. 261–8.

Al-Khalesi, Y. M. 1978. *The Court of the Palms. A Functional Interpretation of the Mari Palace*. Malibu.

Allen, L. 2005a. *The Persian Empire*. London.

——2005b. 'Le Roi Imaginaire: An Audience with the Achaemenid King', in O. Hekster and R. Fowler (eds), *Imaginary Kings. Royal Images in the Ancient Near East, Greece and Rome*. Munich. 39–62.

——2007. '"Chilminarolim Persepolis": European Reception of a Persian Ruin', in C. Tuplin (ed.), *Persian Responses. Political and Cultural Interaction with(in) the Achaemenid Empire*. Swansea. 313–42.

Allsen, T. T. 2006. *The Royal Hunt in Eurasian History*. Philadelphia.

Alster, B. 1997. *Proverbs of Ancient Sumer* (2 vols). Bethesda.

Álvarez-Mon, J. 2009. 'Notes on the Elamite Garment of Cyrus the Great'. *Antiquaries Journal* 89. 21–33.

Álvarez-Mon, J. and Garrison, M. (eds) 2011. *Elam and Persia*. Winona Lake.

Ambrose, T. 2008. *The Nature of Despotism. From Caligula to Mugabe, the Making of Tyrants*. London.

Anderson, M. 1990. *Hidden Power: The Palace Eunuchs of Imperial China*. Buffalo.

André-Salvini, B. 2009. *Babylone. À Babylone, d'hier et d'aujourd'hui*. Paris.

Andrews, P. A. 1999. *Felt Tents and Pavilions. The Nomadic Tradition and Its Interaction with Princely Tentage* (2 vols). London.

Aperghis, G. C. 1998. 'The Persepolis Fortification Texts – Another Look', in M. Brosius and A. Kuhrt (eds), *Studies in Persian History: Essays in Memory of David M. Lewis*. Leiden. 35–62.

Arfa'i, A. 1999. 'La grande route Persépolis-Suse: Une lecture des tablettes provenant des Fortifications de Persépolis'. *Topoi* 9. 33–45.

Arfaee, A. 2008. *The Geographical Background of the Persepolis Tablets*. Phd, University of Chicago.

Asheri, D., Lloyd, A. and Corcella, A. 2007. *A Commentary on Herodotus Books I–IV*. Oxford.

Axworthy, M. 2007. *Iran. Empire of the Mind. A History from Zoroaster to the Present Day*. London.

Azarpay, G. 1994. 'Designing the Body: Human Proportions in Achaemenid Art'. *Iranica Antiqua* 29. 169–84.

Babaie, S. 2008. *Isfahan and Its Palaces*. Edinburgh.

Bahrani, Z. 2001. *Women of Babylon. Gender and Representation in Mesopotamia*. London and New York.

——2003. *The Graven Image. Representation in Babylonia and Assyria*. Philadelphia.

Bailey, R. C. 1990. *David in Love and War. The Pursuit of Power in 2 Samuel 10–12*. Sheffield.

Baker, P. L. 2010. 'Wrought of Gold or Silver. Honorific Garments in Seventeenth Century Iran', in J. Thompson, D. Shaffer and P. Mildh (eds), *Carpets and Textiles in the Iranian World 1400–1700*. Oxford. 158–67.

Balcer, J. M. 1987. *Herodotus and Bisitun. Problems in Ancient Persian Historiography*. Stuttgart.

——1993. *A Prosopographical Study of the Ancient Persians Royal and Noble, c. 550–450 BC*. Lampeter.

Baldwin, J. G. 1984. *Esther. An Introduction and Commentary*. Leicester.

Barjamovic, G. 2011. 'Pride, Pomp and Circumstance: Palace, Court and Household in Assyria 879–612 BCE', in J. Duindam, T. Artan and M. Kunt (eds), *Royal Courts in Dynastic States. A Global Perspective*. Leiden. 27–61.

Battesti, T. 2011. 'Lumière de gloire et royauté en Iran', in Y. Vadé and B. Dupaigne (eds), *Regalia. Emblèmes et rites du pouvoir*. Paris. 165–86.

Beck, P. 1972. 'A Note on the Reconstruction of the Achaemenid Robe'. *Iranica Antiqua* 9. 116–22.

Berghe, L. V. 1993. 'De Skulpture', in F. van Norten (ed.), *Hoftkunst van de Sassanieden*. Brussels. 71–88.

Berlin, A. 2001. *The JPS Bible Commentary: Esther*. Philadelphia.

Bertelli, R. 2001. *The King's Body*. Pennsylvania.

Bickerman, E. J. 1938. *Institutions des Seléucides*. Paris.

Binder, C. 2008. *Plutarchs Vita des Artaxerxes. Ein historischer kommentar*. Berlin.

——2010. 'Das Krönungszeremonial der Achaimeniden', in B. Jacobs and R. Rollinger (eds), *Der Achämenidenhof/The Achaemenid Court*. Stuttgart. 473–97.

Bishop, T. (1998) 'The Gingerbread Host: Tradition and Novelty in the Jacobean Masque', in D. Bevington and P. Holbrook (eds), *The Politics of the Stuart Court Masque*. Cambridge. 88–120.

Boardman, J. 1970. *Greek Gems and Finger Rings. Early Bronze Age to Late Classical.* London.

——2000. *Persia and the West. An Archaeological Investigation of the Genesis of Achaemenid Art.* London.

Booth, M. (ed.) 1996. *Harem Histories: Envisioning Places and Living Spaces.* Durham, NC.

Borchhardt, J. 1976. *Die Bauskulplur des Heroons von Limyra: Das Grabmal Königs Perikles.* Berlin.

Bottéro, J. 2004. *The Oldest Cuisine in the World. Cooking in Mesopotamia.* Chicago.

Boucharlat, R. 1998. 'À la recherche d'Ecbatane sur Tepe Hagmataneh'. *Iranica Antiqua* 33 (= *Neo-Assyrian, Median, Achaemenian and Other Studies in Honour of David Stronach*). 173–86.

Boyce, M. 1983. 'Iranian Festivals', in E. Yarshater (ed.), *The Cambridge History of Iran. Vol. III, Part 2: The Seleucid, Parthian and Sasanian Periods.* Cambridge. 792–815.

Breasted, J. H. 1906. *Ancient Records of Egypt* (4 vols). Chicago.

Bremmer, J. 2008. *Greek Religion and Culture, the Bible and the Ancient Near East.* Leiden.

Brettler, M. Z. 1989. *God Is King. Understanding an Israelite Metaphor.* Sheffield.

Briant, P. 1982. *Etat et pasteurs au Moyen-Orient ancient.* Paris and Cambridge.

——1988. 'Le nomadisme du Grand Roi'. *Iranica Antiqua* 23. 253–73.

——2002. *From Cyrus to Alexander. A History of the Persian Empire.* Winona Lake.

——2003. 'À propos du roi-jardinier: Remarques sur l'histoire d'un dossier documentaire', in W. Henkelman and A. Kuhrt (eds), *A Persian Perspective. Essays in Honour of Heleen Sancisi-Weerdenburg.* (Achaemenid History XIII.) Leiden. 33–49.

——2005. 'Milestones in the Development of Achaemenid Historiography in the Era of Ernst Herzfeld', in A. C. Gunter and S. P. Hauser (eds), *Ernst Herzfeld and the Development of Near Eastern Studies 1900–1950.* Leiden.

——2009. 'Entrées royales et mises en scène du pouvoir dans l'empire achéménide et les royaumes hellénistiques', in A. Bérenger and É. Perrin-Saminadayar (eds), *Les entrées royales et impériales.* Paris. 47–64.

Briant, P. and Chauveau, M. (eds) 2009. *Organisation des pouvoirs et contacts culturels dans les pays de l'empire achéménide.* Paris.

Briant, P., Henkleman, W. and Stolper, M. (eds) 2008. *L'archive des Fortifications de Persépolis.* Paris .

Brisch, N. 2008. *Religion and Power. Divine Kingship in the Ancient World and Beyond.* Chicago.

Brosius, M. 1996. *Women in Ancient Persia (559–331 BC).* Oxford.

——2000. *The Persian Empire from Cyrus II to Artaxerxes I.* (LACTOR 16.) Cambridge.

——2006. *The Persians. An Introduction.* London.

——2007. 'Old Out of New? Court and Court Ceremonies in Achaemenid Persia', in A. J. S. Spawforth (ed.), *The Court and Court Society in Ancient Monarchies.* Cambridge. 17–57.

——2010a. 'The Royal Audience Scene Reconsidered', in J. Curtis and S. Simpson (eds), *The World of Achaemenid Persia.* London. 141–52.

——2010b. 'Das Hofzeremoniell', in B. Jacobs and R. Rollinger (eds), *Der Achämenidenhof/The Achaemenid Court.* Stuttgart. 459–71.

——2011. 'Greeks at the Persian Court', in J. Wiesehöfer, R. Rollinger and G. Lanfranchi (eds), *Ktesias' Welt/Ctesias' World.* Wiesbaden. 69–80.

Brown, J. P. 2001. *Israel and Hellas. Vol. III: The Legacy of Iranian Imperialism and the Individual.* Berlin.

Brown, W. P. 1996. *Seeing the Psalms. A Theology of Metaphor.* Louisville and London.

Brulé, P. 2003. *Women of Ancient Greece.* Edinburgh.

Budin, S. L. 2011. *Images of Woman and Child from the Bronze Age. Reconsidering Fertility, Maternity, and Gender in the Ancient World.* Cambridge.

Bulliet, R. W. 1975. *The Camel and the Wheel.* Cambridge, MA.

Bullough, V. L. 2002. 'Eunuchs in History and Society', in S. Tougher (ed.), *Eunuchs in Antiquity and Beyond.* Swansea and London. 1–17.

Burke, P. 1994. *The Fabrication of Louis XIV.* New Haven.

Calmeyer, P. 1976. 'Zur Genese Altiranischer Motive, V: Synarchie'. *Archäologische Mitteilungen aus Iran* 9. 63–95.

Carney, E. D. 2000. *Women and Monarchy in Macedonia.* Norman.

Cartmill, M. 1995. 'Hunting and Humanity in Western Thought'. *Social Research* 62(3). 773–86.

Casson, L. 1994. *Travel in the Ancient World.* Baltimore.

Chamberlin, J. E. 2006. *Horse. How the Horse Has Changed Civilizations.* Oxford.

Chang, M. G. 2007. *A Court on Horseback. Imperial Touring and the Construction of Qing Rule, 1680–1785.* Cambridge, MA.

Charles-Gaffiot, J. 2011. *Trônes en majesté. L'autorité et son symbole.* Paris.

Cleland, L., Davies, G. and Llewellyn-Jones, L. 2007. *Greek and Roman Dress. From A–Z.* London.

Clutton-Brock, J. 1992. *Horse Power: A History of the Horse and the Donkey in Human Societies.* Harvard.

Collon, D. 1987. *First Impressions. Cylinder Seals in the Ancient Near East.* London.

Cook, J. M. 1983. *The Persian Empire.* London.

Cottrell, A. 2004. *Chariot. The Astounding Rise and Fall of the World's First War Machine.* London.

Cumming, C. G. 1934. *The Assyrian and Hebrew Hymns of Praise.* New York.

Curtis, J. and Simpson, S. (eds) 2010. *The World of Achaemenid Persia*. London.

Curtis, J. and Tallis, N. (eds) 2005. *Forgotten Empire. The World of Ancient Persia*. London.

Curtis, V. S. 1993. *Persian Myths*. London.

Dandamayev, M. A. 1984a 'Royal Paradeisoi in Babylonia'. *Acta Iranica* (2nd series) 23. 113–17.

——1984b. *Slavery in Babylonia*. DeKalb.

——1988. *s.v.* 'Barda and Barda-Dāri', in *Encyclopaedia Iranica*. New York.

——1989. *A Political History of the Achaemenid Empire*. Brill.

Dandamayev, M. A. and Lukonin, V. G. 1989. *The Culture and Social Institutions of Ancient Iran*. Cambridge.

Davaran, F. 2010. *Continuity in Iranian Identity*. London.

Davidson, J. 2006. 'The Greek Courtesan and the Art of the Present', in M. Feldman and B. Gordon (eds), *The Courtesan's Arts. Cross-Cultural Perspectives*. Oxford. 29–51.

Davis, D. 2006. *Shahnameh: The Persian Book of Kings*. New York.

Dayagi-Mendels, M. 1989. *Perfumes and Cosmetics in the Ancient World*. Jerusalem.

Dayagi-Mendels, M. and Rozenberg, S. (eds) 2010. *Chronicles of the Land. Archaeology in the Israel Museum, Jerusalem*. Jerusalem.

de Jong, A. 2010. 'Religion at the Achaemenid Court', in B. Jacobs and R. Rollinger (eds), *Der Achämenidenhof/The Achaemenid Court*. Stuttgart. 533–58.

Deller, K. 1999. 'The Assyrian Eunuchs and Their Predecessors', in K. Watanabe (ed.), *Priests and Officials in the Ancient Near East*. Heidelberg. 303–11.

DelPlato, J. 2002. *Multiple Wives, Multiple Pleasures. Representing the Harem, 1800–1875*. London.

Desroches Noblecourt, C. 2007. *Gifts from the Pharaohs*. London.

De Troyer, K. 1995. 'An Oriental Beauty Parlour: An Analysis of *Esther* 2.2–18 in the Hebrew, the Septuagint, and the Second Greek Text', in A. Brenner (ed.), *A Feminist Companion to Esther, Judith and Sussana*. Sheffield. 47–70.

de Vaux, R. 1961. *Ancient Israel. Its Life and Institutions*. London.

Dodson, A. and Hilton, D. (2005) *The Complete Royal Families of Ancient Egypt*. London.

Driver, G. R. 1956. *Aramaic Documents of the Fifth Century BC*. Oxford.

Duindam, J. (2003) *Vienna and Versailles: The Courts of Europe's Dynastic Rivals, 1550–1780*. Cambridge.

Duindam, J., Artan, T. and Kunt, M. (eds) 2011. *Royal Courts in Dynastic States. A Global Perspective*. Leiden.

Dusinberre, E. R. M. 2003. *Aspects of Empire in Achaemenid Sardis*. Cambridge.

——2005. 'Herzfeld in Persepolis', in A. C. Gunter and S. P. Hauser (eds), *Ernst Herzfeld and the Development of Near Eastern Studies 1900–1950*. Leiden.

Dutz, W. F. 1977. *Persepolis and Archaeological Sites in Fars*. Tehran.

Dutz, W. F. and Matheson, S. A. 2001. *Parsa-Persepolis*. Tehran.

Elias, N. 1983. *The Court Society*. Oxford.

——1994. *The Civilizing Process*. Oxford.

Elton, G. 1983. 'Tudor Government. The Points of Contact III: The Court', in G. Elton (ed.), *Studies in Tudor and Stuart Politics and Government*. Cambridge. 38–57.

Eraly, A. 1997. *The Mughal World. India's Tainted Paradise*. London.

Erskine, A., Llewellyn-Jones, L. and Wallace, S. (eds) 2013. *The Hellenistic Court*. Swansea.

Farrokh, K. 2007. *Shadows in the Desert. Ancient Persia at War*. Oxford.

Finkel, I. L. and Seymour, M. J. (eds) 2008. *Babylon. London*.

Foster, B. R. 2005. *Before the Muses. An Anthology of Akkadian Literature*. Bethesda.

Fowler, M. A. and Marincola, J. (eds) 2002. *Herodotus. Histories Book IX*. Cambridge.

Frankfort, H. 1944. *Kingship and the Gods*. Chicago.

——1954. *The Art and Architecture of the Ancient Orient*. New Haven and London.

Frazer, J. 1911. *The Magic Art. Vol. I*. London.

Fredricksmeyer, E. A. 1997. 'The Origin of Alexander's Royal Insignia'. *Transactions and Proceedings of the American Philological Association* 127. 97–109.

——2000. 'Alexander the Great and the Kingship of Asia', in A. B. Bosworth and E. J. Baynham (eds), *Alexander the Great in Fact and Fiction*. Oxford. 136–66.

Frye, R. N. 1962. *The Heritage of Persia*. London.

——1972. 'Gestures of Deference to Royalty in Ancient Iran'. *Iranica Antiqua* 9. 102–7.

——1996. *The Golden Age of Persia*. New York.

Gabbiani, G. 2009. 'Les déplacements impériaux dans la Chine du XVIII siècle: dimensions rituelles et politiques', in A. Bérenger and É. Perrin-Saminadayar (eds), *Les entrées royales et impériales*. Paris. 255–82.

Garrison, M. B. 2012. 'Les arts visuels du début de l'ère achémenide onts-ils représenté l'autel du feu et le feu sacré zoroastriens?' *Religions and Histoire* 44. 42–5.

Garthwaite, G. R. 2005. *The Persians*. Oxford.

Garvie, A. F. 2009. *Aeschylus. Persae*. Oxford.

Geertz, C. 1983. *Local Knowledge: Further Essays in Interpretive Anthropology*. New York.

Gershevitch, I. 1985. *The Cambridge History of Iran. Vol. II: The Median and Achaemenian Periods*. Cambridge.

Ghirshman, R. 1964. *Persia. From the Origins to Alexander the Great*. London.

Ghirshman, R. and Herzfeld, E. 2000. *Persepolis. The Achaemenians' Capital.* Tehran.

Glassner, J. J. 2004. *Mesopotamian Chronicles.* Atlanta.

Gnoli, G. 1974a. 'Politica religiosa e concezione della regalità sotto gli Achemenidi'. *Gururajamanjarika: Studi in onore di Giuseppe Tucci* 1. 23–88.

——1974b. 'Politique religieuse et conception de la royauté sous les Achéménides', in J. Duchesne-Guillemin and P. Lecoq (eds), *Commémoration Cyrus: actes du congrès de Shiraz 1971 et autres études, rédigées à l'occasion du 2500e anniversaire de la fondation de l'empire perse. Vol. II: Acta Iranica.* Leiden. 117–90.

Goffman, E. 1956a. *The Presentation of Self in Daily Life.* New York.

——1956b. 'The Nature of Deference and Demeanour'. *American Anthropologist* 58. 473–502.

Goldman, B. 1964. 'Origin of the Persian Robe.' *Iranica Antiqua* 4. 133–52.

——1991. 'Women's Robes: The Achaemenid Era'. *Bulletin of the Asia Institute* 5. 83–103.

Gordon, S. 2003. *Robes of Honour. Khil'at in Pre-Colonial and Colonial India.* Delhi.

——2010. 'Khil'a: Clothing to Honour a Person or Situation', in G. Vogelsang-Eastwood (ed.), *Berg Encyclopaedia of World Dress and Fashion. Vol. V: Central and Southwest Asia.* Oxford. 462–7.

Grayson, A. L. 1975. *Babylonian Historical-Literary Texts.* Toronto.

——1995. 'Eunuchs in Power', in M. Dietrich and O. Loretz (eds), *Vom Alten Orient zum Alten Testament. Festschrift W. v. Soden.* Neukirchen-Vluyn. 85–98.

Gressmann, H. 1929. *Der Messias.* Göttingen.

Griffiths, A. 1987. 'Democedes of Croton. A Greek Doctor at the Court of Darius', in H. Sancisi-Weerdenburg and A. Kuhrt (eds), *The Greek Sources.* (Achaemenid History II.) Leiden. 37–51.

Gruber, M. I. 1980. *Aspects of Non-Verbal Communication in the Ancient Near East* (2 vols). Rome.

Gunter, A. C. and Hauser, S. R. (eds) 2005. *Ernst Herzfeld and the Development of Near Eastern Studies, 1900–1950.* Leiden.

Guterbock, H. G. and van Hout, T. 1991. *The Hittite Instruction for the Royal Bodyguard.* Chicago.

Guyot, P. 1980. *Eunuchen als Sklaven und Freigelassene in der griechisch-römichen Antike.* Stuttgart.

Hallock, R. T. 1969. *Persepolis Fortification Tablets.* Chicago.

——1978. 'Selected Fortification Texts'. *Cahiers de la Délégation Française en Iran* 8. 109–36.

——1985. 'The Evidence of the Persepolis Tablets', in I. Gershevitch (ed.), *The Cambridge History of Iran. Vol. II: The Median and Achaemedian Periods.* Cambridge. 588–609.

Hamilton, M. W. 2005. *The Royal Body. The Social Poetics of Kingship in Ancient Israel.* Atlanta.

Handley, P. M. 2006. *The King Never Smiles: A Biography of Thailand's Bhumibol Adulyadej.* New Haven.

Harper, P. O., Aruz, J. and Tallon, F. (eds) 1992. *The Royal City of Susa. Ancient Near Eastern Treasures in the Louvre.* New York.

Harrison, T. (ed.) 2002. *Greeks and Barbarians.* Edinburgh.

——2011. *Writing Ancient Persia.* London.

Hazewindus, M. W. 2004. *When Women Interfere. Studies in the Role of Women in Herodotus' Histories.* Amsterdam.

Head, D. 1992 *The Achaemenid Persian Army.* Stockport.

Henkelman, W. F. M. 1995-6. 'The Royal Achaemenid Crown', *Archäologische Mitteilungen aus Iran* 28. 275-93.

——2003a. 'An Elamite Memorial: The Šumar of Cambyses and Hystaspes', in W. Henkelman and A. Kuhrt (eds), *A Persian Perspective. Essays in Honour of Heleen Sancisi-Weerdenburg.* (Achaemenid History XIII.) Leiden. 101-72.

——2003b. 'Persians, Medes and Elamites: Acculturation in the Neo-Elamite Period', in G. B. Lanfranchi, M. Roaf and R. Rollinger (eds), *Continuity of Empire (?). Assyria, Media, Persia.* Padova. 181-231.

——2008. *The Other Gods Who Are. Studies in Elamite-Iranian Acculturation Based on the Persepolis Fortification Texts.* (Achaemenid History XIV.) Leiden.

——2010a. 'Consumed Before the King. The Table of Darius, Irdabama and Irtaštuna and That of His Satrap, Karkiš', in B. Jacobs and R. Rollinger (eds), *Der Achämenidenhof/The Achaemenid Court.* Stuttgart. 667-775.

——2010b. 'Xerxes, Atossa, and the Persepolis Fortification Archive'. *Annual Report of the Netherlands Institute for the Near East Leiden/The Netherlands Institute in Turkey Istanbul.* 26-33.

——2011a. 'Cyrus the Persian and Darius the Elamite: A Case of Mistaken Identity', in R. Rollinger, B. Truschnegg and R. Bichler (eds), *Herodot und das Persische Weltreich/Herodorus and the Persian Empire.* Wiesbaden. 577-634.

——2011b. 'Parnaka's Feast: *Šip* in Pārsa and Elam', in J. Álvarez-Mon and M. B. Garrison (eds), *Elam and Persia.* Winona Lake. 89-166.

——2012. 'Une religion redistributive. Les sacrifices perses selon l'archive des Fortification de Persépolis'. *Religions et Histoire* 44. 36-41.

Henkelman, W. F. M. and Stolper, M. W. 2009. 'Ethnic Identity and Ethnic Labelling at Persepolis: The Case of the Skudrians', in P. Briant and M. Chauveau (eds), *Organisation des pouvoirs et contacts culturels dans les pays de l'empire achéménide.* Paris. 271-329.

Herzfeld, E. 1941. *Iran in the Ancient East.* London.

Hesker, O. and Fowler, R. (eds) 2005. *Imaginary Kings. Royal Images in the Ancient Near East, Greece and Rome.* Munich.

Hobhouse, P. 2003. *The Gardens of Persia*. London.

Hofstetter, J. 1978. *Die Griechen in Persien. Prosopographie der Griechen im persischen Reich vor Alexander*. Berlin.

Holdsworth, M. and Courtauld, C. 1995. *The Forbidden City. The Great Within*. Hong Kong.

Homan, M. M. 2002. *To Your Tents, O Israel! The Terminology, Form and Symbolism of Tents in the Hebrew Bible and the Ancient Near East*. Leiden.

Hornblower, S. 2003. 'Panionios of Chios and Hermotimos of Pedasa (Hdt. 8.104–106)', in P. Derow and R. Parker (eds), *Herodotus and His World. Essays from a Conference in Memory of George Forrest*. Oxford. 37–57.

Hourani, A. 1991. *A History of the Arab Peoples*. Cambridge, MA.

Huff, D. 2005. 'From Median to Achaemenian Palace Architecture'. *Iranica Antiqua* 40. 371–95.

——2010. 'Überlegungen zu Funktion, Genese und Nachfolge des Apadana', in B. Jacobs and R. Rollinger (eds), *Der Achämenidenhof/The Achaemenid Court*. Stuttgart. 311–74.

Irwin, R. 2010. *Camel*. London.

Jackson, D. 2010. *Lion*. London.

Jacobs, B. 2010. 'Höfischer Lebensstil und materielle Prachtenfaltung', in B. Jacobs and R. Rollinger (eds), *Der Achämenidenhof/The Achaemenid Court*. Stuttgart. 377–409.

Jacobs, B. and Rollinger, R. (eds) 2010. *Der Achämenidenhof/The Achaemenid Court*. Wiesbaden.

Janković, B. 2008. 'Travel Provisions in Babylonia in the First Millennium BC', in P. Briant, W. Henkleman and M. Stolper (eds), *L'archive des Fortifications de Persépolis*. Paris. 429–64.

Jidejian, N. 2006. *Sidon Through the Ages*. Beirut.

Jigoulov, V. S. 2010. *The Social History of Achaemenid Phoenicia*. Cambridge.

Joannes, F. 2004. *The Age of Empires. Mesopotamia in the First Millennium BC*. Edinburgh.

Jones, B. W. 1977. 'Two Misconceptions Re the *Book of Esther*'. *Catholic Biblical Quarterly* 39. 172–7.

Jones, G. H. 1989. 'The Concept of Holy War', in R. E. Clements (ed.), *The World of Ancient Israel*. Cambridge. 299–321.

Jursa, M. 2011. 'Höflinge (*ša rēši, ša rēš šarru, ustarbaru*) in babylonischen Quellen der ersten Jahrtausends', in J. Wiesehöfer, R. Rollinger and G. Lanfranchi (eds), *Ktesias' Welt/Ctesias' World*. Wiesbaden. 159–74.

Kantorowicz, E. H. 1957. *The King's Two Bodies. A Study in Medieval Political Theology*. Princeton.

Kaplan, F. E. S. 2008. 'Politics in an African Royal Harem: Women and Seclusion at the Royal Court of Benin, Nigeria', in A. Walthall (ed.), *Servants of the Dynasty. Palace Women in World History*. Berkeley. 115–36.

Kaptan, D. 2002. *The Daskyleion Bullae: Seal Images from the Western Achaemenid Empire* (2 vols). Leiden.

Keaveney, A. 1998. 'Xerxes' New Suit: Aeschylus' *Persae* 845–851'. *Giornale –Italiano di Filologia.* 15. November. 239–41.

——2003. *The Life and Journey of the Athenian Statesman Themistocles (524–460 BC?) as a Refugee in Persia.* Lampeter.

——2010. 'The Chiliarch and the Person of the King', in B. Jacobs and R. Rollinger (eds), *Der Achämenidenhof/The Achaemenid Court.* Stuttgart. 499–508.

Kelekna, P. 2009. *The Horse in Human History.* Cambridge.

Kennedy, H. 2004. *The Court of the Caliphs. The Rise of Islam's Greatest Dynasty.* London.

Knecht, R. J. 2008. *The French Renaissance Court.* New Haven.

Knight, D. A. and Levine, A-J. 2011. *The Meaning of the Bible.* New York.

Koch, H. 2001. *Persepolis.* Mainz Am Rhein.

Krefter, F. 1971. *Persepolis. Rekonstruktionen.* Berlin.

Kuhrt, A. 1988. 'Earth and Water', in A. Kuhrt and H. Sancisi-Weerdenburg (eds), *Method and Theory.* (Achaemenid History III.) Leiden. 87–99.

——1995. *The Ancient Near East c. 3000–330* BC (2 vols). London.

——2001. 'The Achaemenid Persian Empire (c. 550–c. 330 BCE): Continuities, Adaptations, Transformations', in S. E. Alcock, T. N. D'Altroy, K. D. Morrison and C. M. Sinopoli (eds), *Empires. Perspectives from Archaeology and History.* Cambridge. 93–123.

——2002. *'Greece' and 'Greeks', in Mesopotamian and Persian Perspectives.* The 21st J. L. Myres Memorial Lecture. Oxford.

——2007. *The Persian Empire. A Corpus of Sources from the Achaemenid Period* (2 vols). London.

——2010. 'Der Hof der Achämeniden: Concluding Remarks', in B. Jacobs and R. Rollinger (eds), *Der Achämenidenhof/The Achaemenid Court.* Stuttgart. 901–12.

Kwasman, T. 2009. 'A Neo-Assyrian Royal Funerary Text', in M. Luukko, S. Svärd and R. Mattila (eds), *Of God(s), Trees, Kings, and Scholars. Neo-Assyrian and Related Studies in Honour of Simo Parpola.* Helsinki. 111–25.

Kwasman, T. and Parpola, S. 1991. *Legal Transactions of the Royal Court at Nineveh, Part I: Tiglath-Pileser III through Esarhaddon.* State Archives of Assyria 6. Helsinki.

Lal, K. S. 1988. *The Mughal Harem.* Delhi.

Lal, R. 2005. *Domesticity and Power in the Early Mughal World.* Cambridge.

Lane Fox, R. 2007. 'Alexander the Great: "Last of the Achaemenids"?', in C. Tuplin (ed.), *Persian Responses. Political and Cultural Interaction With(in) the Persian Empire.* 267–311.

Lanfranchi, G. B. 2010. 'Greek Historians and the Memory of the Assyrian Court', in B. Jacobs and R. Rollinger (eds), *Der Achämenidenhof/The Achaemenid Court.* Stuttgart. 39–65.

Lanfranchi, G. B. and Rollinger, R. (eds) 2010. *Concepts of Kingship in Antiquity.* Padua.

Leblanc, C. 1999. *Nefertari: l'aimée-de-Mout: épouses, filles et fils de Ramsès II.* Paris.

Lecoq, P. 1997. *Les inscriptions de la Perse achéménid.* Paris.

Lenfant, D. 2004. *Ctésias de Cinde. La Perse, L'Inde, autre fragments.* Paris.

——2007a. 'Greek Historians of Persia', in J. Marincola (ed.), *A Companion to Greek and Roman Historiography, Vol. I.* Oxford. 201–9.

——2007b. 'On Persian *Tryphē* in Athenaeus', in C. Tuplin, (ed.), *Persian Responses. Political and Cultural Interaction With(in) the Achaemenid Empire.* Swansea. 51–65.

——2009. *Les Histoires perses de Deinon et d'Héraclide. Fragments édités, traduits et commentés.* Paris.

Leonowens, A. H. 1873. *The Romance of the Harem.* Harvard.

Lerner, J. A. 2010. 'An Achaemenid Cylinder Seal of a Woman Enthroned', in J. Curtis and S. Simpson (eds), *The World of Achaemenid Persia.* London. 153–64.

Levy, J. 2011. *Poison. A Social History.* Stroud.

Lewis, D. M. 1977. *Sparta and Persia. Lectures Delivered at the University of Cincinnati, Autumn 1976, in Memory of Donald W. Bradeen [by] David M. Lewis.* Leiden.

——1997a. 'The Persepolis Fortification Texts', in P. J. Rhodes (ed.), *Selected Papers in Greek and Near Eastern History by David M. Lewis.* Cambridge. 325–31.

——1997b. 'The King's Dinner', in P. J. Rhodes (ed.), *Selected Papers in Greek and Near Eastern History by David M. Lewis.* Cambridge. 332–41.

Lewis, R. 2000. 'Harems and Hotels: Segregated City Spaces and Narratives of Identity in the Work of Oriental Women Writers', in L. Durning and R. Wrigley (eds), *Gender and Architecture.* Chichester. 171–87.

——2004. *Rethinking Orientalism. Women, Travel and the Ottoman Harem.* New York.

Lichtheim, M. 1980. *Ancient Egyptian Literature. Vol. III: The Late Period.* Berkeley.

——2003. 'Instruction of Any', in W. M. Hallo and K. L. Younger (eds), *The Context of Scripture.* 110–15.

Lincoln, B. 2007. *Religion, Empire and Torture. The Case of Achaemenid Persia, with a Postscript on Abu Ghraib.* Chicago.

——2012. *'Happiness for Mankind'. Achaemenian Religion and the Imperial Project.* (Acta Iranica 53.) Leuven.

Lindenberger, J. M. 2003. *Ancient Aramaic and Hebrew Letters* (2nd edition). Atlanta.

Livingstone, A. 1989. *Court Poetry and Historical Miscellanea.* State Archives of Assyria 3. Helsinki.

Llewellyn-Jones, L. 2002. 'Eunuchs and the Royal Harem in Achaemenid Persia (559–331 BC)', in S. Tougher (ed.), *Eunuchs in Antiquity and Beyond.* Swansea and London. 19–49.

——2008. 'Achaemenid Persia', in S. Bourke (ed.), *The Middle East. The Cradle of Civilization Revealed.* London. 216–45.

——2009a. 'Ethnic Conceptions of Beauty in Achaemenid Period Seals and Gemstones', in S. Hales and T. Hodos (eds), *Local and Global Identities: Rethinking Identity, Material and Visual Cultures in the Ancient World.* Cambridge. 171–200.

——2009b. '"Help me Aphrodite!" Representing the Royal Women of Persia in Oliver Stone's *Alexander*', in F. Greenland and P. Cartledge (eds), *Responses to Alexander.* Madison. 150–97.

——2009c. 'The First Persian Empire', in T. Harrison (ed.), *Ancient Empires.* London. 65–95.

——2010a. 'The Big and Beautiful Women of Asia: Picturing Female Sexuality in Greco-Persian Seals', in J. Curtis and S. Simpson (eds), *The World of Achaemenid Persia.* London. 165–76.

——2010b. 'Pre-Islamic Dress Codes in the Eastern Mediterranean and Southwest Asia', in G. Vogelsang-Eastwood (ed.), *Berg Encyclopaedia of World Dress and Fashion. Vol. V: Central and Southwest Asia.* Oxford. 24–30.

——2011. 'Hair', in M. Finkelberg (ed.), *The Homer Encyclopaedia. Vol. II.* Oxford. 327–8.

——2012. 'The Great Kings of the Fourth Century and the Greek Memory of the Persian Past', in J. Marincola, L. Llewellyn-Jones and C. Maciver (eds), *Greek Notions of the Past in the Archaic and Classical Eras. History Without Historians.* (Edinburgh Leventis Studies.) Edinburgh. 317–46.

——forthcoming a. 'Empire of the Gaze: Persian Harems and Seraglio Fantasies à la grecque', *Helios.*

——forthcoming b. *The Great King's Body. Corporality and Monarchy in Ancient Persia and the Near East.* Edinburgh.

Llewellyn-Jones, L. and Robson, J. 2010. *Ctesias' History of Persia. Tales of the Orient.* London.

L'Orange, H. P. 1953. *Studies in the Iconography of Cosmic Kingship.* Oslo.

Luckenbill, D. D. 1989. *Ancient Records of Assyria and Babylonia* (2 vols). Chicago.

Mackey, S. 1996. *The Iranians. Persia, Islam and the Soul of a Nation.* New York.

Madhloom, T. A. 1970. *The Chronology of Neo-Assyrian Art.* London.

Maguire, H. 2004. *Byzantine Court Culture from 829 to 1204.* Cambridge, MA.

Marmon, S. 1995. *Eunuchs and Sacred Boundaries in Islamic Society.* New York.

Marr, J. L. 1998. *Plutarch. Life of Themistocles.* Warminster.

Marsman, H. J. 2003. *Women in Ugarit and Israel. Their Social and Religious Positions in the Context of the Ancient Near East.* Leiden.

Matheson, S. A. 1972. *Persia: An Archaeological Guide.* London and Tehran.

McDermott, J. 1999. *State and Court Ritual in China.* Cambridge.

McGovern, P. E. 2009. *Uncorking the Past. The Quest for Beer and Other Alcoholic Beverages*. Berkeley.

Melville, S. C. 1999. *The Role of Naqia/Zakutu in Sargonid Politics*. Helsinki.

——2006. 'Eponym Lists', in M. W. Chavalas (ed.), *The Ancient Near East*. Oxford. 293–8.

Mikasa, T. (ed.) 1984. *Monarchies and Socio-Religious Traditions in the Ancient Near East: Papers Read at the 31st International Congress of Human Sciences in Asia and North Africa*. Wiesbaden.

Milani, A. 2011. *The Shah*. New York.

Miller, M. 1997. *Athens and Persia in the Fifth Century BC. A Study in Cultural Receptivity*. Cambridge.

Mitford, N. 2001. 'Mme de Pompadour's Theatre', in D. Snowman (ed.), *Past Masters. The Best of History Today*. London. 21–9.

Montero Fenollòs, J-L. 2006. 'La "maison de succession" à l'époque néo-assyrienne', in V. A. Troncoso (ed.), *Diodokhos tēs Basileias: La figura del sucesor en la realeza helenística. Anejo IX*. Madrid. 205–22.

Moran, W. L. 1992. *The Amarna Letters*. Baltimore and London.

Morgan, J. 2007. 'Women, Religion, and the Home', in D. Ogden (ed.), *A Companion to Greek Religion*. Oxford. 297–310.

——2010. *The Classical Greek House*. Bristol.

Morris, I. 1979. *The World of the Shining Prince: Court Life in Ancient Japan*. London.

Mousavi, A. 1992. 'Parsa, a Stronghold for Darius: A Preliminary Study of the Defense System of Persepolis'. *East and West* 42. 203–26.

——2002. 'Persepolis in Retrospect: Histories of Discovery and Archaeological Exploration at the Ruins of Ancient Parseh'. *Ars Orientalis* 32. 209–25.

——2012. *Persepolis. Discovery and Afterlife of a World Wonder*. Berlin.

Murphey, R. 2008. *Exploring Ottoman Sovereignty*. London.

Nashat, G. 2003. 'Women in Pre-Islamic and Early Islamic Iran', in G. Nashat and L. Beck (eds), *Women in Iran. From the Rise of Islam to 1800*. Urbana and Chicago. 11–47.

Neale, J. E. 1958. *Elizabeth I and Her Parliaments* (2 vols). New York.

Nelso, S. M. 2003. *Ancient Queens*. Oxford and New York.

Nichols, A. 2011. *Ctesias. On India. Introduction, Translation and Commentary*. London.

Niditch, S. 2008. *'My Brother Esau Is a Hairy Man'. Hair and Identity in Ancient Israel*. Oxford.

Nielsen, I. 1999. *Hellenistic Palaces*. Aarhus.

——(ed.) 2001. *The Royal Palace Institution in the First Millennium BC. Regional Development and Cultural Interchange Between East and West*. Aarhus.

Novotny, J. R. 2001. 'Daughters and Sisters of Neo-Hittite and Aramaean Rulers in the Assyrian Harem'. *Canadian Society for Mesopotamian Studies* 36. 174–84.

Novotny, J. R. and Singletary, J. 2009. 'Family Ties: Assurbanipal's Family Revisited', in M. Luukko, S. Svärd and R. Mattila (eds), *Of God(s), Trees, Kings, and Scholars. Neo-Assyrian and Related Studies in Honour of Simo Parpola*. Helsinki. 167–77.

Oakley, F. 2006. *Kingship*. Oxford.

Oates, J. and Oates, D. 2001. *Nimrud. An Assyrian Imperial City Revealed.* London.

Ogden, D. 1999. *Polygamy, Prostitutes and Death. The Hellenistic Dynasties.* London.

Olmstead, A. T. 1948. *History of the Persian Empire.* Chicago.

Oost, S. I. 1977/8. 'Xenophon's Attitude to Women'. *Classical World* 71.4. 225–36.

Oppenheim, A. L. 1964. *Ancient Mesopotamia.* Chicago.

——1967. *Letters from Mesopotamia.* Chicago.

——1973. 'Note on *ša rēši*'. *Journal of the Ancient Near Eastern Society* 6. 325–34.

Parker, S. B. 1997. *Ugaritic Narrative Poetry.* Atlanta.

Parkinson, R. B. 1999. *The Tale of Sinhue and Other Ancient Egyptian Poems, 1940–1640 BC.* Oxford.

Parpola, S. 1970. *Letters from Assyrian Scholars to Kings Esarhaddon and Assurbanipal. Vol. I: Texts.* Neukirchen.

Parpola, S. and Watanabe, K. 1988. *Neo-Assyrian Treaties and Loyalty Oaths.* State Archives of Assyria 2. Helsinki.

Paterson, J. 2007. 'Friend in High Places: The Creation of the Court of the Roman Emperor', in A. J. S. Spawforth (ed.), *The Court and Court Society in Ancient Monarchies.* Cambridge. 121–56.

Peirce, L. 1993. *The Imperial Harem. Women and Sovereignty in the Ottoman Empire.* Oxford.

Penzer, N. M. 1936. *The Harem. An Account of the Institution As It Existed in the Palace of the Turkish Sultans, with a History of the Grand Seraglio from Its Foundation to Modern Times.* London.

Perrot, J. 2008. 'Beyond Harem Walls: Ottoman Royal Women and the Exercise of Power', in A. Walthall (ed.), *Servants of the Dynasty. Palace Women in World History.* Berkeley. 81–94.

——(ed.) 2010. *Le palais de Darius à Suse. Une résidence royale sur la route de Persépolis à Babylone.* Paris.

Pirngruber, R. 2011. 'Eunuchen am Königshof. Ktesias und die altorientalische Evidenz', in J. Wiesehöfer, R. Rollinger and G. Lanfranchi (eds), *Ktesias' Welt/Ctesias' World.* Wiesbaden. 279–312.

Porten, B. and Yardeni, A. 1987–99. *Textbook of Aramaic Documents from Ancient Egypt.* Jerusalem.

Porter, Y. 2003. *Palaces and Gardens of Persia.* Paris.

Potts, D. T. 1999. *The Archaeology of Elam. Formation and Transformation of an Ancient Iranian State.* Cambridge.

——2008. 'The Persepolis Fortification Texts and the Royal Road: Another Look at the Fahliyan Area', in P. Briant, W. Henkleman and M. Stolper (eds), *L'archive des Fortifications de Persépolis*. Paris. 275–302.

——2010. 'Monarchy, Factionalism and Warlordism: Reflections on Neo-Elamite Courts', in B. Jacobs and R. Rollinger (eds), *Der Achämenidenhof/ The Achaemenid Court*. Stuttgart. 107–37.

——2011. 'The Elamites', in T. Daryaee (ed.), *The Oxford Handbook of Iranian History*. Oxford. 37–56.

Pritchard, J. B. 1969. *Ancient Near Eastern Texts Relating to the Old Testament* (3rd edition with supplement). Princeton.

Rawski, E. S. 1998. *The Last Emperors: A Social History of Qing Imperial Institutions*. Berkeley.

Razmjou, S. 2004. 'The *lan* Ceremony and Other Ritual Ceremonies in the Achaemenid Period'. *Iran* 42. 103–17.

——2010. 'Persepolis: A Reinterpretation of Palaces and Their Function', in J. Curtis and S. Simpson (eds), *The World of Achaemenid Persia*. London. 231–45.

Reade, J. 1988. *Assyrian Sculpture*. London.

Redford, S. 2002. *The Harem Conspiracy. The Murder of Ramesses III*. Deklab.

Rehm, E. 2006. *Pracht und Prunk der Großkönige – Das persische Weltreich*. Stuttgart.

Robins, G. 1993. *Women in Ancient Egypt*. London.

Rodríquez-Salgado, M. J. 1991. 'The Court of Philip II of Spain', in R. G. Asch and A. M. Birke (eds), *Princes, Patronage, and the Nobility. The Court at the Beginning of the Modern Age, c. 1450–1650*. London and Oxford. 206–44.

Rollinger, R. 2004. 'Herodotus, Human Violence and the Ancient Near East', in V. Karageorghis and I. Taifacos (eds), *The World of Herodotus*. Nicosia. 121–50.

——2010. 'Extreme Gewalt und Srtafgericht. Ktesias und Herodot als Zeugnisse für den Achaemenidenhof', in B. Jacobs and R. Rollinger (eds), *Der Achämenidenhof/The Achaemenid Court*. Stuttgart. 557–666.

Root, M. C. 1979. *The King and Kingship in Achaemenid Art: Essays on the Creation of an Iconography of Empire*. Leiden.

——1990. *Crowning Glories. Persian Kingship and the Power of Creative Continuity*. Ann Arbor.

——2003. 'The Lioness of Elam: Politics and Dynastic Fecundity at Persepolis', in W. Henkelman and A. Kuhrt (eds), *A Persian Perspective. Essays in Honour of Heleen Sancisi-Weerdenburg*. (Achaemenid History XIII.) Leiden. 9–32.

——2011. 'Elam in the Imperial Imagination: From Nineveh to Persepolis', in J. Álvarez-Mon and M. B. Garrison (eds), *Elam and Persia*. Winona Lake. 419–74.

Rubinson, K. S. 1990. 'The Textiles from Pazyryk: A Study in the Transfer and Transformation of Artistic Motifs'. *Expedition* 32(1). 49–61.

Rudenko, S. I. 1970. *Frozen Tombs of Siberia: The Pazyrik Burials of Iron-Age Horsemen.* London.

Russell, J. M. 1991. *Sennacherib's Palace Without Rival at Nineveh.* London and Chicago.

Saïd, E. W. 1978. *Orientalism.* London.

Salvesen, A. 1998. 'Trappings of Royalty in Ancient Israel', in J. Day (ed.), *King and Messiah in Israel and the Ancient Near East.* Sheffield. 119–41.

Sánchez, M. G. 2006. 'La figura del sucesor del Gran Rey en la Persia aquemé-nida', in V. A. Troncoso (ed.), *Diodokhos tēs Basileias: La figura del sucesor en la realeza helenística. Anejo IX.* Madrid. 223–39.

——2009. *El Gran Rey de Persia: Formas de Representación de la Alteridad Persa en el Imaginario Griego.* Barcelona.

Sancisi-Weerdenburg, H. 1983. 'Exit Atossa: Images of Women in Greek Historiography on Persia', in A. Cameron and A. Kuhrt (eds), *Images of Women in Antiquity.* London. 20–33.

——1987a. 'Decadence in the Empire of Decadence in the Sources? From Source to Synthesis: Ctesias', in H. Sancisi-Weerdenburg (ed.), *Sources, Structures and Synthesis.* (Achaemenid History I.) Leiden. 33–45.

——1987b. 'The Fifth Oriental Monarchy and Hellenocentrism', in H. Sancisi-Weerdenburg and A. Kuhrt (eds), *The Greek Sources.* (Achaemenid History II.) Leiden. 117–31.

——1989. 'Gifts in the Persian Empire', in P. Briant and C. Herrenschmidt (eds), *Les tributes dans l'empire perse. Actes de la Table Ronde de Paris 12–13 décembre 1986.* Paris. 129–46.

——1995. 'Persian Food: Stereotypes and Political Identity', in J. Wilkins, D. Harvey and M. Dobson (eds), *Food in Antiquity.* Exeter. 286–302.

——1997. 'Crumbs from the Royal Table'. *Topoi* (supplement 1). 332–42.

——1998. 'Bāji', in M. Brosius and A. Kuhrt (eds), *Studies in Persian History: Essays in Memory of David M. Lewis.* Leiden. 23–34.

Scheidel, W. 2009. 'Sex and Empire. A Darwinian Perspective', in I. Morris and W. Scheidel (eds), *The Dynamics of Ancient Empires. Sate Power from Assyria to Byzantium.* Oxford. 255–324.

Schick, I. 2010. 'The Harem as Gendered Space and the Spatial Reproduction of Gender', in M. Booth (ed.), *Harem Histories: Envisioning Places and Living Spaces.* Durham, NC: 69–84.

Schimmel, A. 2000. *The Empire of the Great Mughals. History, Art and Culture.* London.

Schlumberger, D. 1971. 'La coiffure du grand roi'. *Syria* 48. 375–83.

Schmandt-Besserat, D. 1978. *Ancient Persia. The Art of Empire.* Austin.

Schmidt, E. F. 1953. *Persepolis I.* Chicago.

——1957. *Persepolis. Vol. II: Contents of the Treasury and Other Discoveries.* Chicago.

——1970. *Persepolis. Vol. III: The Royal Tombs and Other Monuments.* Chicago.

Schmitt, R. 1977a. 'Königtum im Alten Iran'. *Saeculum* 28. 384–95.

——1977b. 'Thronnamen bei den Achaimeniden'. *Beiträge zur Namenforschung* 12. 422–5.

Scholz, P. O. 1999. *Eunuchs and Castrati. A Cultural History*. Princeton.

Sekunda, N. V. 2010. 'Changes in Achaemenid Royal Dress', in J. Curtis and S. Simpson (eds), *The World of Achaemenid Persia*. London. 256–72.

Sekunda, N. V. and Chew, S. 1992. *The Persian Army*. Oxford.

Shahbazi, A. S. 2003. *Persepolis Illustrated* (2nd edition). Shiraz.

——2004. *The Authoritative Guide to Persepolis*. Tehran.

——2009. s.v. 'Persepolis', in *Encyclopaedia Iranica*. New York.

Shaked, S. 2004. *Le satrape de Bactriane et son gouverneur. Documents araméens du IVe avant notre ère provenant de Bactriane*. Paris.

Shamasastry, R. 1923. *Kautilya's Arthashastra*. Mysore.

Smith, R. 2007. 'The Imperial Court in the Late Roman Empire, c. AD 300–c. AD 450', in A. J. S. Spawforth (ed.), *The Court and Court Society in Ancient Monarchies*. Cambridge. 157–232.

Solvang, E. K. 2003. *A Woman's Place is in the House. Royal Women of Judah and Their Involvement in the House of David*. Sheffield.

Sommer, B. D. 2009. *The Bodies of God and the World of Ancient Israel*. Cambridge.

Spawforth, A. J. S. 2007a. 'The Court of Alexander the Great', in A. J. S. Spawforth (ed.), *The Court and Court Society in Ancient Monarchies*. Cambridge. 82–120.

——(ed.) 2007b. *The Court and Court Society in Ancient Monarchies*. Cambridge.

Spence, K. 2007. 'Court and Palace in Ancient Egypt: The Amarna Period and the Later Eighteenth Dynasty', in A. J. S. Spawforth (ed.), *The Court and Court Society in Ancient Monarchies*. Cambridge. 267–328.

Starkey, D. 1987. 'Court History in Perspective', in D. Starkey (ed.), *The English Court. From the Wars of the Roses to the Civil War*. London. 1–24.

——2008. *Henry: Virtuous Prince*. London.

Stevens, A. 1995. *Private Myths: Dreams and Dreaming*. Cambridge, MA.

Stevenson, R. B. 1997. 'Lies and Invention in Deinon's *Persica*', in H. Sancisi-Weerdenburg and A. Kuhrt (eds), *The Greek Sources*. (Achaemenid History II.) Leiden. 27–35.

——1997. *Persica. Greek Writing about Persia in the Fourth Century BC*. Edinburgh.

Stolper, M. W. 1985. *Entrepreneurs and Empire. The Muraŝû Archive, the Muraŝû Firm, and Persian Rule in Babylonia*. Leiden.

——1988. 'Some Ghost Facts From Achaemenid Babylonian Texts'. *Journal of Hellenic Studies* 108. 196–8.

Stronach, D. 1978. *Parsagade*. Oxford.

——1997a. 'Darius as Parsagadae: A Neglected Source for the History of Early Persia'. *Topoi* (supplement 1). 351–63.

——1997b. 'Anshan and Persia: Early Achaemenid History, Art and Architecture on the Iranian Plateau', in J. Curtis (ed.), *Mesopotamia and Iran in the Persian Period: Conquest and Imperialism 539–331 BC*. London. 35–53.

——2011. 'Court Dress and Riding Dress at Persepolis: New Approaches to Old Questions', in J. Álvarez-Mon and M. B. Garrison (eds), *Elam and Persia*. Winona Lake. 475–87.

Stronk, J. 2004–5. 'Ctesias of Cnidus: From Physician to Author'. *Talanta* 36–7. 101–22.

Strootman, R. 2007. *The Hellenistic Royal Court. Court Culture, Ceremonial and Ideology in Greece, Egypt and the Near East, 336–30 BCE*. Unpublished thesis. Utrecht.

——2011. 'Hellenistic Court Society: The Seleukid Imperial Court Under Antiochos the Great, 223–187 BCE', in J. Duindam, T. Artan and M. Kunt (eds), *Royal Courts in Dynastic States. A Global Perspective*. Leiden. 63–89.

Sumner, W. M. 1986. 'Achaemenid Settlement in the Persepolis Plain'. *American Journal of Archaeology* 90(1). 3–31.

Svärd, S. and Luukko, M. 2009. 'Who Were the 'Ladies of the House', in the Assyrian Empire?', in M. Luukko, S. Svärd and R. Mattila (eds), *Of God(s), Trees, Kings, and Scholars. Neo-Assyrian and Related Studies in Honour of Simo Parpola*. Helsinki. 279–94.

Tavernier, J. 2010. 'Multilingualism in the Fortification and Treasury Archives', in P. Briant, W. Henkleman and M. Stolper (eds), *L'archive des Fortifications de Persépolis*. Paris. 59–85.

Taylor, L. R. 1927. 'The *Proskynesis* and the Hellenistic Ruler Cult'. *Journal of Hellenic Studies* 47. 53–62.

Tilia, A. B. 1972. *Studies and Restorations at Persepolis and Other Sites of Fārs. Vol. I*. Rome.

——1978. *Studies and Restorations at Persepolis and Other Sites of Fārs. Vol. II*. Rome.

Tomes, R. 2005. *'I Have Written to My Lord the King': Secular Analogies for the Psalms*. Sheffield.

Tougher, S. 2008. *The Eunuch in Byzantine History and Society*. London.

Tsai, S-S. H. 1996. *The Eunuchs in the Ming Dynasty*. Albany, NY.

——2002. 'Eunuch Power in Imperial China', in S. Tougher (ed.), *Eunuchs in Antiquity and Beyond*. London and Swansea. 221–33.

Tuplin, C. 1987. 'The administration of the Achaemenid Empire', in I. Carradice (ed.), *Coinage and Administration in the Athenian and Persian Empires*. BAR International Series 34. London. 109–66.

——1996. *Achaemenid Studies*. Stuttgart.

——1998a. 'Review: Women in Ancient Persia'. *Classical Review* 48(1). 104–6.

——1998b. 'The Seasonal Migration of Achaemenid Kings: A Report on Old and New Evidence', in M. Brosius and A. Kuhrt (eds), *Studies in Persian History: Essays in Memory of David M. Lewis*. Leiden. 63–114.

——2004a. 'The Persian Empire', in R. Lane Fox (ed.), *The Long March and the Ten Thousand*. Yale. 154–83.

——2004b. 'Doctoring the Persians: Ctesias of Cnidus, Physician and Historian'. *Klio* 86. 305–47.

——(ed.) 2007a. *Persian Responses. Political and Cultural Interaction With(in) the Achaemenid Empire*. Swansea.

——2007b. 'Herodotus on Persia and the Persian Empire', in R. B. Strassler (ed.), *The Landmark Herodotus*. New York. 792–7.

——2007c. 'Treacherous Hearts and Upright Tiaras: The Achaemenid King's Head-Dress', in C. Tuplin (ed.), *Persian Responses. Political and Cultural Interaction With(in) the Persian Empire*. 67–97.

——2010a. 'All the King's Men', in J. Curtis and St. J. Simpson (eds), *The World of Achaemenid Persia*. London. 51–61.

——2010b. 'All the King's Horses: In Search of Achaemenid Cavalry', in M. Trundle and G. Fagan (eds), *New Perspectives on Ancient Warfare*. Leiden. 101–82.

Uchitel, A. 1997. 'Persian Paradise. Agricultural Texts in the Fortification Tablets'. *Iranica Antiqua* 32. 137–44.

Vale, M. 2001. *The Princely Courts. Mediaeval Courts and Culture in North West Europe*. Oxford.

van de Mieroop, M. 2004. *A History of the Ancient Near East*. Oxford.

Van Selms, A. 1957. 'The Origin of the Title "The Friend of the King"'. *Journal of Near Eastern Studies* 16. 118–23.

Vogelsang, W. 2010. 'Trouser Wearing by Horse-Riding Nomads in Central Asia', in G. Vogelsang-Eastwood (ed.), *Berg Encyclopaedia of World Dress and Fashion. Vol. V: Central and Southwest Asia*. Oxford. 349–54.

von Rad, G. 1991. *Holy War in Ancient Israel*. Michigan.

Walker, E. 2010. *Horse*. London.

Walthall, A. 2008. 'Introducing Palace Women', in A. Walthall (ed.), *Servants of the Dynasty. Palace Women in World History*. Berkeley. 1–21.

Wan, Y. 1988. *Daily Life in the Forbidden City: The Qing Dynasty, 1644–1912*. Harmondsworth.

Watanabe, C. E. 2002. *Animal Symbolism in Mesopotamia. A Contextual Approach*. Vienna.

Waterman, J. 1930. *Royal Correspondence of Assyria* (4 vols). Oxford.

Waters, M. 2011. 'The Oibaras Saga in Ctesias', in J. Wiesehöfer, R. Rollinger and G. Lanfranchi (eds), *Ktesias' Welt/Ctesias' World*. Wiesbaden. 489–506.

Widengren, G. 1951. *The King and the Tree of Life in Ancient Near Eastern Religion*. Uppsala.

——1956. 'Some Remarks on Riding Costume and Articles of Dress Among Iranian Peoples in Antiquity', in A. Furumark (ed.), *Artica*. Studia Ethnographica Upsaliensa XI. Uppsala. 228–76.

——1959. 'The Sacral Kingship of Iran'. *La regalita sacra, contributi alterna dell' VIII Congresso Internazionale de Storia delle Religioni (Roma, Aprile 1955).* Leiden. 242–57.

——1965. *Die Religionen Irans.* Stuttgart.

——1968. *Les religions de l'Iran.* Paris.

Wiesehöfer, J. 1996. *Ancient Persia from 550 BC to 650 AD.* London and New York.

——2009. 'The Achaemenid Empire', in I. Morris and W. Scheidel (eds), *The Dynamics of Ancient Empires. Sate Power from Assyria to Byzantium.* Oxford. 66–98.

——2010. 'Günstlinge und Privilegien am Achaimenidenhof', in B. Jacobs and R. Rollinger (eds), *Der Achämenidenhof/The Achaemenid Court.* Stuttgart. 509–30.

Wiesehöfer, J., Rollinger, R. and Lanfranchi, G. (eds) 2011. *Ktesias' Welt/ Ctesias' World.* Wiesbaden.

Wilber, D. N. 1969. *Persepolis. The Archaeology of Parsa, Seat of the Persian Kings.* Princeton.

Wilkinson, R. H. 1992. *Reading Egyptian Art.* London.

Yamauchi, E. M. 1990. *Persia and the Bible.* Grand Rapids.

Yeazell, R. B. 2000. *Harems of the Mind. Passages of Western Art and Literature.* New Haven and London.

Zega, A. 2002. *Palaces of the Sun King: Versailles, Trianon, Marly; the Châteaux of Louis XIV.* London.

Zhou, M. 2010. 'The Cross-Cultural Comparison of *The Tale of Genji* and *A Dream of Red Mansions'. Journal of Cambridge Studies* 5(2–3). 24–31.

Index